George Sand: An Introduction

by Ellen Moers

And now I'm attached to it, this name of mine.
. . . I was baptized, obscure and carefree, between the manuscript of *Indiana* which was then
my whole future—and a thousand-franc note,
which was then my whole fortune. It was a contract, a new marriage between the poor apprentice poet that I then was and the humble muse
who had consoled me in my difficulties. God defend me from tampering with the dispositions of
destiny. What is a name, anyway, in our revolutionary world? A number for those who do
nothing, a sign or emblem for those who work or
fight. This name I've been given, I made it myself, and I alone, finally, by my labor. I have
never exploited the work of another, never taken,
or bought, or borrowed a page, a line from anyone. Of the seven or eight hundred thousand
francs that I've earned since I was twenty, I have
nothing left, and today as at twenty I live from
day to day, by this name which protects my
work. . . .

(Histoire de Ma Vie, IV, xiv)

What should that famous name "George Sand" mean to us? A reasoned answer, supplied by Joseph Barry's newly translated anthology, is that George Sand was a writer—a nineteenth-century French writer, who for four and a half decades, from 1831 to 1876, wrote with verve, eloquence, and power well over one hundred volumes of prose: fiction, plays, autobiographies, letters, essays. A prolific and successful but not really a popular writer, as Henry James noted with surprise: none of her works was by the standard of her time or ours a "best-seller," not even *Consuelo*, one of her most important novels, which sold only a few thousand copies. Among writers and intellectuals, however, she reached what might be called a "mass market" everywhere around the world, and their tributes to her as spokesman of the age (surpassing even Dickens, Dostoevski insisted) were touched with reverence and gratitude, as well as hyperbole.

The English critic George Henry Lewes wrote in 1842 that Sand was "the most remarkable writer of the present century. . . . George Sand is infinitely more than novelist. She is a Poet, not of the head alone, but of the heart—a Poet, not writing clever verses, but uttering the collective voice of her epoch. . . . No genius was ever recognized by the many; George Sand may comfort herself with the appreciation of the few." Lewes was only a young man then, and just beginning his career as a critic; but his reverence for Sand as a writer was to prove a bond between him and the two great novelists Lewes most influenced, Charlotte Brontë and George Eliot. They too read George Sand as the genius of their age; they too reverenced the poet and the thinker in the novelist.

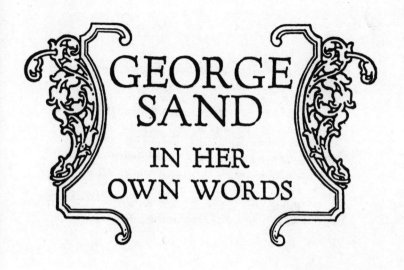

GEORGE SAND
IN HER OWN WORDS

Translated and edited by
JOSEPH BARRY

Introduction by Ellen Moers

QUARTET BOOKS
LONDON   MELBOURNE   NEW YORK

First published in Great Britain by
Quartet Books Limited 1979
A member of the Namara Group
27 Goodge Street, London W1P 1FD
First published in the U.S.A. by
Anchor Press/Doubleday, New York, 1979
Copyright © 1979 by Joseph Barry
Introduction copyright © 1979 by Ellen Moers
ISBN 0 7043 2235 8
Printed and bound in Great Britain by
Billing & Sons Ltd, Guildford and Worcester

To Nathalie Datlof,

*dear friend and founder of
the Friends of George Sand, and to
Georges Lubin, first of Friends*

Contents

CONTENTS

Turgenev, Renan, Heine, Dostoevski, the Brownings, the Carlyles, Mill, Ruskin, Taine, Whitman, Marx, Wilde—all testify that, among nineteenth-century intellectuals, reading Sand was something of an addiction. And almost a Victorian parlor game was marking the influence of Sand's novels on other people's fiction, as Marian Evans (the future George Eliot) saw marks of *François le Champi* on Thackeray's *Henry Esmond.** However, a number of the prominent Victorian addicts of Sand's fiction—Emerson, Whitman, Ruskin, Arnold—were people who otherwise had little use for the novel as a form. Matthew Arnold, the most important literary critic of the century, could barely say a good word for Dickens and, devoted as he was to contemporary French literature, never once mentioned the name of Flaubert; but he went on reading Sand's novels all his life.

When she died in 1876, Arnold predicted that "the immense vibration of George Sand's voice upon the ear of Europe will not soon die away"; he was wrong. Within a quarter of a century intellectuals stopped reading Sand.† Virtual silence descended on the acad-

---

* Patricia Thomson, in her brilliant new study of *George Sand and the Victorians,* assembles evidence for the serious consequences of Sand's influence on the fiction of the Brontës and George Eliot, of Hardy, Meredith, and James, particularly the last. Henry James wrote ten review essays on Sand, and, as some of his apprentice tales and much of *Roderick Hudson,* his first novel, reveal, when he began to write fiction, he was distinctly a Sandiste.

† An exception must be made for the turn-of-the-century women writers who explored Sand's autobiography for parallels to their own writing lives: Edith Wharton, Gertrude Stein, Kate Chopin, Colette, Willa Cather, Virginia Woolf—the last of whom quoted Sand's *Story of My Life* at the end of *Three Guineas.*

emy and the critical journals; no more vibrations. Marcel Proust wrote the experience of reading Sand, as a nineteenth-century child, into his *Remembrance of Things Past,* and George Sand's work slipped, with so much else, into *le temps perdu.*

By a reversal of taste as extreme as any in literary history, and by a process of denigration familiar to experts in women's history, the name of George Sand came to mean to most people not an author at all but a target for labels: transvestite, man-eater, lesbian, nymphomaniac. The very texts of some of her volumes had vanished, as French scholars discovered when they began the massive labor of recovering the writer George Sand, for, predictably, the reversal of literary taste was due to be again reversed and Sand was to return to our own time as a writer, not a caricature.

When the revival of interest in Sand's work started quietly in France in the 1930s, it was once again an intellectual phenomenon, beginning with two eminent Frenchmen, Edouard Dolléans and Alain (pen name of Émile Chartier), who happened to be friends. Dolléans was the historian of nineteenth-century working-class movements in France (he also wrote a history of Chartism in England), and he began to write about Sand with the deepest respect because of her own involvement with working-class poets and politics, because of her influential role as champion of *le peuple.* While the critic Alain turned to Sand because of her love of nature and music, her passion and her prose. Alain is best known outside France as the teacher of philosophy whose students brought him fame, notably Simone Weil and André Maurois. And it was Maurois's biography called *Lélia: The Life of George Sand*

and published in 1952 that gave the Sand revival wide and international currency.

In the 1960s and 1970s, literary scholars in France and Italy prepared definitive new editions of Sand's novels (including *Consuelo, La Comtesse de Rudolstadt, Indiana, Lélia, Mauprat, La Mare au Diable, François le Champi, La Daniella*) and supplied learned introductory studies of Sand's politics, her knowledge of music and history, her use of dialect and regional lore, her place among the Romantics. Georges Lubin, the dean of Sand scholars, edited her autobiographical writings (which include her masterworks) and since 1964 has been editing Sand's correspondence —thirteen volumes of it for the years through June 1856, with two more decades of Sand's life and presumably ten more volumes still to come. The letters are dazzling. Had she written nothing else, George Sand would be securely known as one of the greatest of all practitioners of the form.

Because of the incredible range of Sand's epistolary relationships and concerns, Georges Lubin's scholarship has perforce reached out to include virtually all the politics and all the arts in mid-nineteenth-century Europe, not to mention the day-by-day chronology of Sand's passionate life as writer, lover, mother, friend, and *châtelaine*. His magisterial edition of the *Correspondance* has formed the basis for the two new scholarly lives of George Sand, both widely read and widely hailed, both by Americans: Curtis Cate (1975) and Joseph Barry (1977). Mr. Barry's particular strength as a Sand biographer—a knowledge of her works which is probably unrivaled in the English-speaking world— is also reflected in the present anthology.

Both Cate and Barry know far more about Sand's intimate life than did any of her contemporaries, because the documentation at their command is so enormous. Yet the "new" George Sand who emerges from their biographies is remarkably like the "old" George Sand perceived in her own time by those who knew her or who divined her character from her writings. She has a brilliant, well-stocked mind and a warm heart; she has courage, energy, vitality, generosity, responsibility, good humor, and charm; she has aristocratic distinction combined with bohemian informality; she is a wise, passionate, down-to-earth human being, and disappointingly sane. These days we want our writers to be crazies; in the mid-nineteenth century, people wanted their writers to be great men. Their ideal of a writer was Goethe (to whom Sand was often compared) because of the wholeness and fullness of both his active and spiritual life. "Great Men are the inspired (speaking and acting) Texts of that divine Book of Revelation" called "History," said Carlyle, who worshiped Goethe, who made a cult of the writer as Hero, who privately admitted there was "something Goethian" about George Sand but never would have said so in public, because she was a woman.

She was a woman who was a great man: that is what her admirers most wanted to say about George Sand. But words of gender being what they are, suggestions of abnormality and monstrosity cling to their portraits of Sand, all unintentionally and quite the reverse of what her admirers had in mind. Elizabeth Barrett (later Mrs. Robert Browning) began a sonnet to Sand with the line

Thou large-brained woman and large-hearted man . . .

and what she intended as a tribute to wholeness came out sounding grotesque. Similarly, Balzac wrote down his impressions of Sand after a visit to her home in Nohant: "She is boyish, an artist, she is great-hearted, generous, devout, and *chaste*; she has the main characteristics of a man; *ergo* she is not a woman."

Flaubert, who wrote the novella *Un Coeur Simple* for Sand's approval, wept at her funeral and said: "You had to know her as I did to know how much of the feminine there was in that great man, the immensity of tenderness there was in that genius." And Turgenev: "What a brave man she was, and what a good woman."

Reading George Sand is to encounter a great man who was all woman, not a phenomenon—though that such a life, a spirit, a style were possible struck her contemporaries as phenomenal, for they had never known a literary woman of her kind before. To read Sand is also to return to a Romantic age, to find the lanes greener, the nightingales thicker, the stars brighter, the breezes softer, the colors brighter, and the tones more heavenly, for Delacroix is painting, Viardot is singing, Liszt and Chopin are at the piano; and the hopes of relieving human suffering, of binding all humanity into one golden solidarity, are more dazzling than ever before. Reading Sand, however, is not the ponderous experience that American and English readers might expect from our rather Victorian definition of "greatness of character." George Sand was very French, and she never took herself very seriously.

In 1831, when she was twenty-six, she set out for Paris to become a writer—to support herself and her dependents by writing. High Romanticism was in full sway in France, and the new writers were named Victor Hugo, Lamartine, Musset, Vigny, Balzac, Stendhal, Mérimée, Sainte-Beuve. When she was twenty-seven, George Sand, the author of *Indiana*, was one of the names on that Romantic list. With the speed and energy characteristic of her entire literary career, she accomplished her apprenticeship in journalism and fiction, including the writing of dozens of works and thousands of pages, the making of contacts and finding of markets, all within fifteen months. She also established a dual life-style which makes itself felt throughout all her writings. On the one hand, she was an independent: her officer father and aristocratic grandmother long dead, her mother removed, her maiden name (Dupin) and married name (Dudevant) abandoned, her husband put in his place by a formal contract of separation. She was a Parisian and a cosmopolitan, in touch with all that was new in the arts and in political thought. But on the other hand, she was a countrywoman in residence principally in her province of Berry and enmeshed, voluntarily and wholeheartedly, with human ties: her two children; her country estate of Nohant, with its servants, peasants, neighbors, its spreading regional associations of memory and legend; and her lovers and friends. Friends were, as far as George Sand could manage it, for life; lovers came and went more quickly, but they too long had a claim on her responsibility and generosity.‡

‡ The case of Jules Sandeau, the young poet with whom she lived her first year in Paris, set something of a pattern. She

Indiana, the novel which first made the name of George Sand famous, is in many ways uncharacteristic of her fiction, with its debts to the earlier Romanticism of Madame de Staël and Bernardin de Saint-Pierre, its small cast of mainly wealthy characters, its unlikely Bourbon Island references, its melancholy Englishman. (Yet even Sir Ralph may be forgiven Sand, if, as has been argued, he inspired the relationship between Ralph Touchett and Isabel Archer in Henry James's *Portrait of a Lady*.) But already in *Indiana* the distinctive pleasures of reading Sand make themselves felt, and the first of these are country pleasures: country nights, country solitude, country passions, country journeys, the horses and dogs and pastimes, even the boredom of rainy autumn evenings in the country interior. It was, however, *Valentine*, her second novel, in which Sand's originality as landscapist and country chronicler (and creator of rebellious heroines) overwhelmed readers such as Matthew Arnold. He responded as a young man to what he called "the cry of agony and revolt" in Sand's early

---

supported him, got him to write and publish, financed his military replacement; and when they broke up, she contributed to a trip to Italy to cure him of the doldrums. Such generosity, because unfamiliar to us from the annals of male writers in love, has been called abnormal, and Sand's easy assumption of the maternal role at the height of passion was made to appear a monstrosity, which it was not. Much has been made of the fact that most—not all—of Sand's lovers were younger than she, but little attention paid to her avoidance of married men, her refusal to compete with other wives and mistresses—a scrupulousness which perforce limited her choice of lovers to young bachelors. Sand's lovers were men of talent, even genius, and they flourished rather than faded because of her, Chopin, for example, writing his greatest music during their nine years together. Her love encompassed their health and their work, her writing paid their bills, because she was a woman of energy and character.

fiction; but what Arnold *did* in response was to set off on a journey into Sand's countryside and Sand's interior at Nohant—a pilgrimage on which he has been followed ever since by untold thousands of enthusiasts of Romantic art and Romantic nature.

At her best, no one has ever surpassed George Sand as the novelist of Nature, because her style pulsates with a natural vigor and music and because she was a countrywoman as well as a Romantic. Her range includes not only the mysteries and enchantments of distant horizons and perilous wanderings, of superstition and legend, of ecstatic (and often feminist) solitude; but also the closely observed and dearly loved realities of peasant life: the greeds and frugalities, the labor of the seasons, the farm animals and insects, the stolid silences of illiterate folk radiated with their music and dancing, their enchanting dialect speech. Her *romans champêtres* (*La Mare au Diable, François le Champi, La Petite Fadette, Jeanne, Les Maîtres Sonneurs, Le Meunier d'Angibault*) are those of Sand's novels which have never gone completely out of fashion and to which the English country novelists (George Eliot and Thomas Hardy) were most in debt.

But Sand had something her English imitators did not and that was her grasp of history. "Tout concourt à l'histoire," she wrote, "*tout est l'histoire*, même les romans qui semblent ne se rattacher en rien aux situations politiques qui les voient éclore." Her country tales and her love stories take place in the churning past and the open future of a world of toppling regimes, shifting classes, and clashing ideologies. Even in *Indiana,* Delmare is the husband he is because he is a displaced Bonapartist, Indiana the wife she is because she is the daughter of slaveholding colonials, and Raymon the lover he is because he is an apologist for constitutional monarchy, his political portrait drawn after that of a minister of the July monarchy, which had come into power two years before the publication of the novel. When Sand gives her heroine views on women's education, as in *Valentine*, they are those of an aristocrat who remembers what happened to her sex and class during the French Revolution. Sand places most of her young heroes in generational conflict with their fathers and offers them as typical *enfants du siècle*. She demonstrates that even the illiterate peasant—as in the interesting study of Patience in *Mauprat*—could be touched by the ideas of the Enlightenment. And in some of the most brilliant sections of *Histoire de Ma Vie*, she presents her own childhood as riven by the class and period ideologies held by her grandmother and her mother and seconded even by their maids.

It can be something of a relief to turn from the slow-moving dreamtime of Thomas Hardy and George Eliot to the faster pace of George Sand's European world, a world, as Marx read it and we still read it today, in revolutionary turmoil. Sand was a shrewd, committed, and radical observer of the half-dozen regimes that rose and fell in France during her lifetime. As Minister (without portfolio) of Propaganda, she played an active political role—greater than any woman before her—in the revolutionary government of 1848. Correspondent of Mazzini, of Gutzkow, of Bakunin, she was in touch with most of radical Europe. In all her work, her fiction and nonfiction, ideology remains a principal excitement, never a bore.

Less interesting to us today, I think, than to her contemporaries is Sand on the passion of love; here there
can be the boredom of excess French talk, of impossible chastities, of improbable plots. "I don't care,"
wrote George Eliot, ". . . whether I think the design
of her plot correct or that she had no precise design
at all . . . I cannot read six pages of hers without feeling that it is given to her to delineate human passion
. . . with such truthfulness such nicety of discrimina-
tion such tragic power and withal such loving gentle
humour that one might live a century with nothing
but one's own dull faculties and not know so much as
these six pages will suggest." Sand remains interesting
as the chronicler of passion in the occasional scene
where, as V. S. Pritchett has put it, "her people and
landscapes are silhouettes seen in sheet lightning": for
example, the Noun-Raymon love scene in Indiana's
bedroom, which made Alfred de Musset first admire
before he fell in love with its author.

Today Sand's social thought sustains her love stories
rather than the other way around, for her pairings of
lovers of different ages and places and classes still convey that aspiration toward a new, humane social order
which lifted the hearts of her contemporaries and still
has the power to move even our own. A commonplace
of Romanticism was the use of human love as the
paradigm of social solidarity; but from Friedrich Schil-
ler's (and Beethoven's) *Ode to Joy* to Walt Whitman's
Leaves of Grass, that theme ordinarily centered on
man's love for man, on fraternity. Sand's originality—
and it was this that must have attracted Dostoevski
to her heroines—was to redefine fraternity from the
woman's point of view, as friendship between men

and women. Certainly her ideal of marriage, which she despaired of seeing fulfilled under the legal system of her times, was that of the perfect friendship, without rivalry or dominance, of two beings come together in that state of unity and wholeness which, as she wrote Flaubert, is Nature's supreme law.

Friendship seems to me to be George Sand's greatest theme. It pervades her fiction and her politics, shapes her style and her humor, and makes her *Lettres d'un Voyageur*, those exquisitely worded imaginary dialogues of reflection and criticism, her single greatest work. Even the disarray of her novel plots is sometimes excused by her charming finales of communal life, when groups of lovers settle down together for a friendly sharing of work, talk, child raising, and country pleasures that seems to promise more of ecstasy than all their frenetic lovemaking. At the end of *Valentine*, peasants and aristocrats are so united; at the end of *Les Maîtres Sonneurs*, the workers of the fields are united with their rivals, the wandering foresters. In *Valvèdre*, the late novel (1861) which Arnold ranked among her best, Sand's ultimate programmatic fantasy of communality makes friends of scientist, industrialist, and artist, of "new" woman and old, of Protestant, Catholic, and Jew.

Sand worked hard at her friendships, writing marvelous letters, dispensing generous hospitality. A highly skilled domestic manager, she made Nohant (the locale of her own slavery to ceaseless writing) into a haven of comfort and bohemian relaxation for such as Liszt, Balzac, Juliette Adam, the English actor Macready, Turgenev, Flaubert, Pauline Viardot, Delacroix—who were her friends, not her lovers. But her genius for friendship seems to have originated in childhood, the period of her life which, to the despair of scandalmongers, dominates her *Histoire de Ma Vie*.

There Sand opens what to us seems unusual, but for her was her birthright as a French countrywoman: the friendly association between bastard and legitimate half-siblings, between unrelated children raised by the same wet nurse (the Noun-Indiana relationship), between future peasant and future *châtelaine*. Sand wrote, and there is something to it, that her ideas of utopian communism originated in her girlhood participation in the communality of peasant labors and diversions. Certainly she had not a trace of gentility or snobbery, not a shred of vainglory over being a *propriétaire*. Nohant was where her heart was, but Nohant made her neither proud nor wealthy. It was her writing, not her land, that supported her; and of that she was justly proud.

A talk with friends is the manner of her best tales and memoirs and essays and even political propaganda —a manner which Sand raised to the dignity of the grand style. And it is her style, finally, which makes reading George Sand an addiction. "The taste one develops for Sand," wrote the critic Émile Faguet, "is a kind of sympathy. Her style becomes our friend. And we more easily free ourselves of an enchantment than of a friendship."

Preface

Really to know George Sand, we must read her in her own language—and perhaps in her own time. Perhaps. How many of her period really knew and understood her, though she was the most successful and prolific novelist of the mid-nineteenth century, certainly in French? It has taken several revolutions, not least that of women.

The purpose of this book and the choice of its selections is to present George Sand in her own (translated) words (and we shall confront the sphinx of translation further on). An ancillary purpose has been to try to answer the question: How does one become George Sand? Here the "Chronology," or life, provides the major clue, as her life was her major work—and so it has been placed first.

In a late tale, Isak Dinesen indicated a parallel for us. All we need recall is that Chateaubriand, after reading Sand's Lélia, wrote to her, "You will be the Lord Byron of France." In Dinesen's tale "Second Meeting," Byron encounters his double Pipistrello. They talk of the last frustrating, self-defeating years of the poet which will, however, Pipistrello says, have *their compensation. That my books will still be read in a hundred years? asks Byron wearily.*

No, replied Pipistrello. "In a hundred years your works will be read much less than today. . . . But one book will be rewritten and reread, and will each year in a new edition be set upon the shelf . . . The Life of Lord Byron."

Unfortunately—though more fortunately, we have no excuse for being unaware of it—Histoire de Ma Vie (The Story of My Life) of George Sand is neither the full nor the fully told story. "It will be the story of my life, but not my confessions," she has sufficiently warned us. Begun in her forty-fourth year and taken through her fiftieth, Sand's autobiography is invaluable for the early years but falters with her marriage and fails us completely thereafter. However, no one can have written so much and remain concealed.

Gathered together, Sand's writings would fill at least 150 volumes, twenty-five of which, each a thousand pages long, would contain her letters—and that last great editing chore has reached thirteen volumes, thanks to the meticulous, affectionate, but no less scrupulous work of Georges Lubin. Many of Sand's manuscripts are available, and 687 printed items, including various editions, are listed in the catalogue of the Bibliothèque Nationale, in Paris. Consequently, sources for a fuller, truer story of George Sand are not lacking. (Notes describing them may be found at the head of each section of this book, together with other relevant information.)

But that true story, Henry James has rightly

insisted, "George Sand's real history, the more interesting one, is the history of her mind [which] is of course closely connected with her personal history." And here there is little concealment, but rather projection—one might even say propaganda—as in the numbered days of the revolutionary Republic of 1848 when Sand served its ministries.

Most emphatically, the story of George Sand is not that of her loves, unless they are extended to the passions of the mind, to political engagement, to personal, enduring commitment to the oppressed, whether women or the working class. This she kept far from secret, and for that she had trouble with her publisher. Her writings spread throughout Europe and beyond. Before the 1848 Revolution, the Russian aristocrat, anarchist, and exile Mikhail Bakunin had written her: "Please think occasionally of a man who venerated you even before he met you, for often in the saddest days of his life, you were a consolation and a light." The response of women is part of history. Some of the texts, other than the novels, to which they all responded may be found in the sections devoted to Sand's nonfiction, including her reflections on painting, music and her own trade—writing.

And now the translator's sphinx can no longer be avoided, nor the question she poses: To what extent has he been faithful? The first side step, I must admit, was to shelter in a cliché, however much truth there is in it—namely, that we cannot really know George Sand except in her own language. But to what extent, to reply to a question with a question, can the French

today *read George Sand's romantic prose and appreciate its sensibilities and sentiments, not to mention its
excesses? The translator's—our own—mother tongue
has evolved from Chaucer through Shakespeare and
Melville to Joyce and Stein.*

*It is presumed to be high praise for a translator that
he or she has made George Sand read as if her language had been English, albeit Victorian. But that
would have been the first betrayal: her language was
French and her thinking was far from what we ordinarily consider Victorian, though it was none the
less nineteenth-century. Content forces the form. Her
syntax, her long-breath sentences punctuated with semi-
colons—her style, in short—is, to adapt Schopenhauer's
phrase, "the physiognomy of her mind." To render
that would be indeed a triumph; as for her "liquid
and iridescent prose" (Henry James once more), I
must again take that mincing side step and suggest
that the reader would best read the French text, if he
or she can, or, what is more difficult, can find it,
alongside the English translation.*

Paris   J.B.
1978

Chronology

1804

The future George Sand is born on July 1 in Paris, daughter of Maurice Dupin, twenty-six, and Antoinette-Sophie-Victoire Delaborde, thirty, who were married twenty-six days before, on June 5. She is the descendant on her father's side of a Saxon king of Poland and on her mother's of a French bird seller. Her name as a child is Amantine-Aurore-Lucile Dupin and she is addressed as Aurore.

Napoleon Bonaparte is crowned Emperor of the French in Nôtre-Dame, Paris.

1808

Madame Dupin and Aurore join Maurice Dupin, aide-de-camp of Marshal Murat, in Madrid. The Dupin family returns to Nohant, in central France, where Maurice's mother, the aristocratic Aurore Dupin de Francueil, has an estate. Maurice is thrown from his horse and killed at La Châtre, near Nohant, September 16.

1809

Madame Dupin de Francueil becomes the guardian of

her granddaughter Aurore and quarrels frequently
with Aurore's mother, the plebeian Sophie-Victoire,
who goes off to live in Paris, leaving Aurore at Nohant with her grandmother.

Birth of Edgar Allan Poe.

1818

Aurore enters the Convent of English Augustinians,
Paris, as fashionable, if religious, a finishing school as
any in France. Here Aurore experiences a period of
piety as well as "deviltry."

1820

Aurore leaves the convent for Nohant as her grandmother seeks a husband for her. Aurore prefers horseback riding to the husbands proffered and rides
dressed as a man.

Birth of Charles Pierre Baudelaire and Gustave Flaubert.

1821

Aurore's grandmother dies. Aurore frequently sees
Stéphane de Grandsagne, a medical student.

1822

Sophie-Victoire arrives at Nohant and takes her
daughter Aurore with her to Paris. In April Aurore
meets Casimir-François Dudevant, illegitimate but recognized son of Baron Jean-François Dudevant. In Sep-

tember they are married. In October they settle in the château (actually a manor house) of Nohant.

Death of Percy Bysshe Shelley.

1823

Birth of Maurice Dudevant, June 30, in Paris.

1824

Love fades between Casimir and Aurore as their differences in tastes spread (see the description of Colonel Delmare in *Indiana*) and Aurore's ennui deepens. They travel a good deal about France as some compensation.

1825

The pair vacation in the Pyrenees, where Aurore acquires a platonic lover, the young magistrate Aurélien de Sèze. Casimir eventually plays the complaisant husband, but the triangle proves unsatisfying for Aurore.

1827

Aurore rediscovers the friend of her youth, Stéphane de Grandsagne; they became lovers and meet in Paris.

Death of Ludwig van Beethoven.

1828

Aurore's daughter Solange is born, September 13, at Nohant; her father is most likely Stéphane de Grandsagne, not Casimir Dudevant.

1829

More traveling for the Dudevants. First writing of Aurore—about her travels—not to be published in her lifetime. Aurore sees Aurélien de Sèze from time to time with increasing dissatisfaction. Casimir meantime drinks, hunts, has a mistress or two, including a servant at Nohant.

1830

Aurore meets Jules Sandeau, nineteen, at a friend's château near Nohant in July; they become lovers. In November Aurore discovers and reads her husband's testament, addressed to her and to be opened on his death. "Good God! What a testament! Nothing but maledictions!"[1] she writes shortly afterward to her son's occasional tutor Jules Boucoiran and tells her husband, "I am leaving forever for Paris, and I am leaving the children at Nohant. I insist on an allowance." The allowance—actually money from the Nohant estate which was her grandmother's—is accorded. Aurore is to live six months a year in Paris—three months at a time—and six months in Nohant.

Meanwhile the July revolution of 1830 has driven Charles X into exile and Victor Hugo's *Hernani* has been performed, launching the Romantic revolution.

Stendhal's *Le Rouge et le Noir* (The Red and the Black) appears.

1831

Aurore arrives in Paris in January to live semiclandestinely with Jules Sandeau in a garret on the Left Bank of the Seine. She writes unsigned articles for the new, satirical paper, *Le Figaro*. She returns to Nohant for three months, then returns to Paris from Nohant. Several novelettes appear, signed "J. Sand," written in collaboration with Jules Sandeau. In December the five-volume novel *Rose et Blanche*, by "J. Sand," is announced.

1832

In February and March at Nohant, Aurore writes the novel first called *Noëmi* but later to be titled *Indiana*. She returns to Paris in April, bringing her daughter, Solange. In May, *Indiana*, signed "G. Sand," appears and is a success. Aurore quarrels with the indolent Jules Sandeau; they separate. *Valentine* by George Sand appears in November. Several novelettes by her are also published during the year.

1833

Sand meets actress Marie Dorval; they briefly become, in all probability, lovers (see the passage of *Lélia*, written at this time, describing women in love). A seven-day amorous fiasco follows with Prosper Mérimée, diplomat and author. (Sand: "I wept from the suffering, the disgust, and the discouragement."[2]) Sand meets Alfred de Musset, twenty-two, the golden boy of French poetry; they become lovers and leave for Venice. *Lélia* is published. Several short novels, including *Lavinia*, appear in various reviews.

1834

Sand and Musset alternately fall ill in Venice. A young doctor, Pietro Pagello, is sent for. Musset, cured, plunges into pleasures of Venice—ballets and brothels. Sand becomes lover of Pagello; terrible scenes occur with Musset, now very ill, who leaves for Paris in March, followed by Sand and Pagello in July. There follows a breakup with Pagello and a passionate but brief reunion with Musset. Publications of the year indicate Sand's intense, prolific, and parallel writing, which includes three novels—*Le Secrétaire Intime* (The Private Secretary), *Jacques*, and *Leone Leoni* (published serially in a review)—as well as four *Lettres d'un Voyageur* (Letters of a Traveler). The stay in Venice was paid for by Sand.

1835

There follows a reunion and final rupture with Musset. Sand meets Michel de Bourges, radical republican lawyer; they become lovers. A violent scene at Nohant occurs between Casimir and his wife; Sand sues for separation, with Michel as her lawyer. Publications: *André, Leone Leoni* (in book form), three *Lettres d'un Voyageur*, and other pieces.

1836

Musset's *Confessions d'un Enfant du Siècle* (Confessions of a Child of His Time), fictionally describing the liaison with Sand, among much else, is published. The tribunal at La Châtre decrees separation, which Casimir appeals, then finally agrees to, after a public

trial in Bourges. Sand and her two children join Franz
Liszt and Marie d'Agoult in Switzerland for a vacation. *Simon* and several *Lettres d'un Voyageur* appear.

1837

Liszt and Marie d'Agoult twice visit Nohant, now
Sand's. Sophie-Victoire, Sand's mother, dies; Sand's
daughter Solange is stolen away by Casimir then re-
taken from him. Sand writes and publishes *Mauprat*
(a precursor of Emily Brontë's *Wuthering Heights*),
and *Lettres d'un Voyageur* (in book form); also
Lettres à Marcie (Letters to Marcie), *Les Maîtres Mosaïstes* (The Master Mosaic Workers), and various
short pieces in reviews. (Almost all the novels appear
initially as magazine serials; only book publication
will be mentioned hereafter.)

1838

Honoré de Balzac visits Sand at Nohant. A nine-year
liaison begins with Frédéric Chopin, introduced to
Sand by Liszt. Sand, Chopin, and the children leave
for Majorca in October for the sake of Chopin's
health. They settle in the Charterhouse of Valldemosa. The damp, cold winter is disastrous for Chopin's tuberculosis. *La Dernière Aldini* (The Last Aldini) appears in France.

1839

Chopin, Sand, and the children depart from Valldemosa, arrive in Marseilles in February, and at Nohant in June. Sand and Chopin live together on Rue
Pigalle in Paris. *L'Uscoque, Spiridion,* and a revised

Lélia (one critic had greeted the original *Lélia* in 1833 as "filth and prostitution"[3]) are published.

1840

Son Maurice becomes a disciple of painter and friend Eugène Delacroix. Solange is sent to a boarding school. Sand's play *Cosima* is a failure, but she is already launched on her first proletarian, politically engaged, populist novel, *Le Compagnon du Tour de France* (The Journeyman-Carpenter, or the Companion of the Tour of France), which is published the same year and will greatly influence Walt Whitman in Brooklyn. Also published: *Gabriel, Les Sept Cordes de la Lyre* (The Seven Strings of the Lyre), and *Cosima* (as a novel).

Birth of Émile Zola.

1841

Pauline Viardot, concert singer, and husband visit Nohant. The Christian Socialist *Revue Indépendante* is started by Pierre Leroux, Louis Viardot, and George Sand. *Pauline* is published, as well as various articles and prefaces.

1842

Chopin and Delacroix stay at Nohant. Sand establishes a Paris residence at Square d'Orléans with Chopin. Publications: *Un Hiver à Majorque* (A Winter in Majorca); a second proletarian novel, *Horace;* and volumes 1 and 2 of *Consuelo,* whose protagonist is inspired by Pauline Viardot.

1843

Sand decries the scandal of Fanchette, a feeble-minded girl expelled and abandoned by the hospice of La Châtre. Volumes 3–8 of *Consuelo* are published, also *Fanchette*, and volumes 1 and 2 of *La Comtesse de Rudolstadt*, the sequel of *Consuelo* (often published together and among Sand's most important works, along with *Lélia* and the collected *Correspondance*).

1844

Sand initiates a progressive newspaper for La Châtre, *L'Éclaireur*. The sister and brother-in-law of Chopin visit Nohant. Sand publishes *Jeanne*, first of the pastoral novels, and the last volumes of *La Comtesse de Rudolstadt*, as well as various short pieces, particularly a series of four articles entitled *La Politique et le Socialisme* (Politics and Socialism).

1845

Sand publishes *Le Meunier d'Angibault* (The Miller of Angibault) and shorter pieces.

1846

Chopin's health worsens. So do the relations between Sand and Chopin as a triangular situation develops among Sand, Chopin, and daughter Solange; Chopin, perhaps unconsciously, is infatuated with Solange, who delights in playing the role of her mother's rival. Chopin leaves Nohant for the last time. Publications:

Isidora, Teverino, and *La Mare au Diable* (The Devil's Pool), second of the pastoral novels and written in four days.

Pierre Proudhon's *La Philosophie de la Misère* (The Philosophy of Poverty) appears.

1847

Marriage at Nohant of Solange and sculptor Auguste Clésinger. Painful scenes occur between the couple and George Sand which lead to a rupture between Solange and her mother. Chopin takes Solange's part. Sand and Chopin separate without formality. *Le Péché de M. Antoine* (The Sin of M. Antoine), *Le Piccinino,* and *Lucrezia Floriani,* a novel about Chopin and Sand, are published.

1848

Sand leaves promptly for Paris on hearing of the revolution which overthrew the monarchy in three days of February and drove Louis Philippe into exile. There follows her last encounter with Chopin. She becomes virtual Minister of Propaganda of the new republican government, which includes her friends Étienne Arago, Alexandre Ledru-Rollin, Louis Blanc, and Alphonse de Lamartine. Sand founds the shortlived periodical *La Cause du Peuple* and writes most of the issues of the *Bulletins de la République* (Bulletins of the Republic), which are distributed officially throughout France. *Bulletin* No. 4 extends the idea of republicanism to the extreme of utopian socialism. Another expresses the opinion that women suffer "the heaviest load of oppression."[4] *Bulletin* No. 16 suggests ignoring the coming election if the results are against the Republic. After the failure of the May 15 street demonstration and the arrest of Armand Barbès, Adolphe Blanqui, François Raspail, Pierre Leroux, and others, Sand leaves Paris for the refuge of Nohant. Publications: "Aux Riches" (Letter to the Rich), "Lettres au Peuple" (Letters to the People), and other political writings, including "Socialisme."

The Communist Manifesto of Karl Marx and Friedrich Engels appears.

1849

Birth of Solange's second daughter, Jeanne-Gabriel (the first had died shortly after birth in early 1848). Marie Dorval and Chopin die. *La Petite Fadette* is published. *François le Champi* (François the Foundling) is a success at the Odéon theater in Paris.

1850

The thirty-two-year-old engraver Alexandre Manceau, a friend of Maurice, arrives at Nohant and becomes Sand's secretary and soon her lover. The liaison will last until Manceau's death in 1865. *François le Champi* is published as both a play and a novel (the story of a woman who raises and then marries a foundling, called "the perfect incest" by one critic). Balzac dies.

1851

Several of Sand's plays are performed, with varying success. There is an inauguration at Nohant of a small theater. Publications: *Claudie* (play), *Molière* (play), *Le Château des Désertes*, and *Le Mariage de Victorine* (play).

Coup d'état by Louis Napoleon.

1852

Sand is received by Prince-Président Louis Napoleon; she pleads for amnesty of republican refugees and prisoners. She is criticized by many former republican friends. The Clésinger couple quarrel, leaving their child Jeanne-Gabriel (Nini) with Sand at Nohant. *Les Vacances de Pandolphe* (Pandolphe's Vacation) and *Le Démon du Foyer* (The Household Devil) are published.

Louis Napoleon becomes Napoleon III. In the United States, *Uncle Tom's Cabin*, by Harriet Beecher Stowe, appears and is hailed by Sand.

1853

Michel de Bourges dies. Several plays by Sand are performed, including a dramatization of *Mauprat*. Publications: *Mont-Revêche*, *La Filleule* (The Goddaughter), and *Les Maîtres Sonneurs* (The Master Bellringers).

1854

Sand's granddaughter Nini is bandied back and forth between her parents, to Sand's distress. Clésingers are officially separated. Publications: *Adriani*, *Flaminio*, and volumes 1–4 of *Histoire de Ma Vie* (Story of My Life), a major autobiographical work.

Birth of Arthur Rimbaud. Beginning of the Crimean

War (Russia versus Turkey and her allies, France and England).

1855

Nini, who had been placed by her parents in a boarding school, suddenly dies. Sand cries herself to sleep. She travels to Italy with her son, Maurice, for distraction. Volumes 5–20 of *Histoire de Ma Vie* are published, as well as *Maître Favilla* (play).

1856

Three plays by Sand are performed to mixed receptions. Sand publishes *Evenor et Leucippe*.

End of the Crimean War.

1857

Musset dies. Sand becomes enamored with the little village of Gargilesse, thirty miles from Nohant. Manceau buys a cottage for Sand and himself as an occasional retreat from Nohant and Maurice. Publications: *La Daniella* and *Le Diable aux Champs* (The Devil in the Fields).

Charles Baudelaire's *Les Fleurs du Mal* (The Flowers of Evil) and Gustave Flaubert's *Madame Bovary* appear.

1858

Sand frequently stays at Gargilesse with Manceau. She publishes *Les Beaux Messieurs de Bois-Doré* (The Gallant Lords of Bois-Doré) and *Légendes Rustiques*, with illustrations by Maurice.

1859

Sand does much writing, as usual, during the night, but little else. She publishes *Narcisse; Elle et Lui* (She and He), a novel about Musset and herself (to which Paul de Musset, Alfred's elder brother, will respond with *Lui et Elle*); *L'Homme de Neige* (The Snow Man); *Les Dames Vertes* (The Green Ladies); *Promenades Autour d'un Village* (Promenades About a Village); *La Guerre* (War); and *Garibaldi*. Also a play.

1860

Sand suffers a severe attack of typhus. She publishes *Jean de la Roche* and *Constance Verrier*.

1861

Sand publishes *La Ville Noire* (The Black City), *Le Marquis de Villemer*, *Valvèdre*, and *La Famille de Germandre*.

1862

Maurice marries Lina Calamatta, daughter of an engraver and old friend. Sand publishes *Autour de la Table* (Round the Table), *Souvenirs et Impressions Littéraires*, *Tamaris*, and two plays.

1863

A son, Marc-Antoine, is born to Maurice and Lina. Difficulties between Manceau and Maurice follow. Sand publishes *Mademoiselle La Quintinie*, a very suc-

cessful and controversial novel attacking church ortho-
doxy, and *Pourquoi les Femmes à l'Académie?* (Why
Women in the French Academy?).

1864

Forced to choose between her son Maurice and her
lover Manceau, Sand chooses Manceau. They leave
Nohant to live south of Paris in Palaiseau. In the
meantime, grandson Marc-Antoine, dies to Sand's
great distress. Dramatization of *Le Marquis de Villemer* very well received. Publishes *Théâtre de Nohant.*

1865

Manceau slowly, painfully, dies of tuberculosis on Au-
gust 21, at Palaiseau, despite Sand's devoted care.
Sand publishes *La Confession d'une Jeune Fille* (The
Confession of a Young Girl) and *Laura.*

1866

Aurore is born, the daughter of Maurice and Lina.
Sand visits Flaubert twice at Croisset to knot a grow-
ing friendship and correspondence. She publishes
Monsieur Sylvestre and two plays.

1867

Sand returns to Nohant. She publishes *Le Dernier
Amour* (The Last Love), possibly inspired by her last
lover, the painter Charles Marchal.

Zola's *Thérèse Raquin* appears.

1868

Sand visits a new friend, the young feminist writer Juliette Adam, as well as an old friend, Flaubert. She publishes *Cadio* and *Mademoiselle Merquem*.

1869

Flaubert stays at Nohant. No new books by Sand are published but fifty-five of her old titles are reprinted.

Birth of André Gide.

1870

Last play, *L'Autre* (The Other), not well received at the Odéon theater. Epidemic at Nohant forces temporary withdrawal of Dudevant family. Sand publishes *Pierre Qui Roule* (A Rolling Pierre, or Stone), *Le Beau Laurence,* and *Malgré Tout* (Despite Everything).

The Franco-Prussian War begins, July 19.

1871

Casimir Dudevant dies. Sand loses contact with republican friends; Paris is besieged. Sand writes against the Paris Commune of March, April, and May. She publishes *Césarine Dietrich* and *Journal d'un Voyageur Pendant la Guerre* (Diary of a Voyager During the War).

The Franco-Prussian War comes to an end.

1872

Sand offers to lend Flaubert money. Aged sixty-eight, she swims daily in the Indre. Ivan Turgenev and Pauline Viardot visit Nohant. Sand publishes *Francia* and *Nanou*.

1873

Flaubert and Turgenev visit Nohant. Sand travels one month throughout France despite her age. She publishes *Impressions et Souvenirs* and *Contes d'une Grand-mère* (Grandmother's Fairy Tales).

1874

Flu, rheumatism, and stomach trouble, trouble Sand, yet she manages one short trip to Paris. She publishes *Ma Soeur Jeanne* (My Sister Joan).

1875

Sand makes one last trip to Paris. She publishes *Flamarande* and *Les Deux Frères* (The Two Brothers).

1876

Sand is afflicted with an intestinal occlusion and takes to her bed on May 30, suffering terribly from the blockage. She dies on June 8, just short of her seventy-second birthday and two days before the appearance of *La Tour de Percemont* (The Tower of Percemont). Her *Marianne Chevreuse* was also published that year. Flaubert, who had read them serially, wrote to Sand: *"La Tour de Percemont* pleased me extremely, but *Marianne* has literally enchanted me."[5]

NOVELS

Indiana

(1832)

Indiana *was the first novel signed "G. Sand." Six months before its appearance, a novel written jointly by George Sand (then Aurore Dudevant) and Jules Sandeau,* Rose et Blanche, *signed "J. Sand," had been published with success and some acclaim. The "Rose" of the title was an actress and "Blanche," a nun. Chapters and sections of the novel, such as scenes of the Pyrenees and the English convent, may be identified as Sand's work. Eventually, neither Sand nor Sandeau claimed the novel.*

Possibly aware of the joint authorship, a reviewer in the Paris periodical L'Artiste, *of December 1831, decried the novel's "equivocal, leering head so maladroitly grafted to a pure, decent body."[1] Sand's mother said she was shocked by it. In reply, George Sand wrote: "I agree completely with your criticisms, but I have already told you that the book is not mine alone. There are many farcical parts I disapprove of, but which I accepted in order to satisfy my publisher, who wanted a* spicy *novel. . . . There is nothing like that* in the novel I am now writing, *and this time nothing of my collaborator will be attached to it, except his name."*[2]

The novel in progress, initially titled Noëmi (*see p. 329*), became Indiana. *It was written in two months; there are lapses, repetitions, and a few contradictions (of a trivial nature) which have been left for the reader to discover (he or she might also turn to p. 422 for Sand's own apology). Dots indicate lesser cuts, asterisks greater; together, they account for less than one fourth of the original French text. (The reader might also bear in mind that normally English translated into French expands about fifteen per cent; ideally, French into English should mean a reduction by a similar percentage, however this rarely happens.)*

The two prefaces by George Sand—written ten years apart—are priceless indications of the writer's intentions, realizations, critical receptions, and social impact. The first follows immediately; the second has been placed after Indiana. ❦—

GEORGE SAND'S PREFACE TO THE 1832 EDITION OF *INDIANA*[3]

Should pages of this book incur the grave reproach of inclination toward new beliefs, should severe judges find their tone imprudent and dangerous, one would

have to reply to critics that they do too much honor to
a work of no importance; that to grapple with lofty
questions of the social order, one should feel oneself
endowed with immense spiritual force or great talent;
and that such presumption has nothing to do with so
simple a story, of which the writer created almost
nothing. If, in the course of his task, he happened to
express laments torn from his characters by the social
malaise of which they are victims, if he dared echo
their aspirations for a better existence, let the reader
blame society for its inequalities and destiny for its
whims! The writer is no more than a mirror which
reflects them, a machine which traces them; and he
owes no one apologies if his prints are exact and his
images faithful.

Bear, then, in mind that the narrator did not take as
a subject or slogan some scattered cries of pain and
anger from the drama of human life. He does not for
a moment claim to conceal a profound moral in the
form of a tale; he has not come to add a stone to the
uncertain edifice of the future, nor to throw one at the
crumbling edifice of the past. He knows too well that
we live in a time of moral ruin, when human reason
needs blinders to soften the all too radiant light that
dazzles it. If he had thought himself enough of a
scholar to write a truly useful book, he would have
tempered the truth rather than have exposed it with
its raw colors and cutting lines. Such a book would
have had the effect of dark glasses on tired eyes.

Not that he renounces fulfilling this noble and generous task some day; but young as he is, he recounts

what he has seen without daring to draw conclusions on this immense process between past and future that perhaps no man of the present generation has the competence to judge. Too honest to conceal his doubts but too timid to set them up as certainties, he relies on your reflection and abstains from weaving preconceived ideas and hardened judgments into the fabric of his story. He performs his craft as storyteller with meticulous care. He will tell you all, even that which is outrageously true; but if you deck him in a philosopher's robe, you will embarrass him, simple entertainer that he is, charged with diverting but not with instructing you.

Had he been more mature or more gifted, he would still not have dared touch the gaping wounds of a civilization in agony. One would have to be so sure of healing them before taking the risk of probing them! He would much rather try to reattach you to ancient ruined beliefs, to old lost devotions, than use his talent —if he had any—to trample on overturned altars. However, he knows that with the prevailing spirit of charity, a sensitive conscience is scorned by public opinion as hypocritical reserve—as, in the arts, a timid bearing is ridiculed as quaint decorum; but he knows that there is honor, if not profit, in the defense of lost causes.

To whoever misjudges the spirit of this book, such a profession of faith will sound like a hopeless anachronism. The narrator hopes that after having heard his story to the end, few listeners will deny the *morality* that emerges from its facts, triumphant as in all human affairs. It seemed to him, on finishing his tale, that his conscience was clear. He flattered himself with having portrayed social misery without too much melancholy, human passion without excessive passion. He muted his strings when they sounded too harshly; he tried to stifle those notes of the soul which should remain silent, those voices of the heart one cannot awake without danger.

You will perhaps do him justice by admitting that he has shown how miserable is the creature who transgresses his rightful bounds, how desolate the heart that rebels against the decrees of his destiny. If he did not give the best possible role to the character who depicts the *law*, if he portrayed as more sullen the other who represents *opinion*, you will find a third who represents *illusion* and who thwarts without pity the vain hopes, the mad endeavors of passion. Finally, you will see that if he did not strew rose petals on the patch of ground where the law fences in our wills like sheep, neither did he plant thorns on the road that leads away from it.

That, I think, should suffice to insure this book against the charge of immorality; but if you insist that all novels end like Marmontel's tales, you will perhaps reproach me for the last pages. You will disapprove the fact that I did not plunge into misery and abandon that creature who violated human laws throughout the two volumes. Here let the author reply that before being moral, he wanted to be true; that, feeling too young to write a philosophical treatise on the art of bearing with life, he was content with narrating *In-*

diana, a tale of the human heart with its failings, its cruelties, its rights and wrongs, its virtues and vices.

Indiana—if you insist on explaining everything—is woman herself, that frail creature charged by the author to represent those passions which are repressed or, if you prefer, suppressed by social laws. She is free will grappling with necessity; she is love butting her head blindly against all the obstacles placed before her by civilization. But the serpent wears and breaks its teeth gnawing obstinately on a file, and the powers of the soul are drained in ruthless combat with the reality of life. Such is what you can gather from this anecdote; it was in this spirit that it was told to him who passes it on to you.

Despite his protestations, the narrator expects reproaches. Honest souls and honorable consciences might take alarm at seeing virtue so harsh, reason so dreary, and opinion so unjust. This terrifies him: for a writer fears nothing more than alienating the faith of men of good will, arousing fatal sympathies in embittered souls, poisoning the raw wounds inflicted by society on impetuous and rebel minds.

Nothing is easier to conquer and more dishonorable to court than success based on illicit appeal to the passions of the times. The author of *Indiana* denies ever having dreamed of this. Should it obtain this result, he would destroy his book, notwithstanding that naïve paternal love that pampers rickety creatures in these days of literary miscarriages.

But he hopes to defend himself by saying that he thought he would better serve his principles with authentic examples than with poetic fantasies. With its aura of sad sincerity, the story will—he thinks—move young, ardent minds. They will find it hard to distrust a storyteller who goes his way recklessly in the world of reality, fraternizing left and right with no greater deference for one side than for the other. To describe a cause as odious or absurd is not to combat but to persecute it. The storyteller's art is perhaps nothing more than awakening to their own true stories the fallen he wants to raise up, the suffering unhappy he wants to heal.

To insist on clearing it of all blame would be giving too much importance to a work which is likely to make little stir. The author thus yields completely to his critics. One sole charge is too serious to be admitted: that of having written a dangerous book. He would rather remain unknown forever than erect his glory on the ruins of his conscience. He thus adds a few more lines to deny this charge he fears most.

Raymon, you will say, is society; egoism is morality and reason. Raymon, the author will answer, is that false reasoning, that false morality by which society is governed. He is a man of honor as the world understands it, because the world never looks close enough to see everything. The good citizen stands by Raymon, and you will not say he is the enemy of order; for he sacrifices his happiness, he sacrifices himself, in the name of social order.

You will then say that virtue was not very brilliantly rewarded. Alas!—others will answer—nowadays virtue triumphs only in the *théâtres du boulevard.*

The author will say that he was committed to portraying, not a virtuous society, but one of necessity, and that honor, like heroism, has become rare in these days of moral decadence. Do you think this truth disgusts truly honorable souls? I believe the exact contrary.

PART ONE

I

In the small château of Lagny, in Brie, one cool rainy evening of autumn, three individuals were pensively watching the wood burn in the fireplace and the hands of a clock drag slowly around the dial. Two of the individuals seemed to abandon themselves wholly to the vague ennui weighing upon them, but the third showed signs of rebellion. He squirmed on his seat, half stifled a few weary yawns, and struck at the snapping logs with his tongs as if to do battle with the common enemy.

Much older than the other two, this personage was the master of the house, Colonel Delmare, an elderly retired army officer, once handsome, now gross, gray in the mustache, fierce of eye, and growing bald; an excellent master, in short, before whom all trembled—wife, servants, horses, and dogs.

He quit his chair, obviously irritated by his not quite knowing how to break the silence, and began to stomp up and down the length of the salon, without for a moment losing the rigid bearing of a soldier, balancing his weight on his hips and turning smartly on his heels with the eternal smugness of the parade officer.

But the glorious days were long past when Lieutenant Delmare had sniffed victories in the very air of the camps; a retired field officer forgotten by an ungrateful nation, he now felt sentenced to the punishing consequences of marriage. He was the husband of a young, pretty wife, proprietor of a commodious manor house, and, what's more, a successful manufacturer. But the weather was very damp, the colonel rheumatic and, so, in a foul mood.

He tramped up and down the salon, which was furnished in Louis XV style, occasionally stopping before a door topped by naked, painted cupids leading decorous fawns and tame boar with chains of flowers and sometimes before a panel overcharged with mediocre, maltreated sculptures whose tortuous convolutions wearied the eye. But these passing distractions did not prevent the colonel, as he turned on his heel, from casting a searching look at his two silent companions, shifting his eye from the one to the other, the same watchful eye which had been standing vigil for the past three years over a fragile, priceless treasure—his wife.

For the colonel's wife was nineteen, and if you had seen her huddled under the mantel of that huge fireplace of white marble and burnished copper, if you had seen her, slender, pale, and sad, her elbow on her knee, a young wife alongside an aging husband in an antiquated household, like a flower blooming in a Gothic vase, you would have pitied the wife of Colonel Delmare, and perhaps the colonel even more.

The third occupant of this lonely house was seated in the same corner of the fireplace, at the other end of the burning log. He was a man in the flower and strength of youth, whose rosy cheeks, flowing blond hair, and luxuriant side whiskers clashed with the graying hair, leathering skin, and hard face of the colonel. But the least artistic of men might have preferred the stern, austere look of Monsieur Delmare to the younger man's blander, if more regular, features. . . .

The only cheerful, affectionate face in the group was that of a handsome hunting dog, a large pointer whose head lay full length on the knees of the young man. . . . Half-lighted by the flaring logs, the scene could have been a Rembrandt painting: white, fugitive gleams fitfully brightened the room and the faces, then died down to the rose-glow of the embers, the vast living room darkening into gloom. . . .

From the immobility of the two figures silhouetted against the fire one might have said they dreaded to disturb the very immobility of the scene, that they had become statues, like characters in a fairy tale, that the slightest word or movement might bring the walls of an imaginary city crumbling down upon them. And the glowering master of the house, whose tramping alone disturbed the silent shadows, seemed like a sorcerer who held them under his spell.

At last the pointer, having won a friendly glance

from her master, surrendered to the magnetic power wielded by the eye of man upon animals. A low, affectionate whimper broke from her; with inimitable grace and suppleness she rose and placed two paws on her beloved's shoulders.

"Down, Ophelia, down!"

Gravely and in English the young man reprimanded the gentle creature, who crawled, shamed the repentant, to Madame Delmare as if to beg for her protection. But Madame Delmare did not stir from her reverie; she allowed Ophelia's head to rest on her hands, which were clasped on her knee, but she did not caress her.

"Has that bitch taken over the living room?" demanded the colonel, secretly delighted to have an excuse for ill humor—and simply to pass the time. "Off to the kennel, Ophelia! Out, you stupid beast!"

Had someone closely observed Madame Delmare, he could have perceived in that trivial, vulgar incident of her domestic life the secret sadness of her entire existence. An almost imperceptible shudder sent a wave through her body; her hands which mechanically held the dog's head tightened convulsively around her rough, furred neck as if to defend her. Delmare, drawing his riding crop from the pocket of his jacket, strode menacingly toward the poor beast, which crouched at his feet, closed her eyes, and whimpered. Madame Delmare's pale face whitened, her bosom heaved, and turning her great blue eyes toward her husband, she cried with indescribable dread:

"For pity's sake, sir, do not kill her!"

The exclamation startled the colonel. Anger gave way to chagrin. "That, madame, is a reproach I understand very well," he said. "Since the day I killed your spaniel in a moment of anger, you haven't stopped reproaching me for it. And what a loss *he* was! Forever losing his head and rushing the game! He would have made *anyone* lose his temper! Anyway, you never loved him until he was dead, or paid him any attention. But now that you have a chance to blame me for something—"

"Have I ever reproached you?" asked Madame Delmare with the gentleness we adopt out of generosity when we love and out of self-respect when we do not.

"I never said that," replied the colonel with the tone of one who is half-father, half-husband, "but there are more bitter reproaches in the tears of some women than in all the damnations of others. Blast, madame! You know damn well I don't want weeping about me."

"You never see me weep, I believe."

"Ha! Your eyes are always red! That's worse, by God!"

During the husband-wife conversation, the young man had risen and led Ophelia out with the greatest calm. Then he returned, lit a candle, and sat down opposite Madame Delmare.

This chance act had a sudden effect on the mood of Delmare. When the steadier light of the candle fell upon his wife, he could see the signs of suffering and dejection in her bearing, her general weariness, the long strands of hair falling across her gaunt cheeks, the purplish rings under her tired, inflamed eyes. He took a few turns around the room, then returned to his wife with an abrupt change in manner.

"How do you feel today, Indiana?" he asked, with the clumsiness of a man whose heart and character are rarely in accord.

"As usual, I thank you," she replied, showing neither surprise nor rancor.

"'As usual' is hardly an answer," he said. "Rather, it's a woman's answer, a Norman answer, meaning neither yes nor no, well or sick!"

"Yes, I am neither well nor sick."

"You lie," he said with renewed bluntness. "I know you are not well; you said so to Sir Ralph here. Let's see if it's *I* who am lying. Tell us, did she or didn't she say so, Monsieur Ralph?"

"She did," replied that phlegmatic individual, paying no attention to Indiana's reproachful look.

At that moment a fourth person entered: the steward of the house, a former sergeant of Delmare's regiment. In a few words he explained to the colonel that he had reason to believe that some coal thieves had been prowling in the park at this hour the last few nights and that he wanted a gun when he made his rounds before locking the gates. Delmare, smelling powder in the affair, fetched his shotgun, gave Lelièvre another, and started to leave the salon.

"What!" exclaimed Madame Delmare, dismayed. "You would kill a poor peasant for a few sacks of coal?"

"I'd kill any man like a dog," said Delmare irritably,

"who came prowling about my grounds at night. If you knew the law, madame, you would know my rights."

"It's a terrible law!" Indiana cried impulsively, then immediately repressed the impulse and said in a quieter voice, "Your rheumatism—remember, it is raining and you will suffer tomorrow if you go out tonight."

"You're pretty worried about your old husband!" Delmare retorted, opening the door violently. And he went out, muttering about his age and his wife.

II

The two individuals we have just named, Indiana Delmare and Sir Ralph, or, if you prefer, Mr. Rodolphe Brown, remained facing each other, as calmly and coolly as if the husband were still between them. The Englishman didn't dream of defending himself, and Madame Delmare felt she didn't really have anything for which to reproach him, since he had spoken out of good intentions. At last, breaking the silence with some effort, she mildly rebuked him.

"It wasn't good of you, my dear Ralph," she said. "I had forbidden you to repeat what I had told you under the stress of a moment's illness, and Monsieur Delmare is the last person I would have know I was sick."

"I don't understand you, my dear," replied Sir Ralph. "You are ill and you don't want to take care of yourself. I had to choose between the risk of offending you and the necessity of informing your husband."

"Yes," she said with a sad smile, "so you chose to inform the authorities!"

"Upon my word, you are wrong, wrong to let yourself be so bitter toward the colonel; he is a man of honor, a worthy man."

"But who told you the contrary, Sir Ralph?"

"Why, you do, without intending it. Your sadness, your sickly state, and, as he himself has remarked, your red eyes tell everybody on every occasion that you are unhappy."

"Hush, Sir Ralph, you go too far. I haven't permitted you to know so much."

"I make you angry, I can see, but I can't help it. I am quite clumsy; I don't have the subtleties of your French language, and besides, I have too many similarities to your husband. Like him, I am completely ignorant in French *and* English as to what to say in French *or* English to a woman to console her. . . . It's not the first time that I have noticed how, particularly in France, words count more than ideas. Women more than—"

"Oh, you have a profound contempt for women, my dear Ralph. I am alone here against you two; I must resign myself to being always in the wrong."

"Tell us *we* are wrong, my dear cousin, by being well, by resuming your gaiety, your freshness, your former liveliness; remember Bourbon Island* and our

* Now the French island of Réunion, located in the Indian Ocean.

delightful retreat, Bernica, and our happy childhood, and our old friendship—"

"I remember my father, too," said Indiana, sadly dwelling on the thought, and she put her hand in Sir Ralph's.

They fell again into deep silence.

"Indiana," said Ralph after a pause, "happiness is always within grasp. We have only to reach out to seize it. What do you lack? You have a comfortable life, which is more than great wealth, an excellent husband who loves you with all his heart, and, I dare say, a sincere and devoted friend—"

Madame Delmare pressed Sir Ralph's hand lightly, but her mood did not change; her head still drooped, her moist eyes were still fixed gloomily on the glowing embers.

"Your sadness, my dear friend," Sir Ralph continued, "is pure morbidity. Who of us escapes problems or depressions? Look about you and you can see those who envy you, with reason. Man is made that way: he always wants what he doesn't have—"

I'll spare you a thousand other commonplaces of the good Sir Ralph. . . .

When he saw that Madame Delmare was forcing herself to listen to him, he stopped talking, and all one could hear was the multitude of tiny voices of the fireplace—the plaintive song of a heated, swelling log, the crackling of burned, curling bark, the light phosphorescent explosions with their bluish flame. From time to time, through the cracks of the door, the howling of a dog was heard mingled with the whistling of the wind and the beating of the rain against the window. It was one of the saddest evenings of Madame Delmare's life in the small manor house of Brie.

And I know not what vague premonition weighed on this impressionable soul. . . .

"I am afraid," she said to Sir Ralph with a shiver. "I feel faint."

And her lips became as white as her cheeks. Sir Ralph, more terrified by her deadly pallor than by her premonitions, which he regarded as signs of profound moral fatigue, violently tugged the bell cord for assistance. No one came. As Indiana grew visibly weaker, an alarmed Sir Ralph drew her away from the fire, placed her on a chaise longue, ran for the servants, looked for water or smelling salts, found neither, broke all the bell cords, lost his way in the confusion of dark rooms, and wrung his hands with impatience and anger at himself.

At last he thought of opening the glazed door that gave onto the park, and he cried in turn for Lelièvre and Noun, the Creole maid of Madame Delmare.

A few minutes later Noun came running from one of the darkest paths of the park and urgently inquired whether her mistress was worse than usual.

"Much worse," replied Ralph Brown.

The two returned to the living room and tried to revive the unconscious Madame Delmare, the one with clumsy, useless zeal, the other with the skill and efficiency of a woman's devotion.

Noun was the foster sister of Madame Delmare; raised together, the two young women greatly loved each other. Tall, strong, buoyantly healthy, lively and alert, overfull of passionate Creole blood, Noun's resplendent beauty put further into the shade the pale, frail beauty of her mistress; but their hearts' generosity and the strength of their friendship stifled all sense of feminine rivalry.

When Madame Delmare came to herself, the first thing she noticed was her maid's distressed state—the damp, disordered hair, the agitation betrayed in every movement.

"Don't be upset, my poor child," she said with concern. "My illness seems to affect you more than it does me. Go, Noun, take care of yourself; you've been growing thin, and now you are weeping as if you were dying! My dear Noun, *your* future is bright and joyous."

Noun pressed her mistress' hand to her lips with fervor, and cried in a frenzy, glancing wildly about her: "My God, madame, do you know why Monsieur Delmare is outside in the park?"

"*Why?*" Indiana faintly echoed, losing the little color which had returned to her cheeks. "Wait—what is happening?—You frighten me!"

"Monsieur Delmare," said Noun brokenly, "he says there are thieves in the park. He's looking for them with Lelièvre; they both have guns!"

"And?" asked Indiana, anticipating the worst.

"And . . . ?" repeated Noun, worrying her hands. "How horrible to think they are going to kill a man!"

"Kill a man?" cried Madame Delmare, rising with

the terror of a child frightened by the tales of her nurse.

"Oh, yes! They will kill him!" said Noun, stifling her sobs.

"These two women are mad," thought Sir Ralph, who looked upon the scene with stupefaction. "Then again," he added to himself, "all women are."

"What are you saying, Noun?" Madame Delmare continued. "Do you believe there are thieves out there?"

"If only they were thieves! But they might be some poor peasant who is after a handful of wood for his family."

"Oh! That would be horrible! But it is not likely . . . ?"

Noun was no longer listening; she moved from the window to her mistress' chaise longue, she strained to hear the slightest noise, torn between the yearning to run after Delmare and that of staying with the invalid. Her anxiety seemed so strange, so displaced, that Brown lost his usual gentleness and seized her by the arm, crying: "Have you lost your senses completely? Don't you see you are frightening your mistress with your silly fears?"

Noun did not hear him; she had turned her eyes toward her mistress, who had started in her chair as if she had been shocked by electricity. Almost instantly the sound of a gun rattled the windows and Noun fell to her knees.

"What miserable womanly fears!" cried Sir Ralph, weary of their emotions. "In a minute they will be triumphantly bringing you a dead rabbit, and you will laugh at yourselves."

"No, Ralph," said Madame Delmare, walking with a firm step toward the door. "I tell you, human blood has been spilled!"

With a piercing cry, Noun slumped to the floor. A shout was heard from Lelièvre in the park: "There he is! Good shot, colonel, the beggar is down!"

Sir Ralph stirred. He followed Madame Delmare. A few moments later a bleeding, seemingly dead man was carried onto the porch.

"Stop that noise, enough of that shouting!" said the colonel with rough gaiety to the frightened servants crowding around the wounded man. "It's only a joke; my shotgun was loaded with nothing but salt; I don't think I even touched him."

"But the blood, sir," said Madame Delmare reproachfully. "Did fear make it flow?"

"Why are you here, madame?" cried Delmare. "What are you doing here?"

"My duty, repairing your wrong, sir," she replied coldly, and she went to the wounded man with a courage none present had shown and held a light to his face.

Under the light, instead of the common face and clothes they expected, they saw a young man of noble features, tastefully dressed, albeit in hunting clothes. He had a light wound in one hand, but his torn garments and unconscious state told of a bad fall.

"It certainly was," Lelièvre confirmed. "He fell twenty feet. He was at the top of the wall when the colonel shot and hit him in the hand with the salt, and he couldn't hold on. I saw him fall, and when he hit the ground, poor devil, he couldn't even think of running away."

"How is it possible," said one of the maids, "that a gentleman dressed like him should steal for fun?"

"And his pockets are full of money!" said another, who had loosened the supposed robber's jacket.

"It's very strange," said the colonel, not unmoved as he looked down at the outstretched man. "If the man is dead, it's not my fault. Look at his hand, madame, if you find one grain of lead—"

"I'd like to believe you, sir," replied Madame Delmare, who felt the man's pulse and the arteries of his neck with an unexpected sangfroid and courage. . . .

She ordered the wounded man to be carried to the nearby billiard room. A mattress was placed on benches and Indiana, assisted by her servants, dressed the wounded hand, while Sir Ralph, who knew something about surgery, bled the man profusely.

Meanwhile, the clearly embarrassed colonel found himself in the awkward situation of a man. who had behaved more wickedly than he had intended. He felt obliged to justify himself in the eyes of others, or rather have them justify him in his own. . . . They all agreed with their master, as the gardener quietly drew him aside and assured him that the thief looked exactly like a young landowner, recently installed in the neighborhood, whom he had seen in conversation with Mademoiselle Noun three days before at a country fete.

This news gave another turn to Delmare's thoughts; his bald, glistening forehead throbbed with a suddenly swollen vein, sure sign of an approaching storm.

"Blast!" he exclaimed, clenching his fists, "Madame Delmare is certainly taking an interest in that country dandy who sneaks into my park over the wall!" And he strode into the billiard room, pale and trembling with anger.

III

"Reassure yourself, sir," Indiana said to him. "The man you tried to kill will be all right in a few days. At least, we hope so, although he hasn't yet spoken."

"That's no concern of mine," said the colonel tautly. "What I want to know is the name of that *interesting* patient and how he happened to mistake the wall of my park for the path to my house."

"I have absolutely no idea," replied Madame Delmare with such proud coldness that for an instant her husband was stunned.

However, returning quickly to his jealous suspicions, he said in a low voice, "I will find out, madame; rest assured, I will know."

Then, as Madame Delmare feigned to ignore his fury and continued caring for the wounded man, he left the room so that he might not explode before the servants, and summoned the gardener. "What is the name of that man who, you say, looks like our burglar?"

"Monsieur de Ramière, sir. He just bought the little English house of Monsieur de Cercy."

"What kind of a man is he? A nobleman, a fop, a
dandy?"

"A very fine gentleman, a nobleman, I think."

"That must be our Monsieur de Ramière! Tell me,
Louis," he said, lowering his voice, "did you ever see
that fop prowling around here?"

"Sir," began Louis uncertainly, "last night—I certainly saw—I'm not sure he was a fop—but I'm certain
he was a man."

"And you saw him?"

"As I see you—under the windows of the orangery."

"And you didn't go after him with your shovel?"

"Sir, I was just going to, but I saw a woman in
white come out of the orangery and go to him. So I
said to myself, 'Perhaps monsieur and madame took it
into their heads to take a walk before daybreak.' So I
went back to bed. But in the morning I heard Lelièvre
mention seeing tracks of a thief in the garden, so I
said to myself, 'There's something funny going on.'"

"And why didn't you tell me instantly, stupid?"

"Virgin Mary! There are some things in life, sir—"

"I understand—you dared to think. You are stupid . . ."

Delmare returned to the billiard room, and without
paying attention to the wounded man's stirring, he
began to search the pockets of his jacket hanging on a
chair, whereupon the man stretched out a hand and
said faintly: "You want to know who I am, sir, but it
is useless. I will tell you when we are alone. Until

then, spare me the embarrassment of revealing who I am in this tiresome and ridiculous situation."

"It's really too bad!" said the colonel sourly. "But I must confess I don't give a tinker's damn. However, since I suspect we'll meet again, you and I, I'll wait until then to make your acquaintance. Meanwhile, might I know where you should be taken?"

"To the inn of the nearest village, if you don't mind."

"But Monsieur is in no condition to be moved," said Madame Delmare warmly. "Is it not so, Ralph?"

"The gentleman's condition affects you too much, madame," said the colonel. "Leave the room, the rest of you!" he cried to the servants. "Monsieur is much better, and he will be strong enough now to explain his presence in my house."

"Certainly, sir," replied the wounded man, "and I beg all of you who were so kind as to take care of me to hear me acknowledge my wrong. I feel it is very important that there be no misunderstanding about my conduct, and it is important to me that I do not seem to be what I am not. Let me tell you then what brought me here. You, sir, have installed with the simplest means, known only to you, the finest and most efficient factory in these parts. My brother owns a similar factory in the south, but its maintenance costs enormous sums. His operations had become disastrous, when I heard of your success; so I promised myself to ask your advice as a favor which would not hurt your own interests, since my brother has a different product.

"However, the gate of your garden was kept closed

to me, and when I asked to see you, I was told you allowed no one ever to visit your establishment. Rebuffed by this discourteous refusal, I resolved then to save the honor and life of my brother at the risk of my own: I entered your grounds at night over the wall, and I tried to enter your factory to examine its machinery. . . . And now, sir, if you demand any satisfaction other than my explanation, you shall have it as soon as I am strong enough, and perhaps it will be I who demand it of *you*."

"I believe, sir, we should call it quits," said the colonel, partly relieved of his great anxiety. "The rest of you are witnesses of the gentleman's explanation. I am satisfied with it. Leave us now so we can talk about my business affairs."

The servants departed, but only they believed in the reconciliation. The wounded man, tired by his long speech, was in no state to appreciate the tone of the colonel's last remark. He fell back into Madame Delmare's arms and again fainted. She leaned over him, not deigning to notice her husband's anger, and the two faces above her, that of Delmare, white and crisp with rage, and that of Brown, calm and inscrutable as ever, queried each other in silence.

Delmare didn't need to say a word to indicate his feelings; however he drew Sir Ralph aside, crushed his fingers with a grip, and said: "My friend, it's a finely spun plot. I'm happy, really happy with the young man's quickness of mind in saving my face before the servants. But, by God, he'll pay for what I feel deep down. And that woman who's nursing him and pretends not to know him—how sly those creatures are by nature!"

Sir Ralph, stunned, paced up and down the room three times. On the first round he drew this conclusion: *improbable*; on the second: *impossible*; on the third: *proven*. Then, returning to the colonel with a glacial expression, he pointed to Noun, who stood wringing her hands behind the wounded man, her eyes haggard, her cheeks livid, stiff with despair, fear, and bewilderment. And the colonel was more struck by the violence of Sir Ralph's gesture than by any possible eloquence. . . .

Delmare did not require more evidence; he had only to read the girl's face to see that she alone was guilty. Nonetheless, his wife's zeal in tending the hero of this amorous affair became increasingly displeasing.

"Indiana," he said, "leave us. It is late and you are not well. Noun will take care of this man during the night and tomorrow, if he is better, we'll have him taken to the inn."

There was no denying such unexpected considerateness. . . . An hour later, after all had gone to bed and the house was still, Delmare slipped quietly back to the room, hid behind a curtain, and confirmed his suspicions from their conversation that the young man and the maid were indeed having an affair. The striking beauty of the young Creole had created a sensation at the local balls. Suitors didn't lack even from the best families of the countryside. More than one handsome officer among the lancers garrisoned at Melun went into debt trying to please her; but Noun

was still to know her first love and only the attention
of one man flattered her—that of Monsieur de Ramière.

Colonel Delmare had little interest in further following the evolution of their affair, and so withdrew. . . . In the morning Sir Ralph satisfied himself
concerning the wounded man's recovery. His fall,
however violent, had had no serious consequences; his
wound had already commenced to heal. Monsieur de
Ramière indicated his wish to be taken immediately
to Melun; there he gave his servants money, ad-
monishing them to keep quiet about his misadventure,
so as, he said, not to upset his mother who lived several leagues away. Thus the story only slowly became
known and in a variety of versions. . . . The colonel
and Sir Ralph had the delicacy to keep Noun's secret,
not even letting her know they knew it; and the Delmare household soon ceased to talk about the incident.

IV

You may find it difficult to believe that Raymon de
Ramière, a young, brilliant man of considerable
talents and qualities, who was accustomed to success
in both the salon and the boudoir, had conceived an
enduring passion for the maid of a household in Brie.
Monsieur de Ramière was nevertheless neither fop nor
libertine. He was intelligent—that is, he fully appreciated the advantages of birth. . . . Unfortunately,
what was most striking about him were not his princi-

ples, which he shared with many other white-gloved *philosophes* and which kept him no more than they from inconsistencies, but rather his passions, which his principles could not suppress and which made him a man apart in that decadent society where being different meant the risk of being ridiculous. . . .

Monsieur de Ramière was infatuated with the young Creole of the great black eyes who had filled the countryside with admiration at the Rubelles fete; but he was infatuated, nothing more. He had approached her out of boredom, perhaps, and success had inflamed his desires; the response had been greater than his demand, and on the day of his easy triumph he had returned home in a panic from his victory and, striking his forehead, had said to himself: "God help me if she loves me!"

Only after having accepted all the proof possible of Noun's love had he begun to suspect its very existence. Then he repented, but it was too late; he had to resign himself to the consequences or retreat like a coward. Raymon did not hesitate; he allowed himself to be loved and he returned the love from gratitude; he scaled the walls of Delmare's grounds out of love of danger; he had had a bad fall from clumsiness; and he was so touched by his young, beautiful mistress's grief that he considered himself justified in his own eyes to go on digging the pit into which she must fall.

Once he had recovered his strength, no winter ice, no nocturnal danger, no needling remorse could keep him from crossing a corner of the forest to meet his Creole mistress, swear to her he had never loved anyone but herself, preferred her to all the queens of the earth, and a thousand other hyperboles which will always find an audience among poor, gullible young women.

In January Madame Delmare left for Paris with her husband; Ralph Brown, their good neighbor, withdrew to his estate and Noun, left in charge of the country house, was free to go and come on a variety of pretexts—unfortunately for her, because the facile rendezvous with her lover greatly shortened the ephemeral happiness she would enjoy. The forest with its poesy, its girandoles of frost, its filtered moonlight, the mysterious little garden gate, the furtive departures at dawn when Noun's small feet left fugitive tracks in the snow as she accompanied her lover to the gate—all these accessories of an amorous adventure prolonged the intoxication of Raymon de Ramière.

But when Noun came to him at his home, in her white apron and country-style head scarf, scorning caution and defying danger in her turn, she became nothing more than the maid of a pretty woman, a soubrette for a man's pastime. And yet Noun was very striking; it was dressed like this that he had seen her for the first time at the village dance, when he shouldered his way through the crowd of admirers and carried her off in triumph from twenty rivals. Noun would tenderly remind him of that day: she did not know, poor child, that Raymon's love did not date from then, that *her* day of pride was *his* day of conceit. And besides, the courage with which she sacrificed her reputation, which should have made him love her the more, displeased Raymon de Ramière. The wife of a French lord who would sacrifice herself thus would be a magnificent conquest, but a lady's maid! That which is heroic in the one becomes brazen in the other. With the one a world of jealous rivals envies you; with the other a scrum of scandalized lackeys condemns you. The lady sacrifices twenty former lovers for you; the lady's maid sacrifices only the husband she might have had.

What can you expect? Raymon was a man of modish morality pursuing elegance in life and poetry in love. For him a grisette was not quite a woman, and Noun, because of her incomparable beauty, had taken him by surprise in the easygoing atmosphere of popular gaiety. None of this was Raymon's fault; he had been raised for high society, his thinking had been directed toward an elevated goal, his faculties had been conditioned for priceless pleasures, and it was despite himself that his blood's ardor had driven him into a bourgeois's amorous adventure. . . .

If he had really loved his mistress, he could still have found happiness with her—and consequently given it to her—by sacrificing his future, his family, and his reputation, for love is as good a contract as marriage. But with his ardor already cooled, he felt, what future could he make for her? Should he marry her only to show her daily a sad face, an easily offended heart and a joyless home? Should he marry her in order to make her hateful to her family, contemptible to her peers, ridiculous to her servants; to risk placing her in a social world where she would feel out of place, where humiliation would be her death; and finally to crush her with remorse by making her realize all the troubles she had brought to bear on her lover? . . .

After weighing everything thus, Monsieur de Ramière concluded that it would be better to break the unfortunate tie. Noun's visits had begun to be painful. His mother, who had gone to Paris for the winter, would soon hear about his little scandal. She was already astonished at the frequency of his trips to Cercy, their country house, and his week-long stays. He had claimed to have important work to finish away from the bother of the city, but the pretext was wearing thin. It troubled Raymon to deceive so good a mother, to deprive her of his care; so—how should I put it?—he left Cercy and returned no more.

Noun wept, waited, and, poor wretch, seeing the weeks pass, went so far as to write him a letter. Poor girl! it was the last straw. A letter from a lady's maid! Even though she had taken the satiny stationery and sweet-smelling sealing wax from Madame Delmare's writing desk and the style from her own heart—but the spelling! Have you any idea how much more or less a syllable adds to or detracts from one's sentiments? Alas, the poor half-savage girl from Bourbon Island did not even know languages had rules. She thought she could write and speak as properly as her mistress, and when she saw that Raymon did not return, she said to herself: "My fine letter *should* have fetched him back!"

In fact, Raymon didn't have the courage to read

Noun's letter to the end. It may have been a master-piece of naïve and gracious passion . . . but he hastily threw it into the fire for fear of being too ashamed of himself. And once again, what can you expect? This, too, is a result of education; there is self-love in love as there is self-interest in friendship.

* * *

It was at the Spanish ambassador's ball that Raymon reappeared in society.

"Monsieur de Ramière, I presume," said a pretty woman to her neighbor.

"He's a comet that reappears at irregular intervals," replied the latter. "It's been centuries since we have seen that handsome chap." The speaker was an older woman and a foreigner. Her companion blushed slightly.

"He is indeed good-looking, isn't he, madame?"

"Charming, upon my word," said the Sicilian woman.

"I'll wager," said a dapper colonel of the Guard, "that you're talking about the hero of the *salons éclectiques*, the dashing Raymon."

"He has an interesting face," said the younger woman.

"And what may please you more, perhaps, a wicked mind," said the colonel.

The young woman was his wife.

"Why a wicked mind?" asked the foreigner.

"Southern passion, madame, strong as Palermo's sun."

Two or three young women bent their flower-decked heads the better to hear the colonel.

"He really ravaged our garrison last year," the colonel continued. "We'll have to pick a good quarrel with him to force him out."

"If he's another Lovelace,† too bad!" said a young woman mockingly. "Personally, I can't stand people everybody loves."

A world-weary countess waited until the colonel was at a distance, then she lightly rapped the finger of Mademoiselle de Nangy and said: "Don't talk like that. You have no idea how much we appreciate a man who wants to be loved."

"Do you think all he has to do is to want it?" said the young woman with the sardonic eyes.

"Mademoiselle," said the colonel, approaching her for a dance, "be sure you don't let the *beau* Raymon hear you!"

Mademoiselle de Nangy laughed, but for the rest of the evening her pretty little group did not dare mention Monsieur de Ramière again.

V

Meanwhile with neither distaste nor boredom Monsieur de Ramière was wandering among the undulating waves of the beautifully gowned. . . .

The honors of the evening—and of the moment—

† The seducer of the eponymous heroine of Samuel Richardson's *Clarissa,* a popular English novel.

belonged to a young woman no one knew, whose novel appearance in this society sufficed to fix attention upon her, namely, the simplicity of her dress which put her in bold relief against the diamonds, feathers, and flowers of the other women. The strings of pearls which braided her black hair were her only jewels. The white of her necklace, of her crepe dress and bared shoulders flowed as one; and the heat of the room brought the faintest of flushes to her cheeks, like that of a Bengal rose against the snow. She was a small, pretty, lissome creature, a salon beauty who could be transformed into a fairy by candlelight and dimmed by a single sunbeam. Dancing, she would have been wafted away by a breath, but there was no liveliness, no pleasure in her lightness. Seated, she bent as if her fragile body had no inner strength, and when she spoke, she smiled sadly. Tales of fantasy were then in the very flower of success and the men in that salon admiringly compared her to a ravishing specter evoked by sorcery, who would pale and disappear with dawn, like a dream.

Meanwhile they pressed around her inviting her to dance.

"Hurry," said one dandy to another, "the cock will soon crow! The feet of your partner are no longer touching the floor, and I'll wager you cannot feel the touch of her hand!"

"Look at the dark, strong face of Monsieur de Ramière," said an artistic lady to her neighbor, "and the figure of that pale, slender young woman. Doesn't the

solidity of the one beautifully bring out the fragility
of the other?"

"That young woman," said the female almanac of
social gatherings, "is the daughter of that silly old
man Carvajal, who wanted to play Joseph Bonaparte
and went off to die ruined on Bourbon Island. That
lovely exotic flower, I am told, has made a foolish marriage, but her aunt is well received at court."

Raymon had drawn nearer to *la belle Indienne.*
Hadn't he seen that pale, sad face in one of his
dreams? He had, and his eyes were fixed upon it with
the pleasure of one who has at last found the vision
he had thought lost forever. Raymon's attention troubled its object; gauche and shy, a stranger in this
world, the success she had obtained seemed to embarrass rather than please her. Raymon did a tour of the
salon, finally learned that the woman was Madame
Delmare, went to her, and asked her to dance.

"You do not remember me," he said, once they were
apart from the throng, "but I have been unable to forget you, madame. Just a glimpse of you, through a
cloud, and there you were—so kind, so compassionate."

Madame Delmare started. "Oh, it is you, sir! Yes, I
also recognized you." She flushed as if she feared she
had committed a *faux pas,* and looked around to see
whether she had been overheard. Her shyness added
to her charm and Raymon was touched to the heart by
her Creole intonation, her slightly husky voice, so
gentle it seemed made for a prayer or a blessing.

"I was afraid," he said, "I should never find a
chance to thank you. I couldn't go to you and I knew

you rarely went out. Besides, I was afraid I should see Monsieur Delmare if I went to see you, and our meeting would not be very agreeable in view of the circumstances. How happy I am now to thank you from my heart!"

"It would be more pleasant for me," she replied, "if Monsieur Delmare could share it. If you knew him better, you would know he is as good as he is rough. You would forgive him for his involuntary act, for he was more wounded than you."

"Let's speak no more of Monsieur Delmare, madame! I forgive him with all my heart. I did him wrong, he responded. . . ."

While speaking thus, Raymon held Madame Delmare's hand, preparing to lead her in a dance. He pressed it gently and the young woman's blood rushed to her heart. When he returned her to her seat, her aunt, Madame de Carvajal, was some distance away; many of the others had already left. Raymon sat beside her with the easy manner of an experienced man; it is the violence of our desire, the urgency of our love, which renders us stupid before women. A man who has somewhat sated his emotions is more inclined to please than to love. . . .

In general, as women are well aware, a man who speaks wittily of love is middlingly in love. Raymon was an exception: he expressed passion with art and felt it ardently. However, it wasn't passion which made him eloquent, but eloquence which made him passionate. He sensed a desire for a woman and became eloquent in order to seduce her, and then fell in

love in the process. It was the sentiment of lawyers
and preachers, who weep hot tears because they per-
spire copiously. He had met women sufficiently so-
phisticated to distrust these overheated improvisations,
but Raymon had committed what are called follies,
out of love: he had carried off a young woman of a
fine family; he had compromised women of very high
rank; he had fought three spectacular duels; he had
displayed the disarray of his heart and the wildness of
his thoughts to a theater full of people. A man who
does all this without fear of ridicule or condemnation,
and escapes both, is beyond society's clutch; he can
risk all and hope for everything. Thus the most canny
and resistant woman yielded at the thought that Raymon could be madly in love when he chose to be. In
society, a man capable of the madness of love is a rare
prodigy whom women appreciate.

I do not know how he managed it, but in taking
Madame de Carvajal and Madame Delmare to their
carriage, he succeeded in bringing Indiana's hand to
his lips. Never before had the furtive, burning kiss of
a man touched the fingers of this woman, though she
had been born in a torrid climate and was now nineteen years old—nineteen years on Bourbon Island, the
equivalent of twenty-five in our own land.

Ill and nervous as she was, this kiss almost tore a
cry from her, and she had to be helped into the carriage. Raymon had never known such sensitivity.
Noun, the Creole, was of robust health and *les Pari-*
siennes did not faint when one kissed their hand.

"If I should see her twice," he said to himself, as he withdrew, "I shall surely lose my head." . . .

On the morrow he discovered that Delmare had gone to Brussels on business, that in leaving he had entrusted his wife to Madame de Carvajal, whom he little liked but who was Madame Delmare's only relative. A self-made military man, he came from a poor, obscure family of which he seemed excessively ashamed, since he so often said he was not ashamed of it. But although he spent his time wrongly accusing his wife of looking down at him, he sensed that he should not force her into intimacy with his uncouth relatives. Moreover, despite his dislike for Madame de Carvajal, he could not deny a great respect for her as the descendant of a noble Spanish family . . .

So much for that; let us return to Raymon de Ramière. At the end of three days, he knew all about these family details, so assiduous had been his pursuit of anything that might bring him together with the Delmare ménage. He learned that by winning over Madame de Carvajal he might see Indiana. Thus the evening of the third day he had himself presented to the aunt.

There, in her salon, were four or five *primitives* solemnly playing a Spanish card game—reversi—and two or three young men of "good" families as completely vacuous as it is permitted for those vaunting four generations of nobility. Indiana was patiently finishing the background of a tapestry stretched on her aunt's frame. She was bent over her work, apparently absorbed in that mindless occupation and

perhaps content in this way to escape the empty chatter. I do not know whether behind the long black hair
falling over her tapestry, she was recalling the emotions of that fugitive moment which had opened a
new life before her, when the servitor's voice announcing several guests made her rise. She stood up
mechanically, for she had not listened to the names
and barely lifted her eyes from her tapestry; then a
voice struck her with the effect of an electric shock,
and she had to lean against her work table so as not
to fall.

VI

Raymon did not anticipate that silent salon and its
scattered guests. It was impossible to place a word that
would not be heard in every corner of the room. The
dowagers playing cards seemed there for the sole purpose of annoying the chatting young men, and Raymon thought he could read in their faces the secret
satisfaction of the aged in inhibiting the pleasures of
others. He had counted on a more intimate conversation than he had had at the ball with Indiana, but it
proved the contrary. The unexpected difficulties intensified his desire, the ardor of his glances, and the
vivacity of his remarks to Madame Delmare. The poor
child was a complete novice in this style of attack. She
had no defense, because nothing was asked of her; but
she was forced to listen to the solicitations of an ardent suitor, to hear how much she was loved, to allow

herself to be surrounded by all the dangers of seduction. Her embarrassment grew with Raymon's boldness. Madame de Carvajal, who had some claim to wit and to whom Ramière's wit had been recommended, left her card game to engage him in an elegant discussion of love, into which she poured a great deal of Spanish passion and German metaphysics. Raymon accepted the challenge with relish, and, in the guise of replying to the aunt, told the niece everything she would otherwise have refused to hear. . . .

That night Indiana slept even less than the previous nights; as we said, she had not yet loved, but her heart was ripe for an emotion no man hitherto had inspired. Raised by a bizarre and brutal father, she had never known the happiness affection can give. Monsieur de Carvajal, drunk with political passion, consumed by ambition's disappointments, had become the rudest and most quarrelsome planter of the colonies, and his daughter had cruelly suffered from his bitter temper. However, as a result of continually witnessing the evils of slavery, of undergoing the trials of solitude and dependence, she had acquired an exterior patience that was proof against any trial, an indulgence and kindness toward those in servitude, but a will of iron as well, an incalculable power of resistance to all that would oppress her. In marrying Delmare and coming to live at Lagny, she had simply changed masters, prisons, and solitudes. She did not love her husband, if only, perhaps, because she was told it was her duty to love him, because it had become a second nature, a principle of conduct, a law of conscience, for

her to resist mentally all moral constraints. Blind obedience had been all that anyone had prescribed for
her.

Raised in the desert, neglected by her father, living
in the midst of slaves to whom she could offer nothing
but compassion and tears, she would say to herself:
"A day will come when everything will change in my
life, when I will do good for others, when I will be
loved, when I will give all my heart to the one who
gives me his; meanwhile, let us suffer, hold our silence, and save our love as a reward for our liberator."
That liberator, that messiah, had not come; Indiana
was still waiting for him. . . . That silent, broken
heart was still calling, unknown even to itself, to a
young, generous heart to restore it to life. The being
she had most loved until now was Noun, the cheerful,
courageous companion of her solitude; and the man
who had shown her the greatest fondness was her
phlegmatic cousin, Sir Ralph. What nourishment for
her ravenous mind—a poor girl as ignorant and for-
saken as herself and an Englishman whose only passion was fox hunting!

Madame Delmare's unhappiness was real, and the
first time she felt the burning breath of a young, ardent man in that glacial atmosphere, the first time a
tender, caressing word echoed in her ear and quivering lips pressed like a white-hot iron on her hand, she
thought neither of the duties nor of the prudence
impressed upon her, nor of the future predicted for
her; she recalled only her hateful past, her long suffering, her tyrannical masters. Nor did she think that the

man in her mind might be a liar or a fop. She saw him as she had desired and dreamed him. . . .

Nevertheless a feeling of dread succeeded the feverish joy which had just invaded her heart. She thought of her easily aroused, vindictive husband and she was afraid, not for herself who was hardened against threats, but for the man about to engage in a battle to death with her tyrant. She knew so little of the social world that she transformed her life into a tragic novel; a shy creature who dared not love for fear of risking her lover's life, she gave no thought to the loss of her own.

This then was the secret of her resistance, the reason for her virtue. She resolved the next day to avoid Monsieur de Ramière. That evening there was a ball in the house of one of Paris's leading bankers. Madame de Carvajal, an old woman devoid of any affectionate life, doted on society and wanted to take Indiana to it, but Raymon was expected there so Indiana decided not to go. To avoid her aunt's urging, Madame Delmare, whose only resistance was a sort of *fait accompli,* feigned to accept her proposal; she allowed herself to be dressed; then changed into a dressing gown, installed herself by the fire, and prepared to sit it out. When the old Spaniard, as stiff and bejeweled as a Vandyke portrait, came to fetch her, Indiana pleaded illness and inability to go. Vainly her aunt urged her to make an effort.

"I would dearly like it," she replied, "but you see I can hardly stand. I would only embarrass you tonight.

Go to the ball without me, my dear aunt—your pleasure will be mine."

"Go without you!" exclaimed Madame de Carvajal, who was aghast at the idea of having dressed for nothing and shrank from the horror of an evening alone. "What would I do there, I, an old woman, whom people are nice to only to be near *you*? What would I be without your beautiful eyes beside me?"

"Your wit will do, my dear aunt."

The Marquise de Carvajal, who only asked to be persuaded, finally left. Then Indiana buried her face in her hands and wept, for she thought she had made a great sacrifice and was convinced she had brought the beautiful edifice of the day before tumbling down in ruins.

But Raymon would not permit it. The first thing he spotted at the ball was the marquise's arrogant, tufted crest. In vain he looked about her for the white robe and black hair of Indiana. He approached; he heard her say in a low voice to another woman, "My niece is ill, or rather," she added to justify her presence at the ball, "it's a young girl's caprice. She preferred to be romantically alone with a book in her hand."

"Is she avoiding me?" Raymon asked himself.

At once he left the ball. He arrived at the marquise's home, entered without addressing the concierge, and asked the first servant he met dozing in the antechamber for Madame Delmare.

"Madame is ill."

"I know. Madame de Carvajal has requested me to see how she is."

"I will tell Madame that—"

"It is not necessary. Madame will see me." And Raymon entered without being announced. All the other servants had gone to bed. The empty rooms were melancholic in their silence. A single lamp with a shade of green silk dimly lighted the large salon. Indiana's armchair had its back to the door; completely hidden by it, she sadly watched the burning logs as on the evening when Raymon scaled the walls of Lagny; she was sadder now, because that evening's vague sufferings and desires had been succeeded by a fugitive joy, a glimpse of happiness now lost.

Raymon's dancing slippers made no sound on the soft, deep-piled rug as he approached. He saw that she was crying and when she turned her head, she found him at her feet, forcibly taking her hand, which she strained to free. Then, I must admit, with ineffable joy she saw her resistance fail. She deeply felt that she passionately loved this man who scorned obstacles and brought her happiness despite herself. She blessed heaven for rejecting her sacrifice, and instead of scolding Raymon, she almost thanked him.

As for Ramière, he already knew he was loved. He did not need to see the joy shining through her tears to know he was the master—and might dare anything. He did not give Indiana time to question him; he changed roles with her: he did not explain his uncalled-for presence, he did not try to render himself less guilty than he was.

"You are crying, Indiana," he said. "Why are you crying? I must know."

She started at her name, but his audacity only added to her joy. "Why do you ask?" she said. "I must not tell you."

"Well, I know why, Indiana. I know your whole story, your whole life. Nothing that concerns you is foreign to me, because nothing that concerns you is of indifference to me. I wanted to know everything about you—and I learned nothing that wasn't revealed to me the brief instant I spent with you at Lagny, when they carried me, bloody and bruised, to your feet, and your husband was so angry to see you, so beautiful and kind, give me the support of your soft arms, the balm of your sweet breath. He was jealous! I can understand that; in his place I would have been too, Indiana; rather, in his place I would have killed me; for to be your husband, madame, to possess you, to hold you in his arms and not to deserve it, not to possess your heart, is to be the most miserable or the greatest dastard of men!"

"Heavens, hush!" she cried, covering his mouth with her hand. "No more! You make me guilty. Why do you speak to me of him? Why do you want me to damn him? If he should hear you! But *I* haven't spoken badly of him; I haven't asked you to either. I do not hate him, I respect him, I . . . love him!"

"Say you are terribly afraid of him, because that brute has crippled your soul, and terror has sat at your bedside ever since you became that man's game. . . . I know that if God had wished it, if you had been given to me, unlucky devil that I am, who should have his head broken for coming so late, you would

47

not be ill. I swear on my life, Indiana, I would have
loved you so that you would have loved me as well
and you would have blessed the chain. I would have
carried you in my arms to prevent the ground from
wounding your feet . . . and when you woke from
sleep, Indiana, you would have found me there, at
your feet, guarding you like a jealous master, serving
you like a slave, watching for your first smile, stealing
your first thoughts, your first look, your first kiss."

"Enough, enough!" cried Indiana, all bewilderment
and athrob with emotion. And yet, if one could die of
happiness, Indiana would have died that instant.
"Don't speak to me that way, not to me, I who am.
fated to be unhappy. Don't show one destined to die,
heaven on earth."

"Destined to die!" cried Raymon violently, taking
her into his arms. "*You* die, Indiana, die before you
have lived, before you have loved? No, you will not
die; I will not let you die, your life is bound to mine.
You are the woman I dreamed of, the purity I worshiped, the chimera that has always escaped me, the
bright star that said to me, 'Go on in this miserable
life and God will send you one of His angels to keep
you company.' You were destined for me from the beginning of time, our souls were forever betrothed, Indiana! Men and their iron laws have taken you from
me, the soul mate God would have chosen for me, if
He did not sometimes forget His promises. But what
do we care for men and their laws, if I love you,
though you are still in another's arms, if you can still
love me, cursed and unhappy as I am for having lost

you! You see, Indiana, you belong to me, you are the half of my heart which has long yearned to rejoin the other half. . . . It was your husband, your master, who brought me in obedience to destiny, bleeding in his arms, and threw me at your feet, saying, 'Here he is.' And now nothing can tear us apart."

"*He* can!" Indiana vehemently interrupted, though deliriously transported by her lover's recital. "Alas, you do not know him; he is a man who never forgives and can not be fooled. Raymon, he will kill you!" She buried her face on his chest and wept. Passionately Raymon embraced her.

"Let him come!" he cried. "Let him come and try to take this moment of happiness away from me! I defy him! Stay, Indiana, stay against my heart, it is your refuge and your shelter. Love me and I will be invulnerable. You know he doesn't have the power to kill me; I have already been defenseless before him. But you, my angel, you hovered over me, protecting me with your wings. Do not be afraid, we will know how to turn away his anger; and now, I am not even afraid for you, because I will be there. I also will protect you, when that master of yours tries to beat you down. Do you want me to kill him? Tell me you love me and I will be his murderer, if you sentence him to death!"

"You make me tremble! Hush! If you want to kill someone, kill me! I have lived one whole day—I ask for nothing more."

"Die, then, but let it be from happiness!" cried Raymon, pressing his lips to hers.

But the storm was too strong for so delicate a flower; she turned pale, put her hand to her heart, and fainted.

At first Raymon thought his kisses would bring her blood coursing back through her icy veins, but he covered her hands in vain with his kisses and in vain did he call her the sweetest of names. It was not the willful faint we so often witness. Madame Delmare had been seriously ill for some time and was subject to nervous fainting spells which lasted for hours. In despair, Raymon had to call for help. He rang; a maid appeared, but when she saw Raymon she dropped the flask she was carrying and a cry burst from her throat. Immediately he recovered his composure, drew close to her, and said:

"Silence, Noun! I knew you were here, so I came here to see you; I didn't count on finding your mistress, who I thought was at the ball. When I entered, I frightened her and she fainted. I'm leaving now; be careful!"

Raymon sped away, leaving each of the two women with a secret which would bring despair to the other.

VII

The next morning, on waking, Raymon received a second letter from Noun. This he did not throw away in disdain; rather, he hastily tore it open: it might tell him something about Madame Delmare. It did indeed, but what an embarrassing tangle of intrigues

was now Raymon's! It had become impossible for the
young servant to conceal her secret. Suffering and
fright had already thinned her cheeks, and Madame
Delmare had noticed her ailing state, though not its
cause. Noun dreaded the colonel's harshness, but her
mistress's gentleness even more. She knew very well
that she could obtain her forgiveness, but she would
die of shame and sorrow if she had to confess everything. What would become of her if Raymon failed to
save her from the humiliations about to fall upon her!
He must do something for her, or she was going to
throw herself at Madame Delmare's feet and tell her
all.

Fear of this strongly affected Ramière. His first concern was to separate Noun from her mistress. "Don't
say a word before I tell you to," he wrote. "Try to be
at Lagny this evening; I will be there."

On the way he reflected as to what course he
should take. Noun had enough common sense not to
expect the impossible. She had never dared to mention marriage, and because she was generous and dis-
creet, Raymon regarded himself as less guilty. He told
himself that he had hardly deceived her and that
Noun must have known what was certain to happen.
What bothered Raymon was not the problem of offering the poor girl half his fortune; he was ready to
make her rich, to do everything delicacy demanded.
What was painful for him was telling her he no
longer loved her, because he did not know how to lie.
If his behavior at the moment appeared double-faced
and deceitful, his heart was sincere, as it had always

been. He had loved Noun with all his senses; he loved Madame Delmare with all his soul. Thus far he had lied neither to the one nor to the other. He did not want to begin lying now, but Raymon felt equally incapable of deceiving poor Noun and bringing her to the point of despair. He had to choose between cowardice and cruelty. Raymon was indeed unhappy. He arrived at the gate of Lagny park without having made his choice.

For her part, Noun, who had not expected so swift a response, had recovered some hope. "He still loves me," she said to herself. "He does not want to abandon me. . . ."

After brooding over the seductive temptations offered her lover by society's life of luxury, Noun thought of a way of making herself more appealing to him. She dressed herself in all her mistress' finery, lighted a great fire in Madame Delmare's bedroom, decked the mantel with the most beautiful flowers she could find in the greenhouse, prepared a collation of fruit and fine wines, in short, all the boudoir niceties. . . .

Raymon left his mount at a charcoal burner's hut in the forest and entered the park with his key. This time he ran no risk of being taken for a thief—almost all the servants had left with their masters, he had made the gardener his accomplice, and he knew the approaches to Lagny as well as he knew those of his own estate.

The night was cold; a thick mist enveloped the trees of the park and Raymon could scarcely see the black trunks through the gray mist which wrapped them in diaphanous robes. He wandered for a time on the winding paths until he arrived at the door of the arbor where Noun awaited him, cloaked in a hooded pelisse.

"We can't stay here," she said. "It's too cold. Follow me, but without speaking."

Raymon had a feeling of repugnance about entering the house of Madame Delmare as the lover of her maid, yet he also felt he had to follow her. Noun was already walking away ahead of him and his talk with her would be his last.

She preceded him across the courtyard, quieted the dogs, opened the doors without a sound, and, taking him by the hand, guided him silently down the dark corridors; finally she ushered him into a circular bedroom, simple and elegant, which flowering orange trees filled with their fragrance and upon which translucent candles, burning in the candelabra, cast their light. Noun had scattered the petals of Bengal roses across the parquet floor and covered the divan with violets; a gentle warmth prevailed, wine glasses gleamed among the fruit which rested coquettishly in baskets of green moss.

Blinded by the abrupt transition from darkness to bright light, Raymon was momentarily at a loss, but it wasn't long before he realized where he was. The exquisite taste and chaste simplicity of the furnishings; the novels and books of voyage strewn on the mahogany shelves; the embroidery frame with its lovely work telling of long, patient hours; the harp whose strings seemed still to vibrate with songs of sad longing; the engravings of Paul and Virginia in pastoral love scenes and of the peaks of Bourbon Island and the blue cliffs of Saint-Paul; but above all, the small bed half-hidden behind muslin curtains, white and chaste as a virgin's, the palm branch on the headboard, as if in blessing, perhaps torn the day of her departure from a tree of her native island—all these spoke of Madame Delmare's presence and Raymon felt a strange shiver at the thought that the cloaked woman who had brought him here might be Indiana herself. The wild idea seemed confirmed when he saw in the mirror before him the white phantom of a woman entering a ballroom and throwing aside her cloak to stand, radiant and half-nude, in the brilliant light. But it was a momentary illusion: Indiana would not have been thus naked. Her chaste breasts would be sensed only through three layers of gauze; she might have decorated her hair with camellias, but they would not have tumbled about her head in such provocative disorder; she might have imprisoned her feet in satin slippers, but her chaste gown would not have revealed that shapely leg. . . .

After fixedly studying Noun in the mirror, Raymon turned his eyes instead toward everything that rendered a purer reflection of Indiana—the musical instruments, the engravings, the narrow and virginal bed. He drank in the lingering fragrance of her presence; he quivered with desire as he dreamed of the day when Indiana herself would open her boudoir's delights to him; and Noun looked on ecstatically, thinking him enthralled by the sight of all she had done to please him.

But at last he broke the silence, saying: "I thank you for your pains; I thank you above all for bringing me here, but I have enjoyed this pleasant surprise enough now. Let us leave this bedroom; it is not our place and I must respect Madame Delmare even in her absence."

"That is very cruel," said Noun, not understanding, but she noted his cold, discontented air. "It hurts to have tried to please you and then see your reaction—pushing me away!"

"No, my dear, I'll never push you away; I came here to talk seriously to you and prove my feeling for you. I'm grateful for your wanting to please me, but I like you better in your natural youth and beauty than in borrowed ornaments."

Noun half understood, and she wept. "I am a miserable woman! I hate myself because I don't please you any more—I should have known that you wouldn't love me very long, a poor girl with no education—I don't blame you for anything. I knew you wouldn't marry me, but if you would have continued to love me, I would have sacrificed everything, done anything without a single regret, and you would never have heard me complain—oh, I am ruined, dishonored! I'll be sent away! I am going to give life to someone who will be even more unfortunate than myself, and no one will pity me . . . Everyone will feel he can walk over me—but if you loved me, I wouldn't care—"

For a long moment Noun talked thus . . .

Raymon felt flattered to have inspired such a strong attachment; appreciation, compassion, a bit of vanity, perhaps, gave him a momentary feeling of love.

Noun was choked with tears . . . she was splendid in her sorrow and her love. Overcome, Raymon took her into his arms, drew her beside him on the sofa, pulled the table with the decanters closer, and poured her orange-flower water in a gilded silver cup. Comforted more by this sign of concern than by the calming drink, Noun dried her tears, threw herself at Raymon's feet and passionately embraced his knees.

"Love me!" she pleaded. "Tell me you still love me and I will be cured, I will be saved. Kiss me as you used to and I won't regret ruining myself to give you a few days of pleasure!" She embraced him with her cool, brown arms, she covered him with her long hair; her great black eyes burned with languor; with that hot blood, that Oriental sensuality which overwhelms all efforts of the will, all nuances of thought. Raymon forgot everything—his resolutions, his new love, the very place he was in. He returned Noun's delirious caresses. He drank from the same cup and the heady wines close at hand completed the routing of their senses.

Gradually a vaguely floating memory of Indiana merged with the drunkenness of Raymon. The two facing mirrors which infinitely reflected Noun's image seemed peopled by a thousand phantoms. He looked into the depth of that doubled and redoubled reflection and seemed to see in the last shadowy and confused figure of Noun the slender, graceful form of Madame Delmare. . . . Noun regarded all his transports as tributes to herself, when Raymon, in fact, looking at her, saw only Indiana. When he kissed her black hair, he kissed Indiana's, and it was Indiana he saw in the vapors of the punch warmed by Noun's hand; it was she who beckoned and smiled from behind the white muslin curtains; and it was she he dreamed of on that chaste, unstained bed when, succumbing to love and wine, he led his disheveled Creole to it.

Light was filtering through the cracks of the closed shutters when Raymon woke, and for a long moment he lay without moving, plunged in the uncertainty of surprise, looking about him—at the room, at the bed— as if they were part of the night's dream. Everything had been put neatly into order. Noun had gone to bed queen of the bedchamber and had awakened as a chambermaid. She had removed the flowers and the remains of the meal; the furniture was back in its place; nothing betrayed the night's orgy of love—Indiana's bedroom had recovered its candid, innocent air.

Overcome with shame, Raymon rose to leave, but the door was locked and the window was thirty feet above the ground; he had to remain imprisoned in that room of remorse, like Ixion on his wheel. He fell to his knees, facing that ravaged, disorderly bed which was his shame. "Oh, Indiana!" he cried, wringing his hands. "How I have outraged you! . . . Oh, miserable wretch, miserable, guilty wretch! If only I could wash away with blood the stain I have left on this bed!"

And he bathed it with his tears.

At this point Noun returned in her head scarf and apron; seeing Raymon on his knees, she thought him praying. She did not know that people of his world do not pray. So she waited, standing in silence, until he should deign to remark her presence.

Seeing Noun, Raymon felt both embarrassed and irritated, but without the courage to scold her or the strength to speak kindly. "Why did you lock me in?" he said at last. "Can't you see it's broad daylight and I can't leave now without compromising you?"

"But you need not leave," said Noun lovingly. "The house is empty, no one can see you here. The gardener never comes to this part of the house, and besides, only I have the keys. You'll have to stay with me today; you're my prisoner!"

Raymon despaired at the idea; all he experienced now for his mistress was dislike. Nevertheless he had to submit, or perhaps an irresistible attraction held him, despite what he had suffered in this room. After Noun left to find something for breakfast, he began to examine the mute witnesses of Indiana's solitude. He leafed through the books, opened the albums, then hastily closed them: he was afraid of committing another profanatory act, violating a woman's mystery. Finally he began to walk about the room and observed a large, richly framed portrait covered with two layers of cloth, hanging on the wall opposite Madame Delmare's bed.

Perhaps it was Indiana's portrait, he thought. Avidly curious, Raymon put aside his scruples, mounted a chair, removed the pins and was stunned to see the full-length portrait of a handsome young man.

VIII

"It seems to me I recognize that face," he said to Noun, as she returned, forcing himself to sound indifferent.

"Fie, sir!" said the young girl, placing the breakfast tray on the table. "You should not pry into my mistress' secrets!"

The remark made Raymon pale. "Secrets!" he exclaimed. "If *that* is a secret, you share it, Noun, and so you were doubly guilty in bringing me to this room."

"Oh, no, it is not a secret," said Noun, smiling. "It was Monsieur Delmare himself who helped hang the picture of Sir Ralph. How could Madame have any secrets with a husband who is so jealous?"

"Sir Ralph, you say? Who is Sir Ralph?"

"Sir Rodolphe Brown, Madame's cousin, her childhood friend—I might say mine, too; he's so good!"

Raymon studied the painting with surprise and uneasiness. . . . It was an admirably executed portrait, an authentic family picture, with all its perfection of details, its puerile resemblances, its bourgeois minutiae —a painting to make a nurse weep, dogs bark, and a tailor swoon in rapture. There was only one thing in the world more insignificant than that painting—its subject.

Nevertheless, it infuriated Raymon.

"So this young English sportsman has the rights of entry into Madame Delmare's most secret sanctum!" he said to himself. "This insipid face is always hanging here, looking down coldly on the most intimate acts of her life! . . . That insolent face feasting on her charms! That man in boots presides over her toilet!" He turned to the maid. "Does that cloth usually cover the painting?"

"Always," she replied, "when Madame is away. But don't bother to replace it—Madame is returning in a few days."

"In that case, Noun, you would do well to tell her that face is very impertinent. If I were Monsieur Delmare, I wouldn't let it hang there without blanking out both eyes. How stupid can jealous husbands be? They imagine everything and understand nothing."

"What do you have against the face of the good Monsieur Brown?" asked Noun, arranging her mistress' bed. "He's such a fine master! I never used to like him, because I heard people say to Madame that he was very selfish, but since the day he took such good care of you—"

"I know," Raymon interrupted, "it was he who helped me, I recognize him now. But I owe that to Madame Delmare's concern."

"Because she is so good!" said poor Noun. "Who doesn't become good living with her?"

When Noun spoke of Madame Delmare, Raymon listened with an interest she did not suspect. The day passed quietly, but Noun didn't bring up the subject that most concerned her. Finally toward evening she made the effort, forcing him to declare his intentions. He had no other intention than to rid himself of a dangerous mistress, of a woman he no longer loved. But he wanted to assure her future, and with some fear, he made her the most liberal offers.

It was a bitter affront to the poor girl; she tore her hair and would have beaten her head against the bedroom wall if Raymon hadn't forcibly restrained her. Then, using all the resources of language and intelligence bestowed upon him by nature, he made her understand that it was not for her but for the child she was bearing that he offered to provide.

"It is my duty," he said. "It is his heritage I am giving you, and you would be guilty of a crime against him if, out of false delicacy, you refused my help."

Noun became calmer and she dried her tears. "Very well," she said, "I will accept it, if you promise to continue to love me; doing your duty for the child is not doing it for the mother. Your money will keep him alive, but your indifference will kill me. Can't you take me as a servant? I am not demanding; I don't want anything anyone else in my place might have been able to get. Just let me be your servant. Or your mother's. She'll be pleased with me, I promise you, and even if you don't love me, at least I'll be able to see you."

"What you ask is impossible. You can't dream of

being someone's servant in your present state, and to deceive my mother, to betray her confidence in me, would be too base for me to consent to. Go to Lyons or Bordeaux; I will see to it you have all you need until you are yourself again. Then I will find a place for you with some person I know, in Paris itself, if you want it, if you really want to be near me, but to be under the same roof is impossible—"

"Impossible!" cried Noun, grief-stricken. "I can see that you despise me, that you are ashamed of me—I will not go, alone and disgraced, to die abandoned in some faraway city where you will forget me. What do I care about my reputation! It's your love I want to keep!"

"Noun, if you are afraid I will deceive you, come with me. The same carriage will take us where you wish, I'll follow you anywhere except to Paris or to my mother's home; I will give you anything I owe you."

"Yes, to abandon me the day after you drop me," she smiled bitterly, "a useless burden, in a foreign land. No, monsieur, no. I will remain here: I don't want to lose everything at once. In following you, I would lose the one person I loved most in the world before meeting you, but I am not so anxious about my dishonor as to sacrifice my love *and* my friendship. I will go throw myself at the feet of Madame Delmare, I will tell her everything, and she will forgive me, I know; because she is good and she loves me. We were born almost the same day, we had the same

nurse. . . . She will take care of me, she will take
care of my child, my poor child! . . ."

This resolution plunged Raymon in a terrifying di-
lemma, when suddenly a carriage was heard in the
courtyard. Dismayed, Noun ran to the window.

"It is Madame Delmare!" she cried. "Flee!"

The key to the hidden staircase couldn't be found.
Noun took Raymon by the arm and hurriedly pulled
him into the darkened corridor, but they were not
halfway its length when they heard someone approaching, then the voice of Madame Delmare ten
steps ahead, and a candle held by a servant almost
cast its flickering light on their startled faces. Noun
scarcely had time to turn back, still drawing Raymon
after her, and return to the bedroom.

A dressing room might have offered a few moments'
refuge, but there was no way to lock it, and Madame
Delmare might go to it on arriving. Raymon dashed to
the bedroom alcove and hid behind the curtains. It
was unlikely Madame Delmare would go to bed immediately, and until then Noun could find a way to
help him get away.

Indiana entered the room briskly, tossed her hat on
the bed, and kissed Noun as she would a sister. There
was so little light she did not notice her companion's
agitation.

"You were expecting me, I see!" she said, going to
the fire. "How did you know I was coming?" Without
waiting for a reply, she added: "Monsieur Delmare
will arrive tomorrow. I left at once when I received
his letter. I have reasons to prefer seeing him here

rather than in Paris. I'll tell you about it later, but—
say something—you don't seem as glad to see me as
usual."

"I am unhappy," said Noun, kneeling to remove
her mistress' shoes. "I have something to tell you, too,
afterward, but now let us go to the salon."

"Heaven forbid! What an idea! It's mortally cold
there."

"No, there is a good fire."

"You're dreaming! I just came through it."

"But your supper is waiting for you."

"I don't want to eat; besides, nothing is ready. Go
bring me my boa; I left it in the carriage."

"Later."

"Why not now? Go, go!" As she spoke, she pushed
Noun playfully; the latter, realizing boldness and control were called for, went out for a few seconds. But
she had hardly left the room when Madame Delmare
bolted the door, removed her riding cloak, and lay it
on the bed next to her hat. At that moment, she came
so close to Raymon that he impulsively recoiled, stirring the bed slightly on its rollers. Surprised but not
frightened, since she might have moved it herself,
Madame Delmare drew back the curtains and discovered in the half-light of the fire a man's head outlined
against the wall.

Terrified, she cried out, ran to the mantel, and
reached for the bell cord. Raymon would have preferred to be taken for a thief the second time than be
recognized in such a situation, but if he did not
choose the latter course, Madame Delmare would call

the servants and compromise herself. He put his hope
in her love, hastened to her to stop her cries and keep
her from pulling the bell cord, at the same time saying
in a low voice, lest he be heard by Noun, who could
not be too far distant:

"It is I, Indiana, I! Forgive me! Forgive an unhappy
wretch who has lost his head because of you, who
could not dream of giving you back to your husband
before seeing you once more."

And as he pressed Indiana in his arms, as much to
soften her resistance as to keep her from ringing,
Noun knocked on the door in anguish. Madame Delmare, pushing herself away from Raymon, ran to the
door, opened it, returned, and sank into a chair.

Deathly pale, Noun threw herself against the door
to prevent the scurrying servants from entering upon
the strange scene; even paler than her mistress, her
knees trembling, her back pressed to the door, she
awaited her fate.

Raymon sensed that with some cunning he might
still fool the two women simultaneously.

"Madame," he said, dropping to his knees before
Indiana, "my presence here must seem an outrage to
you; on bended knee I implore your forgiveness. Let
me speak to you just a moment and I will explain—"

"Silence, sir! Leave!" cried Madame Delmare, recovering her dignity. "Leave publicly! Noun, open that
door and let the gentleman pass, so that my domestics
may see him and the disgrace of his behavior fall
upon himself."

Believing she had been discovered, Noun dropped to

her knees beside Raymon. Madame Delmare regarded her in speechless stupefaction. Raymon tried to take her hand, but she pulled it away indignantly. Flushing with anger, she rose and pointed to the door.

"Leave, I tell you! Go! Your conduct is unspeakable! So this is the way you choose to behave! You, sir, hiding in my bedroom like a thief! Has it become a habit for you to introduce yourself into houses this way? Is this the 'pure attachment' you promised me yesterday, the way you want to protect, respect, and defend me? Is this the way you want to 'worship' me! . . ."

Half dead with surprise and despair, Noun had her eyes fixed on Raymon, as if to ask him for an explanation of this extraordinary mystery. Then, wildly trembling, she dragged herself to Indiana, seized her by the arm and cried through clenched teeth:

"What did you say? This man loved you?"

"You must have known it!" said Madame Delmare, pushing her away disdainfully and violently. "You must have known very well why a man hides behind the curtains of a woman's bedroom. Oh, Noun," she said, when she saw the girl's grief, "it was an incredible thing you did. I would never have thought you could do it, sell the honor of somebody who had so much faith in yours!"

Madame Delmare sobbed as much from anger as from sorrow. Never had Raymon seen her so beautiful, but he hardly dared look at her, the hurt pride of an outraged woman made him lower his eyes. He was also appalled, petrified, by Noun's presence. If he had been alone with Madame Delmare, he might have been able to soften her. But Noun's expression was terrifying; her face worked with hate and fury.

A knock on the door startled all three. Again Noun threw herself against it to bar entry to the bedroom, but Madame Delmare thrust her aside with authority and gestured imperiously at Raymon to withdraw to a corner of the room. Then, with that coolness which was remarkably hers in a crisis, she wrapped herself in a shawl, half opened the door, and asked the servant who had knocked what he wished.

"Monsieur Rodolphe Brown has just arrived," he said. "He would like to know if Madame would receive him."

"Tell Monsieur Brown that I am delighted by his visit and I will go down to him. Make a fire in the salon and have some supper warmed. Wait! Bring me the key to the park gate."

The servant left. Madame Delmare remained standing, holding the door ajar, not deigning to listen to Noun and imperiously indicating to Raymon that he keep his silence. In a few minutes the servant returned. Madame Delmare, shielding Raymon with the door, took the key, told the servant to hurry up the supper and, when he departed, addressed herself to Raymon.

"The arrival of my cousin Sir Rodolphe," she said, "saves you from the public scandal I intended for you. He is a man of honor who would defend me warmly, but I would hate to expose the life of a man like him to a man like you. I will allow you to leave quietly.

Noun, who let you in, will find a way to let you out. Go!"

"We shall meet again, madame," replied Raymon, with forced self-assurance, "and though I am guilty, you may regret your severity."

"I trust, sir, that we shall never meet again," she replied, and she coldly showed him the door, together with his poor, trembling accomplice.

Alone in the night-shrouded park with Noun, Raymon braced himself for her reproaches, but Noun never spoke. She led him to the gate; when he tried to take her hand, she had already gone. He called to her in a low voice, he wanted to know where he stood with her, but she made no reply and the gardener, who suddenly appeared, said to him:

"Come, sir, you must away, Madame has arrived and you might be seen."

Raymon departed, sick at heart, but in his sadness at having offended Madame Delmare, he almost forgot Noun and thought only of how he might appease her mistress; he was the kind of man who scorned obstacles and was passionately attached only to what seemed hopeless.

That night when Madame Delmare, who had supped in silence with Sir Ralph, returned to her room, Noun did not come as usual to help undress her. She rang in vain, then concluded the absence was deliberate, closed her door, and went to bed, but she spent a very bad night and at daybreak went down into the park. . . .

Madame Delmare had wept all night; tired, she fell

limply to the grass, which was still white with dew, along the bank of the millstream coursing through the park. March was almost over, nature had begun to reawaken; the morning, though cool, was pleasant; mist still hovered over the water like a scarf and the birds were testing their first songs of love and spring. . . .

The noise of the mill wheel setting Delmare's factory into motion was heard behind the willows on the far bank. The water rushing through the newly opened gates roiled along the surface, and as Madame Delmare followed the swift current with a melancholy eye, she saw floating among the reeds a vague mass of cloth tugged at by the current. She rose, leaned over the water, and could clearly distinguish the clothes of a woman, clothes she knew all too well. Terror froze her, but the water coursed on, slowly dragging a body from the entangling weeds toward Madame Delmare.

A harrowing scream brought the factory workers running to the scene; Madame Delmare had fallen in a faint along the bank, and Noun's body was floating in the stream before her.

PART TWO

IX

Two months have passed. Nothing has changed at Lagny, in that house into which I introduced you one winter evening, save that spring is in full flower around the red brick and white stone walls, the moss-covered slate roofs. The family is scattered about, enjoying the mildness and fragrance of evening; the windows reflect the golden, setting sun and the noise of the factory blends with the sounds of the farm. Delmare sits on the porch steps, shotgun in hand, shooting at flying swallows. Indiana sits at her embroidery frame near the salon window, occasionally casting a sad glance at the colonel's cruel entertainment in the courtyard. Ophelia jumps about and barks, outraged by this kind of hunting; and Sir Ralph, astride the stone balustrade, smokes his cigar, looking on as usual with his impassive eye at the pleasures or problems of others.

"Indiana!" cried the colonel, putting down his shotgun. "Stop your embroidering; you're going at it as if you were paid by the hour."

"It is still daylight," replied Madame Delmare.

"Never mind, come to the window, I have something to tell you."

Indiana obeyed; the colonel went to the window, which was almost at ground level, and said to her with the playful air adopted by aging, jealous husbands: "Since you have worked so hard today and have been so good, I'm going to tell you something that will please you."

Madame Delmare forced a smile, and her smile would have driven a more sensitive man than the colonel to despair.

"You will be happy to know," he continued, "that I have invited one of your humble adorers to lunch tomorrow to keep you from being bored. You will ask me which one, my coquette, because you have quite a collection."

"Our dear old parish priest?" asked Madame Delmare, her melancholy invariably augmented by her husband's gaiety.

"Oh, not at all!"

"Then it must be the mayor of Chailly or the old notary from Fontainebleau!"

"Ah, the slyness of a woman! You know very well it is not those people. Come, Ralph, tell Madame the name she has on the tip of her tongue, but won't let us hear."

"It's not necessary to be so elaborate in announcing Monsieur de Ramière's visit," Ralph said coldly, throwing away his cigar. "I imagine she's completely indifferent to it."

Madame Delmare felt the blood rush to her face; she turned away, pretending to look for something in the salon; her composure somewhat recovered though her legs trembled, she returned and said, "I suppose this is some kind of jest."

"Quite the contrary, it is very serious. He will be here at eleven tomorrow morning."

"What! That man who came here to steal your inventions, whom you almost killed as a thief? You both are remarkably placid to forget so much!"

"You set me the example, my dearest, by welcoming him so cordially at your aunt's when he came to see you."

Indiana paled. "He did not come to see *me*," she

said urgently, "and I feel so little flattered that if I were you, I would not receive him."

"You women are sly little liars out of sheer pleasure! You danced with him all one evening, they tell me."

"They didn't tell you the truth."

"It was your own aunt! Besides, don't defend yourself so strongly; it's not too bad, since your aunt wanted to bring about this reconciliation between us. Ramière has sought it for a long time. Almost without my knowing it, he has helped me a great deal in my business affairs, and since I am not nearly as ferocious as you say and, besides, I don't like to owe anything to a stranger, I thought I'd settle my debt with him."

"How?"

"By making him my friend, by going to Cercy this morning with Sir Ralph. We discovered his mother was a delightful woman . . . Ramière, too, after all, is a good fellow and I have invited him to lunch with us and to visit the factory. . . ."

"You know, my dear Delmare," Ralph said, "that I was never for keeping your machines secret: a good citizen's invention belongs as much to his country as to himself, and if I—"

"Damn! You and your philanthropy, Sir Ralph! You will make me believe that your wealth doesn't belong to you, and if tomorrow the country wanted it, you would exchange your fifty thousand francs a year for a beggar's staff and a few pennies. It's pretty ironical for a chap like you who delights in the comforts of life as much as a sultan to preach contempt for wealth!"

"What I said has nothing to do with philanthropy— it's that selfishness, when it's well understood, leads us to do good to men so they will not do us evil. I am selfish myself, as everyone knows. I have learned not to be ashamed of it: after analyzing the virtues, I found self-interest the basis of them all. Love and devotion, two apparently generous passions, are perhaps the most self-motivated; patriotism no less, believe me. I like men little, but not for anything in the world would I want to show it: my fear of them is proportional to my lack of esteem for them. Thus we are both selfish, but I admit it, you don't."

An argument developed between the two men in which each tried to prove, by all the arguments for selfishness, the selfishness of the other. Madame Delmare took advantage of it by withdrawing to her room and abandoning herself to the reflections such unexpected news gave rise to.

*   *   *

"How miserable I am!" she cried to herself . . . "A curse on that man who came here to bring death and despair! Dear God, why do You permit him to come between me and You, to do as he will with my fate, so that he has only to reach out his hand and say, 'She is mine! I will drive her mad, I will make her life desolate, and if she resists me, I will spread mourning about her, I will ring her with remorse, regret, and alarm!'

Oh God, it is not just for a poor woman to be so persecuted!"

She cried bitterly, for the thought of Raymon led
her to the memory of Noun, more vivid and harrowing
than ever. . . . In weeping thus for her companion,
Indiana was weeping as well, without realizing it, for
the lost illusions of three days which had been the
loveliest days of her life, the only days she had truly
lived; for during those three days she had loved with a
passion which Raymon, had he been even the most
presumptuous of men, would have been incapable of
imagining. But the more violent and blind that love,
the more sharply she had felt the insult; the first love
of a heart such as hers is overfull with decency and
delicacy. . . .

Madame Delmare now sincerely believed that she
hated Raymon.

X

As for Raymon, neither male swagger nor hurt self-esteem impelled him to win Madame Delmare's love
and forgiveness. He believed that both were impossible, that no other woman's love, no other earthly happiness were their equal, so he sought them. He was
made that way. An insatiable appetite for adventure
and emotion consumed his life. He loved society with
its laws and constraints, because it offered him the sustenance of combat and resistance; and if he abhorred
license and debauchery, it was because they offered
tame, facile pleasures. . . .

Raymon exercised an incredible influence over everybody about him, for, take him for what he was
with all his faults and youthful wildness, he was a superior man in society. We have not dwelled on what
his reputation for wit and talent was based upon, because it has been outside our immediate story, but
now is the time to tell you that Raymon, whose
weaknesses you have witnessed and whose flightiness
you have perhaps condemned, is one of the men who
have had the greatest influence over *your* thoughts,
whatever your opinion may happen to be today. You
have devoured his political pamphlets, and, reading
the newspapers of the period, you have often been
captivated by the irresistible charm of his style, the
grace of a courteous, worldly logic of a time already
distant. . . .

Since he was without political passion, Raymon
thought himself above all interests, but he was only
deceiving himself, for society, organized as it then
was, favored him with privileges; it could not be
changed without diminishing his comfort, and that
complete satisfaction with one's social situation, which
communicates itself so readily to one's thinking, is a
wonderful stimulus for moderation. What man is so
ungrateful to Providence as to reproach it for the misfortunes of others, if it smiles upon him? How could
one persuade those young supporters of constitutional
monarchy that the constitution was already outmoded,
that it overburdened the body politic, when they
found the burden full of benefits for themselves?

Who really believes in a poverty he does not personally experience? . . .

Not needing to write for money, thanks to his fortune, Raymon wrote for the pleasure of it and, he said in good faith, from a sense of duty. The talent he possessed of being able to refute seeming truths had made him invaluable to the government, which he served far better by his objective criticisms than others by their blind obedience, and even more invaluable to the young sophisticates, who were willing to renounce the more ridiculous of their aristocratic privileges, but wished to retain all the other advantages. Men such as Raymon were in fact individuals of great talent who supported a society about to crumble into the abyss and who, suspended between two cliffs, fought on calmly and complacently against the hard reality about to swallow them. . . .

Thus Raymon had no sooner rejoined that society which was his element and homeland than he felt its vital, exciting stimulus. The petty interests of love which had preoccupied him gave way for a moment to larger, more brilliant interests. He brought to them the same bravado, the same passion; and when he saw himself more eagerly sought after than ever by the most distinguished personalities of Paris, he felt more than ever that he loved life. . . .

But he had no sooner returned to that life than he felt, as in the past, the profound need to mix thoughts of love and amorous adventure with his political reflections, ambitions, and philosophy. By "ambition" I do not mean the seeking of honors and money, for which he did not lack, but the seeking of reputation and the approval of noblemen.

At first he had despaired of ever seeing Madame Delmare again after the tragic denouement of his double intrigue. But in plumbing the depth of his loss and brooding over the treasure that had escaped him, he simultaneously recovered the hope, will, and confidence to repossess it. He calculated the obstacles before him and concluded that the most difficult, to begin with, would be Indiana herself; he must therefore employ the husband in his defense. It was not a new idea, but it was a sure one; jealous husbands are peculiarly susceptible subjects for this service.

Two weeks after he had conceived this strategy, Raymon was on the road to Lagny, where he was expected for lunch. . . . At this point I should like to draw a quick sketch for you of the colonel.

Do you know what they call an "honest man" in the provinces? It is a man who does not reach for a neighbor's fields, who doesn't demand a penny more than he is owed, who lifts his hat to everyone who bows to him; who does not rape young women on public highways, who does not set fire to another man's barn, who does not rob travelers at a corner of his park. Provided he religiously respects the life and purse of his fellow citizens, they ask nothing more of him than that. He may beat his wife, mistreat his servants, ruin his children—it is no one's affair. Society condemns only those actions injurious to itself; private life is not its business.

Such was the moral philosophy of Monsieur Delmare. He had never studied any social contract other than this: *Each to his own.* He considered all the heart's niceties to be feminine puerilities and sentimental flimflam. A man without wit, tact, or education, he enjoyed a more solid reputation than that won by talent and kindness. He had broad shoulders and a strong wrist; he handled saber and sword to perfection; and with all that, he possessed a quick-tempered touchiness. Since he did not always understand a joke, he was continually obsessed by the idea that people were making fun of him. Incapable of replying in similar style, he had only one defense: to impose silence by threats. His favorite sayings always dealt with flogging and dueling, wherefore the epithet "brave" before his name in the provinces, since military bravura apparently means broad shoulders, sweeping mustache, swaggering oaths, and a touchy sword. . . .

Thus the colonel's character could not have been more antipathetic to that of his wife nor his heart and mind less capable of understanding and appreciating her.‡ And yet, it is certain that her slavery had engendered in her woman's heart a kind of mute, virtuous aversion which was not always just. Madame Delmare overly doubted her husband's heart; he was harsh—she thought him cruel. There was more roughness than rage in his outbursts, more coarseness than insolence in his manners. He was not bad by nature; he had his moments of pity which led him to

‡ Here, as elsewhere, Sand has aspects of her husband, Casimir Dudevant, ex-officer, in mind.

78

repent, and in his repentance he was almost sensitive.
It was camp life that raised brutality to the level of
principle for him. With a less refined, less gentle
woman, he would have been as timid as a tamed wolf;
but this woman's spirit had been drained by her fate;
she did not trouble to try to improve it.

XI

As he stepped down from his gig in the Lagny courtyard, Raymon felt his courage fail him. So he was to
enter once again that house with such terrible memories for him! His reasoning, in harmony with his emotions, might overwhelm his heart's impulses but not
stifle them, and in that instant the feeling of remorse
was as strong as that of desire.

The first person who came forward was Sir Ralph
Brown. Seeing him in his eternal hunting costume,
flanked by his dogs and as sober as a Scottish laird, he
thought he saw the portrait discovered in Madame
Delmare's bedroom walking toward him. Shortly afterward the colonel appeared and lunch was served without Indiana. . . .

"So, Madame Delmare does not choose to come
down?" the colonel said sourly to his factotum Lelièvre.

"Madame has slept badly," replied Lelièvre, "and
Mademoiselle Noun—that devil of a name always
comes out!—Mademoiselle Fanny, I mean, has told me
Madame is resting in bed."

"How is it I just saw her at her window? Fanny is mistaken. Go tell Madame that lunch is on the table. Or wait! Sir Ralph, my dear kinsman, would you mind going up to see if your cousin is really ill?"

If the unhappy name which slipped from the servant's lips painfully jangled Raymon's nerves, the colonel's choice filled him with jealousy and rage. "In her bedroom!" he thought. "He doesn't stop at hanging the man's portrait there, he sends him in person. This Englishman has rights in this house even the husband seems afraid to claim."

As if he had read Raymon's thoughts, Delmare said to him: "Don't be surprised by all this. Monsieur Brown is the family doctor; besides, he's our cousin, a good chap we love with all our heart."

Ralph remained away for ten minutes. Raymon was distraught and ill at ease. He did not eat; he kept looking at the door. At last the Englishman reappeared. "Indiana is truly ill," he said. "I prescribed sleep for her." Calmly he reseated himself at the table and ate with heartiness. The colonel did the same. . . .

"Well, my good neighbor," the colonel finally said. "I must repay my debt to you and keep my promise. The factory is in full operation and the workers are at their jobs. Here are paper and pencil so that you can take notes."

Raymon followed the colonel, examined the factory with an earnest, interested air, and made comments which proved that he was equally at home in chemistry and machinery. . . . He looked at everything, listened to everything, replied to everything, and thought of nothing but the love affair which had brought him to this place.

When they had exhausted the subject of machinery, the discussion turned to the volume and the force of the stream. They went out, climbed to the top of the dam, and charged the overseer with lifting the gates and measuring the different depths.

"Sir," said the man, addressing Delmare, who estimated the maximum depth to be fifteen feet, "excuse me, but we had it at seventeen feet this year."

"When was that? You must be mistaken," said the colonel.

"Excuse me, sir, it was the night you returned from Belgium, the night when Mademoiselle Noun was found drowned; it proves what I said, because her body floated *over* the dike there and stopped here, where the gentleman is standing."

Speaking with animation, the overseer pointed to Raymon. The wretched young man became as pale as death; he looked with horror at the water flowing at his feet; he seemed to see in the reflection of his livid face the still-floating body; he was seized with dizziness and would have fallen into the stream if Ralph had not caught him by the arm and drawn him back.

"Very well," said the colonel, who had noticed nothing and thought so little about Noun that he couldn't have suspected Raymon's state, "but that was an exceptional case and the average force of the current is— But what the devil's going on with you two?"

"Nothing," replied Sir Ralph. "I stepped on the

gentleman's foot when I turned around; I'm very sorry, it must have hurt horribly." Sir Ralph's tone was so even and calm that Raymon himself was convinced he believed what he said. A few polite words were exchanged and the conversation resumed.

Raymon left Lagny a few hours later without having seen Madame Delmare. It had been better than he had hoped; he had feared he would find her cold and indifferent. . . .

Madame de Ramière was at Cercy at this time and Raymon spoke to her of the charms and wit of Madame Delmare; without asking his mother to call upon her, he skillfully planted the thought.

"After all," said Madame de Ramière, "she is the only neighbor whom I haven't met; and since I am the new arrival, it is for me to make the gesture. We will go to Lagny next week together."

The day arrived.

"She cannot avoid me any longer," thought Raymon.

Actually, Madame Delmare could no longer avoid receiving him: when she beheld an unknown elderly lady step from the carriage, she went out on the porch to meet her and then recognized Raymon as the man accompanying her. She realized he must have deceived his mother to induce her to come, and her displeasure gave her the strength to be dignified and poised. . . . Raymon asked leave to join Delmare in the park and left the two women together.

Captured by the charm that a superior intelligence combined with a noble and generous soul extends to the slightest relationship, Indiana slowly became amiable and affectionate, then almost gay. She had never known her own mother and her aunt, Madame de Carvajal, despite her presents and compliments, was far from being one to her—wherefore her heart's fascination with Raymon's mother.

When Raymon rejoined them, as his mother was stepping into the carriage, he saw Indiana raise the offered hand to her lips. Poor Indiana felt the need of having someone to be attached to. She was overjoyed by anything that promised interest and concern for her in her lonely, unhappy life; and besides, she told herself that Madame de Ramière would save her from the trap into which Raymon sought to lead her.

"I will throw myself into the arms of that wonderful woman," she was already thinking, "and if necessary, tell her everything. I will beg her to save me from her son, and she will watch over him and over me." . . . Such was not Raymon's reasoning. "My excellent mother!" he exulted as they returned to Cercy. "Her charm and goodness perform miracles. What don't I owe to them already—my education, my successes in life, my position in society! All that lacks is the happiness of having the heart of a woman like Indiana, and that, too, thanks to her."

Raymon, it can be seen, loved his mother because he needed her for his well-being; and so it is that all children love their mothers.

A few days later, Raymon received an invitation to spend three days at Bellerive, the magnificent country estate of Sir Ralph which lay between Cercy and Lagny, and to join the best hunters of the neighborhood in destroying some of the game devouring Bellerive's woods and gardens. Raymon liked neither Sir Ralph nor hunting, but Madame Delmare acted as hostess for her cousin on such occasions and the hope of seeing her decided Raymon. . . .

He thought it would be inadvisable to show too much eagerness; hints of indifference work very well with women who think themselves loved. But the hunt had been on since morning when he arrived at Sir Ralph's, and Madame Delmare was not expected before dinner. In the meantime he prepared his strategy. He must find a way to justify his behavior, for the moment was approaching. He had two full days before him and he planned the time thus: for the remainder of the day to be impassive, for the next to be persuasive, and for the following day to be happy. He even consulted his watch and calculated almost to the hour when his plan would prove either a success or a failure.

XII

He had been two hours in the drawing room when he heard in the adjoining room the gentle, slightly husky voice of Madame Delmare. In reflecting on his seduction scheme, he had become as cool as an author toward his subject or a lawyer toward his cause; but one could also compare his emotion on seeing Indiana to that of an actor so affected by his role that face to face with his leading lady he can no longer distinguish between stage fiction and reality.

She was so changed that a glimmer of sincere concern penetrated Raymon despite his tenseness. Sorrow and sickness had left such marks that she was hardly pretty and his conquest of her would be more out of pride than pleasure. But Raymon felt he owed it to himself to restore this woman to life and happiness.

Seeing how pale and sad she was, he concluded that he had no strong will to contest against. Could so frail an envelope conceal great moral resistance? He thought it best to interest her in herself to begin with, to frighten her about her depression and declining health in order to open her mind to the desire for a change.

"Indiana!" he cried, masking his assurance with an air of profound melancholy. "To see you like this! I never dreamed that the moment I looked forward to so much would be so painful!" . . .

A French woman of the world would not have lost her head in such a delicate situation, but Indiana was unschooled in the ways of the world; she possessed neither the skill nor the deceit necessary to preserve the advantage of her position. Raymon's words confronted her abruptly with the terrible picture of her sufferings, and tears glistened on her eyelashes.

"I am ill, it is true," she said, seating herself tiredly in the chair offered by Raymon. "I feel very ill, and in your presence, sir, I have a right to complain."

Raymon had not hoped to go so far so quickly. He seized the opportunity by the hair, as the saying goes, and taking her hand, which he found cold and dry, he said: "Indiana! Don't say that! Don't say that I am the cause of your illness or you will drive me mad with grief—and joy!"

"And joy?" she echoed, fixing him with her great blue eyes brimming with sadness and astonishment.

"I should have said hope, for if I have caused you unhappiness, madame, perhaps I can also bring it to an end. Just say one word"—he dropped to his knees on a cushion which had fallen beside her from the sofa—"ask for my blood, my life!"

"Oh, hush!" cried Indiana bitterly, pulling away her hand. "You have hatefully abused your promises. Try to undo the evil you have done!"

"I want to, I will!" he exclaimed, trying to recapture her hand.

"It is too late," she said. "Give me back my companion, my sister! Give me back Noun, my only friend!"

A mortal chill coursed through Raymon. . . . "She knows everything," he thought, "she has found me guilty." Nothing was more humiliating than to see himself accused of a crime by one who had been his innocent accomplice, nothing so ironically bitter as to hear Noun mourned by her rival.

"Yes," said Indiana, lifting her face bathed with tears, "it is you who were responsible"—she paused when she observed Raymon's pallor. It must have been awesome, for never had he suffered so terribly.

All the goodness of her heart and all the involuntary love he aroused in her overwhelmed Madame Delmare. "Forgive me!" she said in distress. "I am hurting you, I have suffered so much myself! Sit down and let us talk of other things."

This swift, sweet, generous response moved Raymon deeply; sobs racked him. He brought Indiana's hand to his lips and covered it with tears and kisses. It was the first time he was able to cry since the death of Noun, and it was Indiana who relieved him of that dreadful weight.

"Oh, if you cry this way," she said, "you who never knew her, how can I continue to reproach you, since you regret so much the hurt you have done me? Let us cry for her together, so that she who is in heaven may see us and forgive us."

A cold sweat broke from Raymon's forehead. If the words "you who never knew her" had delivered him from cruel anxiety, this appeal to the memory of his victim from the innocent mouth of Indiana struck him with superstitious terror. Distressed, he rose and walked agitatedly to the window, leaned against the sill, and took a deep breath. Indiana remained silent, profoundly moved. Seeing Raymon crying like a child and letting himself go like a woman, she felt a kind of secret joy.

"He is good!" she murmured to herself. "He loves me! His heart is warm and kind. He has done wrong, but his repentance makes up for it. I should have forgiven him sooner." She mistakenly took the remorse of a guilty man for the repentance of love.

"Do not cry any more," she implored, going to him. "It was I who killed her, I alone am guilty. It will sadden me all my life. I yielded to an impulse of distrust

87

and anger. I humiliated her, I wounded her to the soul. I poured out on her all the bitterness I felt for you; you alone had hurt me and I punished my poor friend for it. Oh, how hard I was on her!"

"And on me!" exclaimed Raymon, suddenly forgetting the past, being so occupied with the present. . . . He thus recuperated his strength, his determination, his love, his hopes; the sinister moment which had frozen his blood vanished like a bad dream. He awoke from it young, ardent, full of desire, passion, and hope.

"I am guilty, if you hate me," he said, throwing himself at her feet, "but if you love me, I am not, I have never been. Tell me, Indiana, do you love me?"

"Do you deserve it?"

"If, to deserve it," he said, "is to adore you—"

"Listen," she said, offering him her hands and fixing him with her great moist eyes in which a somber flame occasionally flickered, "listen! Do you know what it is to love a woman like me? No, you do not. You thought it was to satisfy a day's caprice. You thought I was like those blasé women you dominate so easily. You don't know that I have never loved, that I will never exchange my untouched virginal heart for a dry, debauched heart, my burning love for a lukewarm affair, my whole life for a passing moment! . . .

"I know you have the art of flattery, but do not hope to move my vanity. I have no need of compliments, only of affection. You must love me and no other, without reserve and forever; you must be ready to sacrifice everything—wealth, reputation, duty, business, principles, family—everything, sir, because I shall put the same devotion into the balance and I want them equal. You see, you cannot love me like that!"

It was not the first time Raymon had seen a woman take love seriously, though it was rare, fortunately for society; but he knew that vows of eternal love do not bind one's honor, again fortunately for society. Sometimes, too, the woman who insisted on these solemn vows had been the first to break them. So he was not afraid of Madame Delmare's demands; rather, he wasted no thought on either the past or the future. He was carried away by the irresistible charm of this slender, passionate woman, so frail in body and so strong in heart and mind. She was so beautiful, so alive and imposing, as she laid down her laws to him that he remained, fascinated, at her feet.

"I swear," he said, "that I will be yours body and soul; I pledge you my life, my blood, my will; take all I have, do with it what you wish—my wealth, my honor, my conscience, my thoughts, my whole being."

"Shh!" said Indiana hastily. "Here is my cousin!"

At this moment the phlegmatic Sir Ralph was entering the room with his usual tranquil air, saying how surprised and happy he was to see her, since he had not expected to. Then he asked if he might not kiss her in gratitude, and bending over her with methodical languor, he kissed her on the lips, as was the custom among children on their island.

Raymon became white with anger, and immediately

after Ralph had left the room he went to Indiana and sought to remove all trace of that impertinent kiss; but Madame Delmare coolly pushed him away and said: "Remember, you have much to make up for before I believe in you."

Raymon did not understand the delicacy of the rejection; he only saw the rejection and was angry with Sir Ralph. A few moments later he observed that when Sir Ralph spoke to Indiana in a low voice, he addressed her with the familiar *"tu,"* and he almost concluded that when Sir Ralph used the formal *"vous"* in public, it was the precaution of an accepted lover. But he blushed inwardly for his suspicions when he met the purity of the young woman's glance.

Raymon was brilliant that evening. There were many guests and they all listened to him. . . . On many occasions Indiana was fascinated by such brilliance, but she said to herself sadly that it was happiness, not glory, which she yearned for. In dismay she asked herself whether this man, for whom life had so many sides, so many enticing interests, could really devote his whole being to her, sacrifice all his ambitions for her. And as he defended step by step doctrines which were purely speculative and interests entirely foreign to their love with such valor and skill, such passion and self-possession, she was horrified to notice that she counted for so little in his life while in hers he was all. She said to herself in terror that for him she was a three-day caprice while he for her was the dream of an entire life.

As he offered his arm when they were leaving the

drawing room, he whispered a few words of love into her ear, but she answered sadly: "You have a brilliant mind!"

Raymon understood the reproach and spent all the next day at Madame Delmare's side. The other guests, occupied with hunting, left them completely free.

Raymon was eloquent; Indiana had such a hunger to believe that half his eloquence would have been enough. Women of France, you do not know what a Creole woman is like; *you* would have been less easily convinced, for you are not among those easily duped and betrayed!

XIII

When Sir Ralph returned from the hunt and felt Madame Delmare's pulse as usual, Raymon watched him closely and observed the faintest shade of surprise and pleasure on his placid features. And then, by I know not what secret impulse, the eyes of both men met, the light blue eyes of Sir Ralph fastened like an owl's on the dark eyes of Raymon and beat them down. The rest of the day the English baronet's glances at Madame Delmare, though barely perceptible through his imperturbability, had a touch of something one would call concern in a more expressive face. But Raymon's effort to ascertain whether it was fear or hope which dominated Ralph's thoughts was in vain; Sir Ralph was impenetrable.

Suddenly, as he stood several paces behind Madame

Delmare's chair, he heard Ralph say in an undertone: "It would be good for you to go riding tomorrow, cousin."

"But you know I have no horse just now," she replied.

"We will find you one. Will you hunt with us?" . . .

"If you agree to, madame," interrupted Raymon, "you will encourage me to follow your example. I like hunting very little, but to have the pleasure of being your squire—"

"In that case, I will go!" Indiana cried impulsively.

She exchanged a meaningful look with Raymon, but quick as it was, Ralph caught it, and for the remainder of the evening Raymon could not look at her or say a word to her without meeting the eye or ear of Sir Ralph. . . .

The following morning before breakfast, Raymon was surprised to see his host, solemn faced, entering his bedroom. His manner was stiffer than ever and Raymon's heart beat faster with an impatient desire for a challenge. But the visit dealt only with a horse which Raymon had brought to Bellerive and had said he wished to sell. In five minutes, without bargaining, Ralph purchased the horse and coldly counted out the sum on the mantelpiece, not deigning to pay attention to Raymon's assurances that there was no need for such haste. Then, as he was leaving, he turned and said: "The horse, sir, is mine from this morning!"

Raymon thought that meant his host wished to prevent him from joining the hunt, and he rather cuttingly remarked that he had no intention of following it on foot.

"I am well aware of the laws of hospitality," Sir Ralph replied with a shade of pomposity, and withdrew.

Going down to the courtyard, Raymon saw Madame Delmare, dressed for riding *en amazone,* playing with her dog Ophelia who was tugging at her handkerchief. Her cheeks had recovered their faint, rosy tint, her eyes shone with a long-absent brilliance. She had become pretty again, her curly black hair tumbled from beneath her little hat, her trim riding habit, buttoned to the chin, outlined her fine, supple figure. . . .

Struck by her charms, Raymon sensed a thrill of conquest and paid her the least banal compliment he could find in his repertoire.

"You were worried about my health," she said to him in a low voice. "Can't you see now how I want to live?"

His reply was a happy, grateful glance. Sir Ralph himself brought his cousin her horse, which Raymon recognized as the one he had just sold.

"What!" exclaimed Madame Delmare, for she had seen him trying it the day before in the courtyard. "Is Monsieur de Ramière lending me his own horse out of politeness?"

"Didn't you admire its beauty and gentleness yesterday?" asked Sir Ralph. "It is yours from today. I am sorry I couldn't offer it to you sooner, my dear."

"You are becoming facetious, cousin," said Madame

Delmare. "I don't understand this joke at all. Who should I thank, Monsieur de Ramière, who consents to lend me his horse, or you, who perhaps asked him to do so?"

"You must thank your cousin," said Colonel Delmare. "He bought the horse for you as a present."

"Is it really true, my dear Ralph?" asked Madame Delmare, caressing the beautiful creature with the joy of a schoolgirl receiving her first jewels.

"Didn't we agree that I would give you a horse in exchange for a piece of your embroidery? Come, get on the horse, don't be afraid. He's gentle, I tried him this morning."

Indiana threw her arms around Sir Ralph, leaped to the back of Raymon's horse, and pranced about the courtyard. . . .

"How happy I am!" she called to Raymon, beckoning him to her side. "My dear Ralph must have known what I would like most in the world. And you, Raymon, aren't you happy, too, that I'm riding the horse you rode? Oh, how I will take care of him! What is his name? Tell me! I don't want to give him any other name."

"If any man is happy here," replied Raymon, "it is your cousin, who gives you presents and receives your kisses." . . .

"Oh, fiddlesticks! Jealousy doesn't become you! How can our ordinary bourgeois intimacy make you envious, you who should be beyond ordinary life and create an enchanted world—you of all men!" . . .

"Forgive me, forgive me, Indiana! I was wrong! I

am not worthy of you, my sweet, gentle angel! But I confess I have suffered terribly from the liberties he has taken."

"Taken? Ralph?! Don't you know what sacred obligation binds us to him? Don't you know that his mother was my mother's sister, that we were born in the same valley, that he was my childhood protector, that he was my only support, my only teacher, my only companion on Bourbon Island, that he has followed me everywhere, that he left the land, which I left, to live where I lived, that he is the only being who loves me and is concerned about my life?"

"The devil take him! Everything you tell me is a knife in the wound. So he loves you, this Englishman! Do you know how much I love you?"

"Oh, no comparison! If it was the same kind of affection which made you rivals, I should have to choose the older one. But never fear, Raymon, that I shall ask you to love me as Ralph loves me."

"Tell me about that man, please. One can't penetrate his mask of stone." . . .

"I must tell you one thing about his life which might explain his character. He had the misfortune of having a brother whom his parents openly preferred; this brother had all the brilliance he lacks. He learned easily, he was talented and sparkled with wit; his face was less regular than Ralph's but more expressive. He was affectionate, eager, lively, in a word, lovable. Ralph, on the contrary, was clumsy, melancholy, undemonstrative; he liked solitude, learned slowly, and never displayed what he knew. When his parents saw how different he was from his older brother, they treated him badly. They did worse; they humiliated him. So, child though he was, his character became gloomy, given to dreams, and an insurmountable shyness paralyzed all his faculties. They had succeeded in inspiring him with an aversion and contempt for himself; he became discouraged with life, and at the age of fifteen he was attacked by depression, a malady which is wholly physical under the foggy skies of England and wholly spiritual under the sunny, life-giving skies of Bourbon Island. He often told me about the day he had left his house to throw himself into the sea, but as he stood and brooded on the shore, he saw me coming toward him in the arms of the Negress who had nursed me. I was then five. I was pretty, they say, and showed a liking for my cousin that no one else did. It is true; he was kind to me, as no one else was in my father's house. Since we were both unhappy, we understood each other. He taught me his father's language and I babbled to him in mine. That mixture of Spanish and English is perhaps the expression of Ralph's character. Once when I hugged him, I saw he was crying, and without knowing why, I began to cry, too. Then, he told me a long time afterward, he pressed me to his heart and swore to himself that he would live for me, an almost abandoned if not hated child; thus I gave his life some purpose and became the first and only tie in his sad existence. Since that day we were scarcely ever separated; we spent the days together in the mountain solitude, feeling free and alive— But perhaps these stories of

my childhood bore you and you would prefer joining
the hunt and having a gallop."

"Foolish girl!" said Raymon, holding onto the bridle
of her horse.

"All right, I'll continue," she said. "Edward Brown,
Ralph's older brother, died at twenty; his mother died
of grief and his father was inconsolable. Ralph would
have liked to lessen his sorrow, but the coldness with
which he was met by Mr. Brown deepened his natural timidity. He passed whole hours in sad silence beside that broken man, never daring to say a word or to
make an affectionate gesture, fearing it would be mis-
placed or futile. His father accused him of insensi-
tivity, and so Edward's death left Ralph more miserable and misunderstood than ever. I was his only
consolation."

"I cannot pity him, whatever you say," Raymon interrupted, "but there is one thing in both your lives I
don't understand: why didn't you marry?"

"I will give you a very good reason," she rejoined.
"When I was old enough, Ralph, who was ten years
older than I—an enormous difference of age in our climate, where the childhood of women is very short—
was already married."

"Is he a widower? I never heard his wife mentioned."

"Never mention her to him. She was young, rich,
and beautiful, but she had loved Edward, she had
been destined for him, and after he died, she was
made to marry Ralph for family reasons and she didn't
even try to hide her dislike. He had to leave for Eng-

land with her; and when he returned to Bourbon Island after the death of his wife, I was married to Monsieur Delmare and about to set off for Europe. Ralph tried to live alone, but solitude aggravated his misery. Though he has never spoken to me about his wife, I have every reason to believe that he had been even more unhappy living with her than in his father's house and that the memory of it added to his natural melancholy. Again he was attacked by depression; so he sold his coffee plantations and installed himself in France. The way he introduced himself to my husband was original, and it would have made me laugh, if the terribly dignified Ralph had not touched me deeply. 'Sir,' he said, 'I love your wife; it is I who raised her; I regard her as my sister and even more as my daughter. She is the only relative remaining to me, the only tie of affection in my life. Allow me to settle close to you, so that we three can spend our lives together. They say you are a bit jealous of your wife, but they say you are an honorable and honest man. When I give you my word that I have never loved her other than the way I have told you, and never will, you can look on me with as little concern as if I were really your brother-in-law. Is it not the truth, sir?' My husband, who takes pride in his reputation of having a soldier's frankness, received this straightforward declaration with a show of confidence. But several months of watchfulness had to pass before the confidence became as real as he claimed it to be. Nor is it as unshakable as Ralph's steadfast heart."

"Are you absolutely sure, Indiana," said Raymon,

"that Ralph is not deceiving himself a bit when he swears that he never loved you?"

"I was twelve when he left Bourbon with his wife for England; I was sixteen when he returned and found me married, and he showed more joy in that than unhappiness. Now Ralph is an old man."

"At twenty-nine?"

"Don't laugh! His face is young, but his heart has aged from suffering, and Ralph loves nothing that might make him suffer."

"Not even you?"

"Not even me. . . . His protection, which was once so courageous in the face of my father's despotism, has become lukewarm and careful before my husband's. He never reproaches himself when I suffer, so long as I am near him; he doesn't ask himself whether I am unhappy; he is satisfied to see me alive. He does not want to do anything to ease my lot if it will disturb his serenity, because it creates trouble with Monsieur Delmare. By constantly repeating to himself that his heart is a desert, he has convinced himself of it, and his heart has dried up from the inaction in which, out of distrust, he lets it slumber. He is a man who might have developed from the affection of another, but it was withheld from him and he has withered. Now he says that happiness is in repose and pleasure is in comfort. He prefers not knowing about problems which are not his; it must be said: Ralph is selfish."

"Well, so much the better," said Raymon. "I'm no longer afraid of him; I might even learn to like him, if you wish."

"Yes, love him, Raymon!" she replied. . . .

The sound of a nearby hunting horn warned them to be on the lookout; it was Sir Ralph, who saw them —or did he?

XIV

Raymon was astonished at the change in Indiana when the hounds were set loose. Her eyes and cheeks sprang to life; her nostrils quivered; and suddenly, digging her spurs into her horse's flanks, she left him and dashed after Ralph.* Raymon had no way of knowing that hunting was the only passion that Ralph and Indiana had in common. Nor did he suspect that in that frail, seemingly timid woman resided a courage beyond a man's, a kind of delirious intrepidity which sometimes appears to be a nervous explosion in nature's weaker creatures. Women rarely have the physical courage which consists in struggling against pain or danger from sheer inertia, but they often have the spiritual courage which is exalted by peril or suffering. Indiana's delicate fibers responded above all to the noise, the swift movement and excitement of the chase, that miniature image of war with its fatigues, ruses, calculations, combats, and hazards. Her dreary, ennui-burdened life had great need for these excitements; she then seemed to wake from leth-

* See p. 309 for Sand's description of her own love for riding and what it meant for a woman to be astride a horse, dressed as a man, and "dominating the landscape."

argy and expend in a single day all the energy which had fermented in her blood for a year.

It terrified Raymon to see her ride away so tempestuously, surrendering herself without fear to the high spirits of a horse she hardly knew, racing him through the thickets, agilely ducking the branches lashing at her face, leaping over ditches without hesitation, boldly defying the slippery clay slopes, risking the breaking of a slender limb, anxious only to be first on the smoking track of the boar. So much determination appalled and almost disgusted him with Madame Delmare. Men, above all lovers, fatuously prefer to protect the weakness, rather than to admire the courage, of women. Shall I confess it? Raymon was terrorstricken by the boldness and tenacity in love such intrepidity indicated. This was not the resigned love of poor Noun, who preferred to drown herself rather than struggle against her misfortune.

"If there's as much high spirit and passion in her affection as in her taste for play," he thought, "if her will fixes itself on me, fierce and throbbing, as her caprice fixes on the flanks of that boar, then society will have no fetters for her, laws no force; my destiny will have to succumb and my future be sacrificed to her present."

Raymon was torn from his reflections by wild cries of distress, among which he could distinguish Indiana's voice. He urgently spurred his horse forward but was quickly overtaken by Ralph, who asked if he had heard the cries. At the same time, several terrified hunters came up, shouting incoherently that the boar had charged and knocked Madame Delmare to the ground. Other hunters, even more terrified, rode up, calling for Sir Ralph's medical aid.

"It's no use!" cried the last arrival. "There's no hope, your help is too late!"

In that moment of horror, the eyes of Raymon turned to the white, gloom-stricken face of Sir Ralph. He did not cry out, he did not rage, he did not wring his hands; he simply drew his hunting knife and coolly put it to his throat; but Raymon snatched it from him and pulled him in the direction of the cries.

Ralph seemed to wake from a bad dream when he saw Madame Delmare hurrying toward him, urging help for the colonel, who was lying as if lifeless on the ground. Ralph hastened to bleed him, once assured he still lived; but Delmare's leg was broken and he had to be carried to the château.

As for Madame Delmare, in the confusion her name rather than her husband's had been called— rather, had been heard by Ralph and Raymon, since it had interested them most. Indiana was unhurt, but fright and consternation had momentarily paralyzed her. Raymon supported her in his arms, reconciled to her by this womanly concern for the misfortunes of a husband whom she had much to forgive before she pitied him. Sir Ralph had already recovered his usual calm, but an extraordinary pallor revealed what a shock he had experienced; he had almost lost one of the two people he loved. . . . However, Raymon never mentioned Ralph's attempted suicide to Indiana. In this ungenerous act of Raymon there was something selfish and hateful, but you might prefer to forgive it as the consequence of jealousy.

Six weeks passed before the colonel could, with difficulty, be moved to Lagny, but more than six months were required before he could walk, for rheumatism had attacked the injured leg before the fractured femur had knit, condemning him to pain and immobility. His wife cared for him devotedly, never leaving his bedside, never protesting his ill-tempered, fault-finding, sickly complaints.

Despite the depressing ennui of such a life, Indiana's health flourished and happiness repossessed her heart. Raymon loved her, he really loved her. He came every day; he permitted nothing to keep him from her, whether the colonel's infirmities, Ralph's coldness, or the constraints put on their conversations. One look from Raymon filled Indiana's heart with joy for a whole day. She no longer dreamed of complaining about her life; her heart was full; her youth was served; her moral force was fed.

Gradually, the colonel began to feel very friendly to Raymon, believing in his simplicity that Raymon's many calls were out of concern for his health. Madame de Ramière also paid occasional visits, sanctioning the liaison of her son by her presence, and Indiana developed a very warm attachment to Raymon's mother. Finally, the wife's lover became the husband's friend.

Constantly thrown together, Raymon and Ralph arrived at a sort of intimacy; they called each other "my dear chap"; they shook hands morning and evening. If they had a small favor to ask, they would say, "I count on your friendship," and so on. When they spoke of each other, they said, "He is my friend."

And yet, though as frank as one can be in this world, they didn't like each other the slightest. They disagreed about everything; nothing united them; their love for Indiana was so different that it resulted in an even greater division. They took a singular delight in contradicting each other and in disturbing each other's humor with criticisms which, though clothed as generalizations, were no less acid and sharp, most often beginning with politics and ending with morals. . . .

For my part, I believe that a man's political opinion is the man entire. Tell me what your heart and your head are and I will tell you your political point of view. No matter what our social rank or political party by accident of birth, our character ultimately prevails over our prejudices and received beliefs. You may find me too absolute, but how can I be optimistic about a mind that clings to certain theoretical systems which human generosity rejects? Show me a man who asserts the advantages of capital punishment and, however conscientious or enlightened he may be, I defy you to establish any sympathetic link between us. If such a man wished to present facts unknown to me, he would fail, because I cannot have confidence in him.

Ralph and Raymon differed on everything, though before they knew each other they hadn't yet reached final opinions. But as soon as they argued, each took a position to the contrary of the other's and arrived at absolute, unshakable conclusions. Raymon invariably was the champion of the *status quo;* Ralph attacked it at every point. . . .

Thus Ralph always put forward his vision of a republic from which he would exclude all abuses, all prejudices, all injustices, a vision based entirely on the hope for a new race of men. Raymon maintained his doctrine of a hereditary monarchy, preferring, he said, to endure abuses, prejudices, and injustices to seeing the erection of scaffolds and a reign of revolutionary terror.

The colonel was almost always initially on Ralph's side. He hated the *ancien régime* of the Bourbons and put all his animosity into his opinions. But soon Raymon would artfully win over the old Bonapartist soldier by proving to him that *his* monarchy was much closer in principle to the empire of Napoleon than to Ralph's republic. Ralph had such little talent of persuasion—he was so candid and maladroit, the poor baronet!—his frankness was so rough, his logic so dry, his principles so absolute! He spared no one, he softened no hard truth. . . .

As for the colonel, he hadn't advanced a step since the battle of Waterloo. He was a conservative type, as encrusted and opinionated as the émigrés at Coblenz, the unfailing objects of his scornful irony. An aging, overgrown child, he understood nothing in the great drama of Napoleon's downfall. He had seen nothing but the fortunes of war in an event that witnessed the triumph of the people's opinion. He talked continually of treason and of a country sold out to the enemy, as if an entire nation could betray a single man, as if France could have let herself be sold by a few generals! He accused the Bourbons of tyranny and regretted the good old days of Napoleon's empire, when men were torn from the soil and bread taken from families. He declaimed one minister's police and extolled another's. He was still a man of the day after Waterloo. . . .

Before Raymon's arrival there had been an unspoken agreement between Delmare and Ralph to avoid controversial, mutually wounding subjects, but Raymon had introduced all the subtleties of language, all the treacherous pettiness of culture. He taught them that anything can be said, any reproach or defense made, under the pretext of honest discussion. He introduced the milder salon form of discussion which had succeeded the passionate debates of the Hundred Days of Napoleon's return, but the colonel was still held by those passions and Ralph made the great mistake of thinking he might listen to the voice of reason. Delmare daily became more sour toward him and drew closer to Raymon, who knew how to assuage the colonel's ego without making too many concessions to his thinking.

But it is very imprudent to introduce politics as a pastime into family life. . . . The little château had defended itself in vain for years against this fatal invasion; it finally lost its insouciance, its active, interior life, its long evenings of silent meditation. Noisy disputes woke the sleeping echoes; bitter, threatening words terrified the faded cherubs who had smiled through the dust of the hangings for a hundred years.

The passions of the day penetrated that old dwelling place and its antiquated splendors; all those relics of a period of pleasure and levity witnessed in dismay the coming of our own epoch of doubt and grand proclamations, represented by three people who closed themselves up together every day to quarrel from morning until night.

XV

Despite the incessant disputes, Madame Delmare indulged herself with the confidence of her years in the dream of a happy future. It was her first happiness. . . . Love was a novel, generous passion in her heart; a thousand noble, delicate feelings were embraced by it and gave her a strength Raymon could not understand.

He himself was annoyed at first by the constant presence of husband or cousin. He had hoped to deal with this love affair as with others, but very soon Indiana compelled him to rise to her level. Her resigned acceptance of surveillance, her happy air when she glanced discreetly at him, her eyes which spoke to him mutely and eloquently, her sublime smile when, during a conversation, a sudden allusion united their hearts—all these soon became exquisite pleasures which Raymon appreciated, thanks to the refinement of his mind and education. . . .

Indiana was opposed to the so-called interests of civilization's simple laws of common sense and humanity;

her objections had a natural freedom which sometimes embarrassed Raymon and always charmed him with its childlike originality. He set to work seriously to bring her around gradually to his beliefs, his principles. He would have been proud to dominate a conviction so conscientious and naturally enlightened, but he had some trouble in attaining it. Ralph's liberal theories, his stiff hatred of the vices of society, his sharp preference for the rule of other laws and other morals were sentiments to which the childhood memories of Indiana responded. But Raymon suddenly demolished his opponent by demonstrating that his aversion for the present was the result of selfishness; he depicted his own predilections with warmth—his devotion to the royal family, which he had the skill to embellish with the heroism of an endangered loyalty, his respect for the persecuted beliefs of his ancestors, the religious sentiments which he did not care to subject to reason, he said, and to which he clung by instinct and need. . . .

There were moments, however, when Raymon almost forgot his love and thought only of his antipathy. When he was with Madame Delmare, he saw nobody but Sir Ralph, who presumed with his rough, cold common sense to attack him, the superior man who had vanquished such greater adversaries. He was humiliated to see himself engaged in combat with so paltry an opponent and would bear down on him with all the weight of his eloquence; he would attack with all the resources of his talent and Ralph, bewildered and slow in collecting his thoughts, and slower still in expressing them, would be made painfully aware of his weakness.

At such moments it seemed to Indiana that Raymon had wandered away from her; she had sensations of anxiety and terror when she suddenly thought that perhaps all those grand and noble sentiments so eloquently declaimed were nothing but the pompous parading of words, the ironical fluency of a lawyer listening to himself and playing to his audience for surprise and effect. She trembled particularly when their eyes met and she seemed to see gleaming in his, not the pleasure of being understood by her, but the triumphant conceit of one who argues brilliantly. She was afraid at such times and thought of Ralph, the egoist, to whom they may have been unjust; but Ralph did not know how to enlarge her doubts and Raymon was adroit in dissipating them. . . .

Despite his strength of character, Ralph was sometimes discouraged with virtue. He hated Raymon and could have, with one word, driven him from Lagny, but he didn't utter it, because he had one belief, one only which was more powerful than Raymon's thousand. It was not the Church, the monarchy, society, reputation, or law which dictated his sacrifices and courage; it was his conscience.

He had lived so alone he had become accustomed to not counting on others, but he had learned in his isolation to know himself. . . . This wholly interior life with its completely private sensations gave him all the outward appearance of selfishness; and perhaps nothing resembles it more closely than self-respect.

However, as often happens when, trying too hard, we fail to do enough, Sir Ralph made the great mistake of being overscrupulous and so caused Madame Delmare a great injury. That mistake was failing to tell her the true reason for Noun's death. Undoubtedly she would then have reflected on the dangers of loving Raymon; but we shall see later why Sir Ralph did not dare enlighten his cousin and what painful scruples made him keep his silence about so important a matter. When he would decide to talk, it would be too late; Raymon would have had time to consolidate his conquest.

An unexpected event occurred which clouded the future of the colonel and his wife—a commercial house in Belgium, on which Delmare's factory depended, suddenly went bankrupt, and the colonel, barely recovered from his accident, left hastily for Antwerp.

Seeing him so weak and ill, his wife said she wanted to accompany him, but Delmare, threatened with complete ruin and resolved to honor all his obligations, feared that his trip would then be construed as flight and so decided to leave his wife at Lagny as a guarantee of his return. He even declined the company of Sir Ralph, beseeching him to remain and support Madame Delmare in case of trouble from anxious or pressing creditors. . . .

Raymon, who had hoped to profit from Delmare's absence, was disappointed when he saw that Sir Ralph seemed determined to replace the colonel in his vigil, that he arrived at Lagny in the morning and did not depart before night; moreover, Ralph affected a maddening politeness in timing his departure with Raymon's on the grounds that they had the same route of return to their respective residences. This constraint soon became unbearable for Raymon de Ramière, and Madame Delmare saw in it not only a suspicion insulting to her but also an intent to assume despotic control.

Raymon did not dare ask for a secret meeting; each time he had attempted it, Madame Delmare had recalled the conditions they had agreed upon. Meanwhile, a week had passed since the colonel had departed; he might be back soon; the present moment must be seized. To concede victory to Sir Ralph would be a dishonor for Raymon. One morning he slipped this note into Madame Delmare's hand:

"Indiana, don't you love me as I love you? My angel! I am miserable and you do not even notice it. I am sad, worried about your future, not my own: wherever you are, there will I live and die. But the thought of poverty for you alarms me. How could you endure it, sick and weak as you are? You have a rich generous cousin; perhaps your husband will accept from him what he refuses from me. Ralph will be helping you, I shall not!

"You see, my dear, I have a reason for being disheartened. You are heroic, you laugh at everything, you don't want me to worry. Oh, how I need your sweet words, your gentle glances, to keep up my courage! But by some inconceivable fate, these days which

I had hoped to spend freely with you have brought an intolerable restraint.

"Say one word, Indiana, that will allow us to be alone together at least one hour, that I may let my tears fall and tell you how much I suffer so that you might console me. Also, Indiana, I have a child's yearning, the true lover's yearning, to enter your bedroom. Oh, don't be frightened, my sweet Creole!" . . .

Madame Delmare read the letter in her bedroom; she replied to him immediately and gave him the reply together with the key: "I, fear *you*, Raymon? Oh, no, not now. I know only too well that you love me; I am all too happy believing it. Come then, I am not afraid of myself either; if I loved you less, I might be less calm, but I love you as you yourself do not realize. Leave early, so Ralph will not be suspicious. Come back at midnight. You know the park and the house; here is the key to the small gate; lock it after you enter."

This ingenuous confidence in him embarrassed Raymon; he had sought to inspire it only to betray it; he had counted on the dark, the danger, the occasion. If Indiana had shown any fear, she would have been lost, but she was calm, she put her trust in his good faith; he vowed he would not give her reason to repent. The important thing was to spend the night in her bedroom so that he would not be a fool in his own eyes, so that Ralph's prudence would be nullified, so that he could laugh at him inwardly. That was the personal satisfaction he hungered for.

XVI

But that evening Ralph was really insupportable; never had he been heavier, colder, more tiresome. He could say nothing relevant and, to top it all, he showed no sign of preparing to leave as the evening lengthened. Madame Delmare began to feel uneasy; she alternately looked at her clock, which registered eleven, the door, which creaked in the wind, and the inexpressive face of her cousin, who placidly watched the fire without appearing to suspect that his presence was unwanted.

Sir Ralph's inscrutable mask, however, his immobile face, concealed at that moment a deep, poignant emotion. He was a man nothing escaped, because he coolly observed everything. He had not been duped by Raymon's simulated departure; he clearly perceived Madame Delmare's anxiety at that moment. He suffered more than she and hesitated irresolutely between the desire to give her a saving warning and the fear of yielding to feelings he disavowed; at last his cousin's interests led him to summon his courage and break the silence. . . .

"Do you remember, Indiana," he said, "that you felt more ill than usual that night just a year ago? I recall your words as if they were still ringing in my ears. 'You will call me mad,' you said, 'but there is some danger ahead of us—threatening me, I'm sure.' . . . You were a prophet that night, Indiana. A great danger did threaten us, a fatal influence invaded our peaceful dwelling."

"Good Lord, I don't understand you!"

"You will, my poor, dear friend. That was the evening Raymon de Ramière was brought here. Do you remember in what state?"

Ralph paused for several seconds, but did not dare lift his eyes to his cousin's face; when she did not reply, he continued: "I was told to revive him, which I did, as much to satisfy you as to obey humane instinct, but in truth, Indiana, it was a misfortune for me to have saved that man's life! It was I who did all the harm."

"I don't know what you mean!" said Indiana through parched lips. She was profoundly affected.

"I mean the death of that unfortunate creature," said Ralph. "If not for him, she would be still alive today; if not for his fatal love, that good, beautiful girl whom you cherished would still be at your side."

Madame Delmare did not yet understand. She was deeply angered by the strange, painful time taken by her cousin to reproach her for her attachment to Monsieur de Ramière.

"That's quite enough," she said, rising.

But Ralph did not seem to hear. "What has always astonished me," he continued, "was that you never guessed what made Monsieur de Ramière climb over your wall."

A sudden suspicion struck Indiana; her legs trembled and she sat down. Ralph had plunged a knife and opened a ghastly wound. He no sooner saw the effect than he was horrified by what he had done; he now thought only of the wound he had just inflicted on the one he loved most in the world; he felt his heart break. He would have cried, if he had known how to cry, but the unhappy man did not have the gift of tears; he had no way of translating the heart's language; the seeming coldness with which he executed the cruel operation gave him the air of a hangman in Indiana's eyes.

"This is the first time," she said bitterly, "that I have seen your antipathy for Monsieur de Ramière lead you to employ weapons unworthy of you, but I don't see how it adds to your act to stain the memory of one who was dear to me and whose tragic end should have made sacred to us. I have not asked you any questions, Sir Ralph; I don't know what you are trying to tell me. Permit me to hear no more."

She rose and left Sir Ralph bewildered and broken in spirit. . . . He quit Lagny in despair and wandered blindly through the forest.

It was midnight; Raymon was at the park gate. He opened it, but on entering he felt a foreboding chill. What was he doing, keeping this rendezvous? He had made virtuous resolutions, but would he be repaid by a chaste chat, a sisterly kiss, for the torments he was subjecting himself to at that moment? For if you remember the circumstances of his previous clandestine passage along these paths, you will understand that it required a certain degree of moral courage to go in pursuit of pleasure along the same way with such haunting memories.

Late in October the climate of Paris's environs become foggy and damp, especially in evening around the streams. By chance, the mist that night was as dense as that of the preceding spring and Raymon walked with uncertainty between the mist-enveloped trees. He skirted a summer pavilion which housed geraniums in the winter. He cast an uneasy glance at the door and his heart beat faster at the wild thought that it might open to disclose a woman wrapped in a cloak. Raymon forced a smile at the idea and went on. Nevertheless he was profoundly chilled by it and he felt his chest tighten as he approached the Lagny stream.

He had to cross it to reach the flower garden bordering the house and the only crossing at that point was a small wooden bridge . . . He was halfway across when an indistinct human figure rose at the railing's end as if in wait. He was seized by confusion, reason fled him; he retreated and hid among the trees and stared fixedly and in terror at that shadowy apparition hovering like the mist and shimmering like a moonbeam. He tried to reassure himself that his harried imagination had played tricks on him, lending a human form to a tree trunk or a shrub, when he distinctly saw the figure move and walk toward him.

At that moment, had his legs not failed him he would have fled like a child from a cemetery at night hearing ghostly footsteps on the grass. But he was half-paralyzed and grasped the trunk of the willow tree behind which he was hiding for support. Then

Sir Ralph, enveloped in a light cloak, brushed by and took the path Raymon had just left.

"Clumsy spy!" thought Raymon as he watched Ralph looking for his footprints. "I will escape your damnable vigilance, and while you are standing guard here, I will be enjoying myself there!"

He crossed the bridge with the lightness of a bird and the brazenness of a lover. . . .

"Poor Ralph," he thought as he went up the secret staircase with a bold, tripping step. "It is you who asked for it!"

PART THREE

XVII

After leaving Sir Ralph, Madame Delmare had locked herself into her bedroom, a thousand stormy thoughts raging in her breast. It was not the first time that a vague suspicion had cast a sinister light on the frail edifice of her happiness. . . . One particular circumstance might have enlightened her, if she had not closed her mind to all mistrust.

They had found a very costly ring on Noun's finger, which Madame Delmare had seen her wear shortly before her death and which Noun claimed to have found. Madame Delmare now wore that ring as a token of sorrow, and she had often observed Raymon turn pale when he took her hand to put it to his lips. Once he had begged her never to mention Noun, because he viewed himself as responsible for her death; and when she had sought to relieve him of that painful thought by blaming herself, he had replied: "No, my dear Indiana, do not accuse yourself. You do not know how guilty I am."

These words, uttered in a bitter, somber tone, had frightened Madame Delmare. She had not dared to insist, and although she was now beginning to understand the various fragments of the truth, she did not yet have the courage to put them together.

She opened her window and, looking out on the calm night, the pale, lovely moon behind the silvery mist, recalling that Raymon would soon come, that perhaps he was already in the park—and, thinking of all the joy she had promised herself in that hour of love and mystery, she cursed Ralph, who with a word had poisoned her hope and had forever destroyed her peace of mind. She even felt hatred for him, that unhappy man who had been as a father and had sacrificed his future for her sake; for his future was Indiana's friendship; it was his only possession, and that, too, he had resigned himself to losing in order to save her. . . .

Suddenly one of those strange, inchoate ideas came to her which only the restless and the unhappy know. She gambled her whole fate on a singular, fragile test against which Raymon could not be on guard. She had scarcely prepared it when she heard his footsteps on the secret staircase. She ran to unlock the door, then returned and sat down, so emotionally stirred she felt on the edge of fainting, but as in all the crises of her life, she held tightly to her clarity and strength of mind.

Raymon was pale and breathless when he pushed open the door, impatient to see the light, the tangible world once again. Indiana had her back turned to him; she was wrapped in a fur-lined cloak. By a strange quirk, it was the same pelisse Noun had worn when she last went to meet Raymon in the park and when, you might recall, he had the illusion that the cloaked, hidden woman was Madame Delmare. Now, when he again saw that very apparition drooping sadly in a chair in the pale, flickering light of a lamp, in the same place of so many memories, in that bedroom he had not entered since the bleakest night of his life, he recoiled involuntarily and stood stark still in the doorway, fastening his terrified gaze on that motionless figure, trembling like a poltroon, for fear that when it turned, it would show him the livid features of a drowned woman. . . .

But on recognizing the woman he had come to seduce, he forgot the one he had seduced and walked toward her. . . . At that moment he noticed that Madame Delmare held something which she seemed to spread before him with an affectation of gravity. He bent over it and saw a mass of black hair, cut roughly and in haste, which Indiana was smoothing with her hand.

"Do you recognize it?" she asked, fixing him with her clear blue eyes in which he glimpsed a strange, piercing gleam.

Raymon hesitated, studied the scarf tied around her

head in Noun's fashion, and thought he understood. "Naughty child!" he said, taking the locks in his hand. "Why did you cut your hair? It was so beautiful and I loved it so much!"

"You asked me yesterday," she said with the ghost of a smile, "whether I would sacrifice it for you."

"Oh, Indiana!" cried Raymon. "You know you will be more beautiful to me than ever. Give it to me! I will not regret your cutting the hair I admired now that I can caress it every day. Give it to me, so that I shall have it always."

But in gathering the great mass in his hand, some of whose strands reached the floor, Raymon fancied it felt drier and rougher than the hair of Indiana he had stroked. He also experienced I know not what nervous shiver as he felt the cold weight of the hair, as if it had been cut a long time ago and had lost its fragrant moistness and vital warmth. Then he looked more closely and searched in vain for the blue sheen which gave Indiana's hair the look of a crow's blue-black wing; this hair was that of a Negro, black, with an Indian texture, a lifeless heaviness.

The clear, cutting eyes of Indiana followed Raymon's as he involuntarily directed them toward a half-open ebony box from which several locks of the same hair hung. "These are not yours!" he cried, and he untied Indiana's head scarf.

Her hair had not been shorn: it tumbled over her shoulders in all its abundant splendor. But she pushed him away and still pointing to the other locks, she said: "Don't you recognize these? Didn't you ever admire, ever caress them? Has one damp night robbed them of their perfume? Have you no memory, no fear for her who wore this ring?"

Raymon sank into a chair; Noun's locks slipped from his trembling hand. So much painful emotion had exhausted him. He was a man of violent, bilious temper whose blood flowed rapidly, whose nerves were easily exacerbated. He shivered from head to foot and fell in a faint to the floor.

When he regained consciousness, he found Madame Delmare on her knees beside him, her face bathed in tears, begging his forgiveness. But Raymon no longer loved her.

"You have hurt me terribly," he said, "irreparably. You will never restore my confidence in you. You have shown me how cruel you can be. Poor Noun, poor unfortunate girl! It was to her I did wrong, not to you; it was she who had a right to vengeance, but she did not take it. She sacrificed her life for my peace. It is not you, madame, who would have done so much! Give me her hair, it is mine, it belongs to me, it is the sole thing left of the only woman who really loved me!" . . .

Madame Delmare did not reply. Motionless, pale, hair disheveled and eyes staring, she moved Raymon to pity. He took her hand.

"And yet," he said, "my love for you is so blind that I can still forget the past and the present, the crime that has scarred my life and the crime you have just committed. So love me, and I will forgive you."

Madame Delmare's despair reawoke desire and

pride in her lover's heart. . . . He pretended to be overwhelmed by somber, melancholy reverie for a few moments; he scarcely responded to Indiana's tears and caresses. He waited until her heart would break from her sobs, until she would foresee with dread the horrors of being abandoned, until she would be exhausted by the wrenching emotions; and then finally when he saw her at his feet, utterly worn out, awaiting death at a word from him, he seized her with a convulsive fury and crushed her in his arms. She surrendered like a child; she gave him her lips without resistance. She was almost dead.

But suddenly, awaking as if from a dream, she tore herself from his burning embrace, fled to the end of the room where the portrait of Sir Ralph was hanging; and as if putting herself under the protection of that grave, calm personage, she huddled against the painting, quivering, distraught, and seized by a strange fear. This made Raymon believe that she had been profoundly moved by his embrace, that she was afraid of herself, that she was now his. He hurried to her, drew her forcefully from her refuge and declared that he had come with the intention of keeping his promises, but that her cruelty had freed him from his vows. . . .

Indiana trembled. So ignorant of life was she that she believed resistance impossible; she was ready to yield out of fear what she would refuse out of love, but as she struggled weakly in Raymon's arms, she said to him despairingly: "Are you capable of using force on me then?"

Raymon halted, struck by a moral resistance stronger than any physical force. He pushed her away smartly. "Never!" he cried. "I would rather die than hold you against your will!" . . . And when he saw that she did not surrender, he gave in to necessity—he reproached her for not loving him. It was a commonplace device he scorned, one that made him secretly smile, almost ashamed of having anything to do with a woman so naïve that she didn't laugh at it herself.

But that reproach sped more deftly to Indiana's heart than all the declarations with which Raymon had embroidered his speech. Then suddenly she remembered.

"Raymon, she who loved you so much—the one we just talked about—she refused you nothing?"

"Nothing!" exclaimed Raymon, exasperated by this awkward reminder. "You, who are always recalling her to me, would do better to make me forget how much she loved me!"

"Listen to me," Indiana resumed gravely and thoughtfully. "Don't be shocked, but I must ask you something else. Perhaps you haven't been as guilty toward me as I thought. I would like to be able to forgive you for what I thought was a deadly insult—so tell me . . . when I surprised you here—whom did you come to see, her or me?"

Raymon hesitated, then convinced Indiana would soon learn the truth, or perhaps knew it already, replied: "Her."

"Well, I prefer it that way," she said sadly. "I prefer infidelity to insult. Be honest to the end, Raymon.

How long had you been in my bedroom when I arrived? Remember, Ralph knows everything, and if I wanted to ask him—"

"There is no need for Monsieur Brown's testimony, madame. I had been here since the night before."

"And you spent the night in this bedroom?—Your silence is enough for me."

The two remained wordless for a time; then Indiana rose and was about to speak when a rap on the door chilled her blood. They scarcely dared to breathe.

A paper was slipped under the door. It had been torn from a notebook. On it was scrawled in pencil, almost illegibly:

Your husband is here.
Ralph

XVIII

"That's a wretched lie!" said Raymon, as the sound of Ralph's footsteps faded away. "Sir Ralph needs a lesson and I'll give him one—"

"You will not," said Indiana coldly and decisively. "My husband is here; Ralph has never lied. We are lost, you and I. There was a time when such a thought would have frozen me with fear; today, what does it matter!"

"Very well," said Raymon, taking her into his arms, "since death is at our door, be mine! Forgive me for everything. At this supreme moment, let your last word be one of love and my last breath one of joy."

"This moment of terror and courage might have been the most beautiful moment in my life," she said, "but you have spoiled it for me."

The rumble of carriage wheels was heard in the courtyard; the gate bell was jangled by a strong, impatient hand. "I know that sound," said Indiana coolly and attentively. "Ralph did not lie; you have time to escape. Go!"

"I will not!" cried Raymon. "I suspect some contemptible betrayal and you will not be the only victim. I am staying; my body will protect you—"

"There was no betrayal—you can hear the servants; they'll be opening the gate. Go! The trees in the garden will hide you; the moon is low. Not another word; go!"

Raymon was forced to obey, but Indiana accompanied him to the bottom of the staircase and looked searchingly about the garden. All was silent and calm. She stood a long time on the last step, listening in terror to the sound of his boots on the gravel, heedless of her husband's arrival. His suspicions, his anger, didn't matter, so long as Raymon was out of danger!

As for him, he swiftly crossed the stream and the park, reached the gate, and in his nervousness had trouble opening it. Outside he met the waiting Sir Ralph, who said to him as coolly as at a party: "The key, please. If there's a search for it, it would be better to find it on me."

Raymon would have preferred an insult to this irony. "I am not one to forget a sincere favor," he said, "but rest assured, I'll avenge an insult and punish a betrayal."

Sir Ralph altered neither his tone nor his expression. "I do not want your thanks," he said, "and I await your vengeance tranquilly, but this is no time for talk. Here's your path; think of Madame Delmare's good name." And he disappeared.

That agitated night had so upset Raymon's thinking that he would gladly have believed in black magic at that moment. He arrived at dawn at Cercy and went to bed with a fever.

As for Madame Delmare, she did the honors at breakfast for her husband and cousin with immense calm and dignity. She had not yet reflected on her situation; she was entirely under the influence of instinct, which told her to be cool and self-possessed. The colonel was gloomy and preoccupied, but it was his business which absorbed him and no jealous suspicions found room in his thoughts.

Toward evening Raymon recovered the strength to turn *his* thoughts to love, but that love had greatly diminished. He liked to hurdle obstacles but he balked at being bothered, and he envisaged a great deal of annoyance now that Indiana had the right to reproach him. Finally he decided that his honor demanded that he inquire about her, so he sent a servant to lurk around Lagny and find out what might be going on. The servant returned with a letter from Madame Delmare which read:

"I had hoped last night that I would lose my senses or my life. Unfortunately I lost neither, but I will not

complain; I deserve my sufferings; I chose this turbulent life; it would be cowardly to retreat from it now. I
don't know whether you are guilty or not; I don't
want to know. We will never return to that subject,
shall we? It makes us both suffer too much, so let this
be the last time we mention it.

"You said one thing which gave me a cruel joy.
Poor Noun! Forgive me, you who are in heaven! You
no longer suffer, you no longer love, perhaps you pity
me! You told me, Raymon, that you sacrificed her for
me, that you loved me more than her. . . . But today
it can no longer be the same; the future can only
mean a horrifying parallel between Noun and myself!
Oh, to be loved no more than she! If only I believed
it! And yet she was more beautiful, far more beautiful
than I! Why did you prefer me? You must have loved
me in another way, and better. This is what I wanted
to tell you. Will you renounce being my lover the way
you were hers? In this event, I can still esteem you,
believe in your regret, in your sincerity, in your love;
if not, forget me; you will see me no more. I may die
as a result, perhaps, but I would rather die than descend to being your mistress."

Raymon did not know how to reply. Her pride
offended him; he had never thought a woman who
had thrown herself into his arms could resist him thus
openly and find reasons for her resistance. "She
doesn't love me; her heart is dry, her character is
haughty."

From that moment he no longer loved her. She had
hurt his vanity. . . . Spitefully he swore he would tri-

umph over her, but he swore in a spirit of vengeance rather than pride. It was no longer a case of filching a new pleasure but of punishing an affront, not of possessing a woman but of seducing her. He swore he would be her master, if only for one day, and then discard her for the pleasure of seeing her at his feet.

Immediately he wrote Indiana a letter. . . .

"You admit you almost lost your senses last night; I lost mine entirely. I was guilty—no, I was insane. Forget those hours of suffering and delirium. I am calm now; I have thought things over, I am still worthy of you. Bless you, my angel, for having saved me from myself, for having reminded me how I should love you. Now, Indiana, command me! I am your slave; you know it. I would give my life for one hour in your arms; I would suffer a lifetime for one smile from you. I am your friend, your brother, nothing more. . . . One word from you and I will shoulder as much remorse as I can bear; for you I would abandon my own mother; for you I would commit any crime. Oh, Indiana, if only you realized how much I love you!—"

The pen dropped from Raymon's hand; he was very tired and he was falling asleep. He forced himself to reread his letter to make sure his sleepiness had not affected his writing, but he was so exhausted it was impossible for him to follow his own reasoning. He rang for his servant, told him to go to Lagny before daybreak, and then slept that profound, refreshing, voluptuous sleep which only those completely satisfied with themselves really know. Madame Delmare had

not gone to bed; she was unconscious of her fatigue;
she spent the night writing; when she received Raymon's letter, she replied to it on the spot:

"Thank you, Raymon, thank you! You give me back
my strength and my life. Now, I can face anything,
endure anything, because you love me and nothing
frightens you. Yes, we will see each other again, we
will face everybody together. Ralph can do what he
will with our secret. I am no longer worried about
anything, because you love me; I am no longer afraid
even of my husband.

"I forgot to mention his business affairs yesterday,
and yet they have taken a turn important to me. We
are ruined. There is a question of selling Lagny and
going to the colonies. But what does it really matter? I
can't even bring myself to think about it. I know we
will never be separated: you have sworn it, Raymon. I
count on that, on your courage. Nothing can frighten
me, nothing can stop me; my place is at your side and
only death can tear me from it."

"A woman's extravagance!" thought Raymon, crum-
pling the note. "Romantic projects! . . . To read this,
who would think she counts her kisses and haggles
over her caresses!"

That day he went to Lagny. Ralph was not there.
The colonel received Raymon in a friendly fashion
and spoke to him in confidence. He took him into the
park to be more at ease and told him he was completely ruined and would put up his factory for sale
the following day. Raymon offered generously to help;
Delmare refused the offer. "No, my friend. . . . I

made my little fortune once, I can begin again. I owe it to my wife, who is young; I can not leave her in poverty. She still possesses a small estate on Bourbon Island. I intend to go there and start a new business. In a few years, in ten years at most, I hope we will meet again."

Raymon pressed the colonel's hand, smiling inwardly at his confidence in the future, at his talking of ten years as if they were one day, when his bald head and aging body spoke of an approaching end. Nevertheless he pretended to share the same hopes. "I'm glad to see that you don't permit yourself to be downcast," he said, "thanks to your manly courage. But does Madame Delmare have the same courage? Aren't you afraid she might have some objection to your project of leaving the country?"

"I would be sorry," rejoined the colonel, "but women are made to obey and not to give advice. I haven't told Indiana it was definite. Except for you, I don't know what she would miss in leaving, and yet I expect tears and headaches if only out of contrariness. Blast women! All the same, I count on you, my dear fellow, to make my wife listen to reason. She trusts you; use your influence to keep her from crying; I hate tears."

Raymon promised to return the next day to tell Madame Delmare about her husband's decision.

"You'll be doing me a great favor," said the colonel. "I'll take Ralph to the farm, so that you will be free to talk to her."

"Well, good luck to us all!" thought Raymon as he left.

XIX

Delmare's plans accorded perfectly with Raymon's desires. . . . So he returned to Lagny the following day to provoke subtly but to the utmost the unhappy woman's enthusiasm for the departure.

"Do you know, Indiana," he said on arrival, "what role your husband has imposed on me concerning you? A strange one, believe me! I'm supposed to beg you to go to Bourbon Island with him, to entreat you to leave me, to tear out my own heart and my life. Do you think he chose his advocate well?"

Madame Delmare's heavy gloom affected Raymon's cunning, imposing a kind of respect. "Why do you come to tell me this?" she asked. "Are you afraid I will be overwhelmed? Are you afraid I will obey? Reassure yourself, Raymon; I've made up my mind: I've spent two nights looking at it from all sides; I know what I am exposing myself to; I know what I must face, what I must sacrifice, what I must discard; I am ready to confront this difficult moment in my life. Will you not be my support and my guide?"

Raymon was inclined to take fright at such coolness and to take the mad threats seriously, but he returned to the opinion that Indiana did not really love him and was simply applying to her situation the inflated sentiments derived from her reading. He

strived for a passionate eloquence, a dramatic sponta-
neity to remain on the level of his romantic mistress,
and thus succeeded in prolonging her error. . . .

Raymon, who had, however, some fear she might
carry out her promises if he did not carefully under-
mine her plans of resistance, persuaded her to pretend
submission or indifference until she might rebel
openly. Before speaking out, he said, they should have
left Lagny in order to avoid a scandal in front of the
servants and the dangerous intervention of Ralph in
the affair.

Ralph, however, did not abandon his unfortunate
friends. Vainly he offered his entire fortune, his Bellerive château, his English income, the sale of his plantations; the colonel remained inflexible. . . . Ralph
closed his Bellerive house and followed his friends to
Paris.

Lagny was put up for sale, together with the
factory. The winter passed sadly and somberly for
Madame Delmare. Raymon was in Paris; he saw her
every day; he was attentive and affectionate; but he
stayed no more than an hour with her. He would arrive at the end of dinner and leave at the same time as
the colonel, the latter on business, Raymon on the pretext of some social function. You see, society was his
element, his life; he needed the noise, the bustle, the
crowd in order to breathe, to exercise his wit, his social ease, his superiority. In privacy he knew how to
be likable; in society he became brilliant; and then he
was no longer the man of a small clique, the friend of
this one or that, but rather the man of intelligence

who belonged to all, for whom society is the homeland.

And then, as we have noted, Raymon was a man of
some principles. When he saw the colonel extend him
so much confidence and friendship, regard him as a
model of honor and sincerity, establish him as the me-
diator between himself and his wife, he resolved to
justify that confidence, merit that friendship, reconcile
that husband and wife, repulse any attachment to the
latter which might imperil the peace of mind of the
former. Once again he became moral, virtuous, and
philosophical. You will see for how long.

Indiana, who did not understand this conversion,
suffered horribly to see herself neglected; yet she still
experienced the comfort of not knowing that her
hopes were in complete ruin. She was easily deceived;
she asked for nothing else, her life was so bitter and
desolate! Her husband had become almost unbearable. In public he affected the courage and stoical insouciance of a brave man; returned to the privacy of
his household, he was little more than an irritable,
demanding, ridiculous child. Indiana was the victim of
his troubled situation, and, I admit, it was largely her
fault. . . . A woman of a more common class would
have dominated a man of his vulgar sort; she would
have echoed his sentiments and enjoyed her own
thoughts in private, feigned respect for his prejudices,
and secretly trampled them underfoot; she would have
kissed him and deceived him. Indiana saw many
women who behaved in this manner, but felt so far
above them that she would have blushed to imitate

them. Virtuous and chaste, she believed herself under no obligation to flatter her master with words, so long as she showed respect for him in her actions. She did not want his affection, because she could not return it. She would have considered herself far more guilty in showing love for a husband she did not love than in granting it to the lover who had inspired it in her. To deceive—that was the crime in her eyes, and twenty times a day she was ready to declare her love for Raymon; only the fear of ruining him restrained her. Her cold obedience irritated the colonel much more than an adroit rebellion might have done. If his self-esteem would have suffered on his ceasing to be master in his own house, it would have suffered much more from being master in an odious and ridiculous fashion. He would have liked to convince but he simply commanded, to reign but he only governed. . . .

So, had he been in Smyrna or Cairo, he would have killed his wife. And yet with all his heart he loved that frail woman who lived in dependence on him and kept secret his wrongs to her with religious prudence. He loved her, or perhaps he pitied her—I do not really know which. He would have liked to be loved by her, for he was proud of her breeding and superiority. He would have risen in his own eyes if she would have stooped so low as to capitulate to his ideas and principles. When he went to her room in the morning to pick a quarrel, he sometimes found her asleep and did not dare to wake her. . . .

That woman, whom he could have broken with one hand if he had wished, lay there, a poor thing, dreaming perhaps of another before his very eyes and defying him even in her sleep. He was tempted to strangle her, to drag her by the hair from bed, to trample on her until she shrieked for mercy and begged for forgiveness; but she was so pretty, so fetching, and so fair that he would suddenly pity her, as a child is impetuously moved to pity by the bird it meant to kill. And he would weep like a woman, that man of bronze, and steal away so that she might not enjoy the triumph of seeing him weep. In truth, I do not know which was the unhappier, he or she. She was cruel out of virtue, he was kind out of weakness; she had too much patience, he had not enough; she had the faults of her qualities and he had the qualities of his faults. . . .

Ralph had the good sense not to meddle in their differences. . . . But it seemed to Indiana that his conduct in this respect was only the result of his egoism; that he loved her still, though he esteemed her less; that he sought her society only for his diversion, for the niceties of her home and the attentions to which she had accustomed him. Besides, she believed, he did not wish to trouble himself with finding faults with either her husband or herself.

"You can see in that his contempt for women," she thought. "In his eyes they are nothing but domestic animals, good for keeping house, preparing meals, and serving tea. He does not honor them with discussion; their faults do not affect him, provided they are not personal and do not disturb his comfort. Ralph has no need of my heart; so long as my hands can prepare his pudding or play the harp for his pleasure, what does he care for my love for another man, my secret sufferings, my deadly squirming under a crushing yoke? I am his domestic; he asks nothing more of me."

XX

Indiana no longer reproached Raymon; he had defended himself so badly she was afraid she would find him all too guilty. The one thing she feared more than being deceived was to be abandoned. She could no longer go on without believing in him, without trusting in the future he had promised, for the life she led with Delmare and Ralph had become too hateful and if she had had no hope in escaping their domination, she too would have drowned herself. She thought of it often; she told herself that if Raymon treated her as he had Noun, there would be no other way out for her than to join Noun. That somber thought pursued her everywhere and she took pleasure in it.

In the meantime, the date of their departure drew nearer. The colonel seemed to have no inkling of the resistance his wife was weighing; every day he made some progress in his affairs, every day he paid off a debt; Madame Delmare regarded these preparations with a tranquil eye, so sure she was of her courage. She was preparing, too, for her forthcoming struggle. . . .

Raymon worried not at all as to what might become

of Indiana. Their love affair had already touched the lowest level of distaste for him—deadly boredom. To cause boredom is to descend to the very bottom of the loved one's heart. Fortunately, for the last days of her illusion, Indiana had no suspicion of it.

Early one morning, as he returned from a ball, he found Madame Delmare in his bedchamber. She had arrived at midnight; she had awaited him for five long hours. It was one of the coldest days of the year; she was sitting in that fireless room, her head in her hands, enduring the cold and anxiety with the brooding patience of a lifetime's upbringing. She lifted her head when she saw him enter, and Raymon, stunned with surprise, saw no expression of anger or reproach in her pale face.

"I came to you," she said gently, "because for three days you had not come to me and because several things have happened in the meantime which you should know about without delay. I came here last night to tell you about them."

"It's an incredible imprudence!" exclaimed Raymon, carefully locking the door behind him. "And my servants know you are here! They just told me."

"I didn't try to hide," she said coldly. "As for the word you choose, I think it is badly chosen."

"I said 'imprudence'; I should have said 'madness.'"

"I would have said 'courage.' But never mind: listen to me. Monsieur Delmare is going to Bordeaux in three days and from there to the colonies. It was understood between us that you would shield me from violence if he employed it; there is no doubt he will,

because I told him what I intended to do last evening
and he locked me in my room. I escaped through a
window; my hands, you see, are still bleeding. They
may be looking for me this moment, but Ralph is at
Bellerive and won't be able to suggest where I am. I
am determined to remain in hiding until my husband
leaves without me. Have you thought about a hiding
place for me? It is so long since I have seen you
alone. . . . Tell me, do you accept my sacrifices?"

The crisis was so pressing that Raymon no longer
had the brazenness to go on pretending. Desperate, furious at finding himself caught in his own trap, he lost
his head, and himself, in brutal, vulgar cursing.

"You are insane!" he cried at last, hurling himself
into an armchair. "Wherever did you find your dream
of love? In what novel for chambermaids have you
learned about society, pray?"

Then he paused, realizing he had gone too far and
racking his brain for a way of saying the same things
in another fashion and sending her away without further insults.

But she remained calm, like one prepared to listen
to anything.

"Continue," she said, folding her arms over a heart
whose pounding had slowly subsided. "I am listening
to you; no doubt you have more than that to say to
me."

"Another effort of the imagination, another love
scene to perform," reflected Raymond. Then, aloud,
rising to his feet energetically: "Never, never will I
accept such sacrifices! When I told you I would have

the strength to do it, Indiana, I was boasting—rather, I was doing myself an injustice, for only a scoundrel would consent to dishonoring the woman he loved. In your ignorance of life, you didn't understand the importance of such an act, and I, in my despair at losing you, did not choose to reflect—"

"Your capacity for reflection has returned very suddenly," she said, withdrawing the hand he tried to take.

"Indiana," he resumed, "can't you see you are attributing dishonor to me, while reserving heroism for yourself, and condemning me because I want to remain worthy of your love? Could you continue to love me, simple, ignorant woman that you are, if I sacrificed your life for my pleasure, your good name for my selfish interest?"

"You are saying things which are very contradictory," said Indiana. "If my being with you makes you happy, why are you afraid of public opinion? Are you more concerned about that than about me?" . . .

"Oh, it is not for myself that I am concerned, Indiana!"

"Then it is for me? I expected your scruples and to free you from any remorse; I took the initiative; I did not wait for you to come and take me away from my home; I did not even consult you before I left my husband. That decision has been made and your conscience cannot reproach you for it. Right now, Raymon, I am dishonored. Waiting for you, I counted the hours on that clock which recorded my disgrace; and now, though the dawn of a new day finds me as stainless as yesterday, I am a lost woman in public opinion. Yesterday there was still compassion for me in the hearts of women; today there is nothing but contempt. I weighed all this before acting."

"Admirable foresight of a woman!" thought Raymon. And then, fighting against her as he would against a process server who had come to seize his furniture, he said in a caressing, fatherly tone: "You exaggerate the importance of what you have done. No, my dear friend, all is not lost because of one rash act. I will make sure my servants don't talk."

"And mine, who are undoubtedly looking for me? And my husband—do you think he will be kept quiet? Do you think he will want to receive me tomorrow, after I have spent the entire night under your roof? Will you advise me to return and throw myself at his feet and ask him, as a sign of his forgiveness, to kindly put back the chain around my neck which has devastated my life and deprived me of my youth? You would consent without regret to see the woman you love return to the yoke of another man, when you are master of her fate, when you can keep her in your arms for eternity, when she is in your power, offering to remain there forever! You would not feel any repugnance, any unease in surrendering her now to the pitiless master who might be waiting for her only to kill her!"

A thought flashed through Raymon's mind. The time had come to tame that feminine pride, or it would never come. She had just offered him all the sacrifices he did not want, and she stood there before him with the high confidence that she ran no other risks than those she had foreseen. Raymon conceived a way to rid himself of her demanding devotion or to derive some profit from it. He was too good a friend of Delmare, he owed too much consideration to the man's trust in him, to carry off his wife; he must content himself with seducing her.

"You are right, Indiana," he cried warmly. "You bring me back to my senses, you revive the rapture which the thought of your danger and the fear of your injury had cooled. Forgive my childish concern and try to understand how much love and tenderness it contains. Your sweet voice makes my blood tingle, your burning words pour fire into my veins; forgive me! Forgive me for having ever thought of anything but this exquisite moment when at last I possess you. Let me forget all the dangers threatening us and thank you on my knees for the happiness you bring me; let me live entirely in this delicious hour spent at your feet, for which all my blood could not pay. Let him come, that stupid husband who locks you up and goes to sleep on the bed of his vulgar brutality; let him come and try to tear you from my arms, my treasure, my life! From now on you do not belong to him; you are my beloved, my companion, my mistress—"

Pleading thus, Raymon by degrees became more excited, as was his habit when "making a case" for his passions. The situation was a powerful, romantic one; it offered tempting risks. Raymon loved danger, like a true descendant of doughty knights. Every sound from the street seemed to herald the coming of the husband to reclaim his wife and demand his rival's blood. To seek love's delights in the rousing emotions of such a situation was a pleasure worthy of Raymon. For a quarter of an hour he passionately loved Madame Delmare; he lavished on her the seductions of fervent eloquence. He was truly powerful in his language and authentic in his behavior, this man whose ardent mind treated the making of love as one of life's accomplishments. He played at passion so well he deceived himself. Shame on that stupid woman! She surrendered herself in ecstasy to those deceptive gestures; she felt happy, she radiated hope and joy; she forgave him all, she almost gave him everything.

But Raymon defeated himself by his haste. Had he prolonged his artful pursuit twenty-four hours more, lengthening the situation in which Indiana had risked herself, she might have been his. But day was breaking, bright and glowing, flooding the room with light, and the noise of the street grew louder with every second. Raymon glanced at the clock: it was seven.

"It is time to put an end to it," he thought. "Delmare may appear at any moment, and before that I must persuade her to return home."

He became more pressing, less tender; his lips' pallor betrayed an impatience more demanding than delicate. His kisses became brusque, almost angry. Indiana took fright. A good angel spread its wings over that wavering, troubled soul; she shook herself and repulsed the cold, selfish, vicious attacks.

"Let me be," she said. "I will not yield from weakness what I would grant out of love or gratitude. You

cannot lack for proof of my affection; my presence is
enough and I bring the future with me. But let me
hold on to all the strength of my conscience so I can
confront the obstacles that still keep us apart; I need
tranquillity and calm."

"What are you talking about?" angrily demanded
the unheeding Raymon, furious at her resistance. Losing his head completely in the torment and wrath of
that moment, he pushed her roughly from him and
paced the room, bosom heaving, face aflame; then he
poured and drank a glass of water, calming his nerves
and cooling his passion. He looked at her ironically
and said:

"Come, madame, it is time for you to leave."

A ray of light had at last laid bare the soul of
Raymon. "You are right," she said and walked toward
the door.

"Your coat and your boa," he said, retaining her.

"Of course," she responded. "They might compromise you."

"You are a child," he said paternally, helping her
with her coat. "You know I love you, but really, you
take pleasure in torturing me, driving me mad. Wait
until I call you a carriage. If I could, I would take you
home, but that would ruin you."

"Don't you know that I am ruined already?" she
said with bitterness.

"No, my love," replied Raymon, who asked nothing
better than to persuade her to leave him in peace.
"Nobody has noticed your absence, since they haven't
come here to inquire about you. Although I should be

the last to be suspected, it would be natural to ask for you at the homes of all your acquaintances. Besides, you can go to your aunt and place yourself under her protection; indeed, that's what I advise you to do; she will arrange everything. People will believe you spent the night with her—"

Madame Delmare was not listening; she was dumbly staring at the sun as it rose huge and red above the glistening roofs. Raymon tried to stir her from her immobility. She turned her eyes in his direction but didn't seem to recognize him. Her cheeks had a greenish cast, her dry lips seemed paralyzed.

Raymon took fright. He recalled the suicide of the other, and in his fear, not knowing where to turn, dreading to be twice a criminal in his own eyes but feeling too exhausted mentally to be able to deceive her yet again, he carefully seated her in his armchair, locked the room, and went upstairs to his mother.

XXI

. . . Because his mother believed herself created to safeguard him from all sorrows and to sacrifice her interests to his, Raymon had accustomed himself to believe that the whole world had been created for him and would meekly place itself in his hand at a word from her. Out of selfless generosity, she had only succeeded in forming a selfish soul.

She turned pale, the poor mother, and sitting up in bed, looked at him anxiously. Her glance said to him: "What can I do? Where must I run for you?"

"Mother," he said, seizing the dry, opaline hand she held out to him. "I am terribly unhappy, I desperately need your help. Save me! I love Madame Delmare, as you know—"

"I did not know it," said Madame de Ramière with tender reproach.

"Don't try to deny it, Mother dear," said Raymon, who had no time to lose. "You did know it, but your admirable delicacy kept you from mentioning it first. Well, that woman is driving me to despair; I'm losing my mind."

"Tell me everything!" exclaimed Madame de Ramière with the youthful vivacity of maternal love.

"I don't want to hide anything from you, since I am innocent this time. For several months I have been trying to restrain her romantic spirit and return her to a sense of her duty, but my efforts only increase her thirst for risks, that craving for adventure which ferments in the minds of all the women of her part of the world. She is here right now in my room, against my will, and I don't know how to get her to leave."

"Poor child!" said Madame de Ramière, hastily dressing. "She is so shy and gentle! I will go and talk to her! Isn't that why you came to me?"

"Yes, yes!" said Raymon, moved by his mother's goodness. "Go, make her understand the language of reason! She will appreciate it from your mouth; she may yield to your caresses; she will come to herself, poor thing! She suffers so much!"

Raymon hurled himself into a chair and burst into tears, so shaken was he by the morning's emotions.

His mother wept with him and would not go down until she had forced him to take a few drops of ether.

She found an unweeping Indiana, who rose calmly and with dignity on seeing her. She so little expected such a dignified, noble bearing that she felt embarrassed before the younger woman, as if she had lacked consideration by taking her by surprise in her son's bedroom. She gave way to the deep emotion of her heart and impulsively held out her arms. Madame Delmare threw herself into them; her despair found relief in racking sobs and the two women cried at length in each other's arms. But when Madame de Ramière started to speak, Indiana stopped her.

"Do not say anything to me, madame," she said, drying her tears. "Nothing you could say would not cause me pain. Your concern and your embrace are enough to prove your generous affection; my heart is as comforted as it can be. I shall go now; I do not need your urging to know what I must do."

"But I did not come to send you away—only to comfort you."

"I cannot be comforted. Love me, that will help me somewhat, but do not speak to me. Adieu, madame; you who believe in God, pray for me."

"You will not go alone!" cried Madame de Ramière. "I will go with you myself to your husband to justify you, to defend and protect you."

"Generous woman!" said Indiana, embracing her warmly. "You cannot do that. You are the only one who doesn't know Raymon's secret. All Paris will be talking about it tonight, and you would play an unsuitable part in such a story. Let me bear the scandal by myself; I shall not suffer long."

"What do you mean? Would you commit the crime of taking your own life? Dear child, you too believe in God!"

"And so, madame, I shall leave for Bourbon Island in three days."

"Come into my arms, my dear child, come and let me bless you! God will reward your courage."

"I hope so," said Indiana, looking upward.

Madame de Ramière wanted at the least to send for her carriage, but Indiana resisted. She wished to return alone and without fanfare. In vain Raymon's mother expressed her fear of so long a walk in Madame Delmare's exhausted and agitated state.

"I have the strength," she replied. "One word from Raymon sufficed to give it to me."

She wrapped herself in her cloak, lowered her black lace veil, and left the house by the hidden door showed her by Madame de Ramière. With her first steps in the street she felt her legs trembling under her and she was barely able to walk. At every moment she seemed to feel the rough hand of her furious husband seize her, throw her to the ground, and drag her in the gutter. But soon the noises of the street, the indifference of passers-by and the penetrating cold of early morning restored her strength and calm, but it was a pitiable strength and a calm as foreboding as that which hovers over the waters of the sea, alarming the sailor more than the tempest's heaving waves. She walked along the quay from the Institut to the Corps

Législatif, but she forgot to cross the bridge and continued along the Seine, absorbed in numb reverie, in meditation without thought, walking on and on without a goal.

Unconsciously she drew closer to the river, which dashed chunks of ice at her feet, scattering them on the stones along the bank with a dry, cold sound. The green, brackish water exercised a hypnotic power on Indiana's senses. One becomes inured to terrible ideas; accepting them, one begins to take pleasure in them. For months the thought of Noun's suicide so appeased her own despair that suicide had become a tempting, even sensual pleasure. One sole thought—religious scruple—had prevented her from undertaking it, but at this moment no clear thought informed her exhausted brain. She scarcely remembered that God existed, that Raymon had ever lived, and she walked on and on, drawing ever closer to the Seine, submitting to the instinct of unhappiness, the magnetism of suffering.

When she felt the biting cold of the water on her feet, she awoke as if from sleepwalking, and, staring about to discover where she was, she saw Paris behind her and the Seine rushing past her, bearing on its oily surface the reflections of gray-white houses and slate-gray skies. The water's movement and the earth's immobility became reversed in her bewildered mind and it seemed as if the water was standing still and the earth slipping past. In that moment of dizziness she leaned against a wall and bent forward toward what seemed a solid mass—but the sudden bark of a dog, who was jumping about her, interrupted the accomplishment of her unconscious design. A man, guided by the dog, came up, seized her by the waist, dragged her back, and laid her in the wreck of an abandoned boat. She looked blankly at him. He knelt, removed his coat, and wrapped her in it, took her hands in his to warm them and called her name. But her brain was too weak for her to respond; for forty-eight hours she had not eaten.

However, when warmth had returned to her limbs, she recognized Ralph kneeling beside her, holding her hands, and watching her return to her senses.

"Did you meet Noun?" she asked him. "I saw her go by there," she pointed to the river, "and I tried to follow her, but she was walking too fast for me. It was like a nightmare."

Ralph looked at her in distress. He too felt his skull bursting, his brain exploding. "Let us go," he said. "Let us go," she echoed, "but first, please find my feet; I lost them among the stones."

Ralph saw that her feet were soaked and paralyzed by the cold. He carried her in his arms to a nearby house where a kindly woman cared for her. Meanwhile Ralph sent word to Delmare that his wife had been found, but the colonel had not yet returned home. He was still searching in a frenzy of anxiety and wrath. Ralph, more perceptively, had gone to Ramière's place, but he had found Raymon, ironic and cool, in bed. It was then he thought of Noun and followed the river in one direction, his servant in an-

other. Ophelia had quickly scented her mistress and
had led Ralph to her.

When Indiana could recall what had happened
that dreadful night, she tried to remember her moments of delirium, but it was in vain. She could not
explain to her cousin what had driven her in that last
hour, but he guessed at the truth and understood the
state of her heart without need for any questions. He
simply took her hand and said gently but gravely:

"Cousin, I ask only one promise from you: it is the
last proof of friendship I shall ever request of you."

"Ask it," she replied. "Obliging you is the only
pleasure left me."

"Well, then, swear to me you will never resort to
suicide without letting me know. I swear to you on
my honor that I will never oppose it in any way. All I
ask is to be told; as for the rest, I care as little for life
as you, and you know that I often have the same inclination."

"Why do you talk of suicide?" demanded Madame
Delmare. "I have never wanted to take my own life. I
fear God; if not for that—"

"Just before, Indiana, when I clutched you in my
arms, when this poor beast"—he stroked Ophelia—
"caught you by the dress, you had forgotten God and
the entire universe, your cousin Ralph along with all
the others."

Tears filled her eyes. She pressed his hand. "Why
did you stop me?" she asked sadly. "I should be in
God's arms now, for I was innocent, I did not know
what I was doing."

"I saw that, and I thought it was better to kill one-self after proper reflection. But we will talk about it when you—"

Indiana shuddered. The cab bearing them had stopped in front of the house where she would meet her husband. She didn't have the strength to go up the stairs; Ralph carried her to her room. The servants had been reduced to a single maid, who had gone off to gossip with the neighbors about Madame Delmare's flight, and Lelièvre, who had gone in despair to the morgue to look at the bodies brought in that morning. So Ralph remained to take care of Madame Delmare. She was shaking convulsively when the bell sounded violently, announcing the colonel's return. A shiver of terror and hate ran through her. She grasped her cousin's arm.

"Listen, Ralph," she said. "If you have the slightest feeling for me, spare me the sight of that man now. I don't want his pity; I prefer his anger. Don't open the door— Or send him away—tell him I haven't been found yet—"

Her lips trembled, her arms clasped Ralph to retain him. Torn between two conflicting emotions, the poor baronet did not know which way to go. Delmare was jerking the bell as if to break it; his wife seemed to be dying in her chair.

"You are thinking only of his anger," Ralph said finally. "You don't think of his anxiety, his torment. You still believe he hates you; if you had seen his grief this morning—"

Indiana dropped her arms, drained of all strength; Ralph went down and opened the door.

"Is she here?" cried the colonel as he entered. "Ten thousand devils! I have run around enough after her. I'm deeply obliged to her for that! The devil take her! I don't want to see her! If I did, I might kill her!"

"You forget she can hear you," said Ralph in a low voice. "She's in no state to be excited. Control yourself."

"Twenty-five thousand curses!" thundered the colonel. "I have endured enough myself since this morning. It's a good thing I have nerves of iron. Which of us is the more upset, the more tired, who has the better right to be sick, she or I? And where did you find her? It's her fault if I insulted that foolish old woman Carvajal, who spoke nonsense and blamed me for the idiocies of this charming creature! Blast! I'm worn out!"

As he shouted hoarsely, Delmare flung himself into a chair in the antechamber; he wiped his forehead of the sweat that streamed from it despite the bitter cold; he swore, as he grumbled about his fatigue, his worry, his suffering; he asked a thousand questions and fortunately didn't listen to the answers, for poor Ralph couldn't lie and he could think of nothing that would calm the colonel. So he sat on a table, as mute and unmoving as if he were absolutely indifferent to the anguish of these two, though he was far more unhappy in their misery than they were themselves.

Madame Delmare, as she listened to her husband's curses, felt stronger than she had expected. She preferred the anger which reconciled her with herself to a generosity which would have aroused her remorse. She wiped away the last trace of tears and called on the last of her strength, only too glad to exhaust it completely, so unbearable had her life become.

Accosting her in his harsh, imperious voice, her husband suddenly changed his manner and tone and became embarrassed before her, quelled by the superiority of her character. He then tried to be as calm and dignified as she, but could not bring it off.

"Will you deign to tell me, madame, where you spent the morning and perhaps the night?"

The "perhaps" told Madame Delmare that her absence had been remarked rather late. Her courage rose. "No, sir," she replied, "I prefer not."

Delmare turned livid with anger and surprise. "Do you really hope to hide it from me?" he bleated.

"I do not care one way or the other," she returned icily. "If I refuse to reply, it's for the principle. I want you to know that you have no right to ask me the question."

"I have no right, for God's sake! Who is master here, you or I? Which of us wears the petticoat and must do the spinning? Do you propose plucking my beard? You'd look fine trying it, little woman!"

"I know that I am the slave and you are the master. The laws of this country make you my master. You can bind my body, lash my hands, dictate my conduct. You have the right of the stronger and society confirms it; but as for my will, sir, you can do nothing; God alone can bend it and break it. So try to find a law, a dungeon, an instrument of torture that can give you control of it! You might as well try to seize the air and grasp space."

"Shut up, you silly, impertinent creature! Your literary phrases bore us!"

"You can make me keep quiet, but you can't keep me from thinking!"

"Idiotic pride! Pride of a woman! You abuse the pity I have for you! But you'll see that this great will of yours can be tamed without much trouble."

"I don't advise you to try it. It wouldn't be easy and your dignity would gain nothing by it."

"Do you think so?" he said, crushing her hand contemptuously between his forefinger and thumb.

"I think so," she said, with no change of expression.

Ralph stepped forward, gripped the colonel's arm with his own hand of iron and bent it like a reed, saying quietly, "Don't touch a hair on that woman."

Delmare wanted to lunge at him, but he felt in the wrong and hated nothing more than to be shamed. He pushed Ralph away, saying only, "Mind your own business!" Then he turned to his wife, his hands rigid at his sides so as not to strike her:

"So, madame, you are in open revolt against me, you refuse to go to Bourbon Island with me, you want a separation? Very well, damn it, so do I!"

"I want it no longer," she replied. "I did yesterday; it was my will; it is not this morning. You used violence, locking me in my room. I escaped through the window to show you that dominating a woman is absurd if you fail to reign over her will. I spent several hours away from your domination; I went off to breathe the air of freedom, to show you that you are not morally my master and that I depend upon no one on earth but myself. As I walked, I reflected that I owed it to duty and conscience to return and put myself again under your patronage. I did it of my free will. My cousin *accompanied* me here, he did not *fetch* me back. If I had not chosen to follow him, he could not have forced me to it. So, monsieur, don't waste your time disputing my determination; you will never change it; you lost all right when you tried to assert it by force. Prepare the departure; I am ready to help you and to follow you, not because it is your will, but because it is mine. You may command me, but I will never obey anyone but myself."

"I pity your madness," said the colonel, shrugging his shoulders. And he went to his room to arrange his papers, well content with Madame Delmare's resolution, anticipating no further obstacles, for he respected the word of this woman as much as he despised her ideas.

XXII

. . . Raymon was highly pleased with *his* Providence, for he had one all his own in whom he believed like a good son, and upon which he counted to arrange everything to everybody else's disadvantage rather than his own. That Providence had treated him so well thus far that he chose not to doubt it. To foresee the consequences of his wrongs and be concerned about them would have been crimes in his eyes against the good Lord who took care of him.

* * *

"Why am I destined," he said wearily [later that day], "to become bored so quickly with this invaluable freedom of mine which I had to buy back so dearly? When I feel caught in a woman's net, I long to break out so I can regain my peace and tranquillity. May I be damned if I sacrifice my peace in such a hurry again! The trouble those two Creoles have caused me will serve as a lesson; from now on it's those gay lighthearted Parisian women, true women of the world, for me! Perhaps I should get married and put an end to it—"

He was plunged in such comforting, bourgeois thoughts when his mother entered, tired and visibly moved.

"She is better," she said. "Everything has gone well; I hope she will become calmer—"

"Who?" asked Raymon, waking with a start from his dream of castles in Spain.

However, he decided on the following day that he still had a task to perform, namely, to regain that woman's esteem, if not her love. He did not want her to boast of having left him; he wanted her to be persuaded that she had yielded to his good sense and generosity. He wanted to dominate her even after he had rejected her, and so he wrote to her in praise of her sense of sacrifice, and concluded:

". . . Be off, therefore, my beloved; go and harvest the fruits of virtue and religion under another sky. God will reward us for such an effort, for God is good. He will reunite us in a happier life, and perhaps even— but the very thought is a crime, though I cannot prevent myself from hoping! Adieu, Indiana, adieu! You can see that our love is a crime! Adieu, my heart is broken! Oh where can I find the strength to say good-by to you!"

Raymon himself took the letter to Madame Delmare's, but she shut herself up in her room and refused to see him. He quit the house after slipping the letter to her servant and cordially embracing the husband. Leaving the last step behind him, he felt lighter-hearted than usual: the air was finer, the women prettier, the shops more sparkling. It was a memorable day in the life of Raymon.

Madame Delmare tucked the letter, still sealed, into a box she would not open until she reached the colonies. She wanted to go and say good-by to her aunt, but Sir Ralph was absolutely opposed. He had seen Madame de Carvajal; he knew she would heap Indiana with reproaches and scorn; he was himself scornful of such hypocritical severity and could not bear the thought of Madame Delmare exposing herself to it.

The following day, as Delmare and his wife were about to leave for the public coach, Sir Ralph said to them with his customary coolness: "I have often told you, my friends, that I want to accompany you, but you have refused to understand or to reply. Would you permit me to leave with you?"

"For Bordeaux?" asked Delmare.

"For Bourbon Island," replied Sir Ralph.

"You cannot think of it," returned Delmare. "You cannot move your home about at the whim of a ménage whose future is uncertain and whose situation is precarious. It would mean taking advantage of your friendship to accept this sacrifice of your whole life and of your social position. You are rich, young, free—you must remarry, start a family—"

"That is not the question," said Sir Ralph coldly. "Since I cannot hide what I think when I speak, let me tell you frankly what I am thinking. It has seemed to me that in the last six months the friendship you both had for me has decidedly fallen off. Perhaps I have made mistakes which my stupid blindness has prevented me from realizing. If I am wrong, one word from you can reassure me; allow me to go with you. If I have disappointed you, tell me; you shouldn't, by abandoning me this way, leave me with the feeling that I have failed to repair my errors."

The colonel was so touched by this naïve, generous appeal that he forgot all the hurts to his pride which had estranged him from his friend. He held out his hand, swore that his friendship was more sincere than ever and that he refused Ralph's offer only from decency.

Madame Delmare maintained her silence. Ralph made an effort to have a word from her. "And you,

Indiana," he said in a choked voice. "Have you any friendship left for me?"

That plea reawoke all the filial affection, all the childhood memories, all the old intimacies which had made their hearts one. They threw themselves with tears into each other's arms, and Ralph nearly fainted, for powerful emotions were always at work in that robust figure, in that controlled and reserved man. He sat down lest he fall and remained without speaking for a long moment; then he grasped the colonel's hand with one of his and his wife's with the other.

"At this moment of separation, perhaps forever, be frank with me. Do you refuse my proposal to accompany you on my account, and not on yours?"

"I give you my word of honor," said Delmare, "that in saying 'no,' I am sacrificing my happiness for yours."

"For my part," said Indiana, "you know that I want never to leave you."

"God forbid that I should doubt your sincerity now!" replied Ralph. "Your word is enough. You have made me happy." And he disappeared.

Six weeks later, the brig *Coraly* set sail from the port of Bordeaux. Ralph had written to his friends that he would be there toward the end of their stay, but, as usual, in such a laconic style that it was impossible to know whether he intended to say good-by for the last time or to accompany them. Vainly they waited for him until the last moment. When the captain gave the signal to cast off, he had still not appeared. Gloomy forebodings added to the dull pain gripping

Indiana's heart as the last houses of the port were slowly lost in the greenery along the shore. She shivered at the thought that she was henceforth alone in the world with a husband she hated, that she must live and die with him—without a friend to console her, without a brother to protect her from his brutal domination—

But as she turned her eyes from the shore, she saw on the deck behind her the calm, kindly face of Ralph smiling into her own.

"So you have not deserted me after all!" she cried, throwing her arms around his neck and letting the tears flow.

"Never!" replied Ralph, pressing her to his heart.

XXIII

Letter from Madame Delmare to Mr. de Ramière

Bourbon Island, 3 June 18—

I had resolved to worry you no more with thoughts of me, but after reading the letter you sent me just before I left Paris, I feel that I owe you a reply because, in my terrible state, I went too far. I was mistaken about you and I owe you an apology, not as a *lover*, but as a *man*.

Forgive me, Raymon, for calling you a monster in that most wretched moment of my life. A word, a look from you forever banished all trust, all hope from my heart. I know I can never be happy again, but I still hope I will not be reduced to despising you; that would be the last blow for me.

Yes, I took you for a coward, for the worst thing in the world, an *egoist*. You became a horror. I regretted that Bourbon was not so far from you as I would have wished to fly; and indignation gave me the strength to see things to the bitter end.

But since I read your letter, I feel better. I don't miss you, but I no longer hate you and I do not want your life to be haunted for having ruined mine. Be happy, be carefree, forget me; I still live and perhaps I shall live a long time.

In fact, you are not guilty; it is I who was insane. Your heart was not a desert, but it was closed to me. You did not lie to me; it was I who was mistaken. You were never a liar nor an insensitive man; you simply did not love me. . . .

I won't entertain myself by refuting your letter; it would be too easy. I will not reply to your remarks about my duties. Rest assured, Raymon, I know them, and I did not love you so little as to betray them without reflection. It was not necessary to say that the price of my fall from grace would have been the scorn of society; I knew it very well. I knew, too, that the stain would be deep, indelible, and biting; that I would be rejected on all sides, damned, covered with shame; and that I wouldn't find a single friend to pity and comfort me. The only mistake I made was to feel confident that you would shelter me in your arms and that you would help me to forget the scorn, the misery, the desertion of the others. The only thing I could not foresee was that you might refuse to accept my sacrifice after it was a *fait accompli*. That I had thought was impossible. . . .

I was mad; as you cynically put it, I had learned life from novels written for chambermaids, from those lightheaded, puerile fictions which enlist the reader's heart in wild enterprises and impossible felicities miraculously achieved. What you said, Raymon, is horribly true! What terrifies and crushes me is that you were right.

But what I cannot understand as well is why the impossibility is not the same for both of us; why I, a weak woman, found enough strength in my exalted feelings to place myself, alone, in the improbable situation of a novel, and why you, a courageous man, could not find enough courage in your strength of will to follow me. And yet you had shared my dreams of the future, you had consented to my illusions, you had fed that hope in me which was unrealizable. . . . Have you men no courage except the physical courage that defies death? Are you not capable of the moral courage equal to misfortune? Will you, who can explain everything so admirably, explain me that?

Perhaps your dream was not like mine; in my case, courage was love. You fancied that you loved me; and you woke surprised to find that you had made such a mistake, on the very day I came to you trusting in the shelter of *my* mistake. Good God, what a strange illusion must have been yours, since you didn't anticipate all the obstacles that met you when the time had come to act! Since you didn't even mention them to me until it was too late! . . .

Perhaps I loved you too well, perhaps my emotion was too importunate, too tiring. You were a man, you loved your independence, your pleasure. I was a burden for you. Sometimes I tried to put claims on your life. Alas, those were petty offenses for such a cruel abandonment!

So, enjoy the freedom you have bought with my life; I will not trouble it any longer. Why didn't you give me this lesson sooner? The hurt might have been the less; for you, too, perhaps.

Be happy; that is the last wish of a broken heart! But do not exhort me to think of God; leave that to the priests who have to soften the hard hearts of the guilty. I have more faith than you; I do not serve the same God, but I serve Him better and with more purity. Yours is the God of men, the king, the founder and upholder of your species; mine is the God of the universe, the support and hope of all creatures. Yours made everything for you alone; mine made all species, the one for the other. You believe you are the masters of the world; I believe you are only its tyrants. You think that God protects you and authorizes you to usurp the empire of the earth; I think that He suffers that only for a brief time and that the day will come when His breath will scatter you like grains of sand. No, Raymon, you do not know God; or rather, let me repeat what Ralph said to you one day at Lagny: you believe in nothing. Your upbringing and your need for an irresistible power to meet the brute strength of the people have led you to the uncritical acceptance of the beliefs of your ancestors, but the sense of God's existence has never touched your heart. I doubt if you have ever prayed to Him. As for me, I have only one belief, and surely the only one you have not: I believe in Him. But the religion you have invented I reject: all your morality, all your principles are simply the interests of your social class which you have elevated to law and which you claim emanate from God Himself, just as your priests have instituted the rites of the Church in order to establish their power and wealth over nations. . . .

No, do not talk to me of God, you of all people, Raymon; do not invoke His name to cast me into exile and reduce me to silence. In submitting as I do, I yield to the power of men. If I listened to the voice which God has placed in the depth of my heart and to the noble instinct of a bold, strong nature which perhaps is the true conscience, I should flee to the desert; I should learn to get along without help, protection, and love; I should go and live for myself deep in our great mountains; I should forget the tyrants, the unjust, and the repulsive. But, alas, man cannot do without his fellow men, and even Ralph cannot live alone.

Farewell, Raymon, may you be happy without me! I forgive you the harm you have done me. Speak of me sometimes to your mother, the best woman I have ever met. Know that there is neither anger nor vengeance in my heart for you; my sorrow is equal to the love I felt for you.

Indiana

* * *

XXIV

Madame Delmare's household, however, had become more peaceable. With their false friends had disappeared many of the difficulties which, in the hotbed of those officious meddlers, had become envenomed by the very warmth of their zeal. Sir Ralph with his silence and apparent noninterference was more adept than all of them in bringing to earth the inflated trivia of intimate relationships buoyed by the breeze of gossip. Indiana, moreover, lived virtually alone. Her house was situated in the mountains above the town and every morning Delmare, who had a warehouse in the port, went down for the day to oversee his commerce with France and the East Indies. Sir Ralph, who had no other home than theirs, but who found ways to add to its comfort without calling attention to his house gifts, busied himself with nature study or the management of the plantation; Indiana, returning to the languor of Creole life, spent the torrid hours in her wicker armchair and the long evenings walking in the solitude of the mountains.

Bourbon Island is, in truth, only an immense cone, whose base is about forty leagues in circumference and whose great peaks are ten thousand feet high. From almost every point of that imposing mass one can see in the distance, beyond the needle-sharp rocks, the narrow valleys, and towering forests, the smooth line of the horizon girdling the azure sea. From the windows of her bedroom Indiana could perceive, between the twin peaks of a wooded mountain opposite, the white sails skimming the Indian Ocean. During the day's quiet hours the spectacle held her eye and tinged her melancholy with despair. That splendid sight, far from casting a poetic light on her dreams, rendered them dark and bitter; and she would lower the raffia curtain at her window and shun even the daylight in order to shed acid, scalding tears in the secrecy of her heart. . . .

Ralph, for his part, was drawn in his walks to gloomy, secluded places where the sea winds could not touch him, for the sight of the ocean had become as antipathetic for him as the thought of crossing it again. France occupied an unwelcome place in his heart's memory. There he had been hopelessly unhappy, he who was armed against unhappiness and stoical before misfortune. He sought with all his force to forget it; for although he was disgusted with life, he wanted to live as long as he felt needed. He was careful, consequently, to say not a word recalling the time he had spent in that country. What would he not have given to wrench that ghastly memory from Madame Delmare's mind! But he was so modest, he felt so inept, so lacking in eloquence that he fled from her instead of trying to divert her. In the excess of his delicate reserve, he continued to present the appearance of self-centered indifference. He went off to suffer alone, and to see him scouring the woods and the mountains in search of bird and insect specimens, you would have taken him for a naturalist absorbed in his innocent passion and thoroughly detached from the emotions of the heart stirring in his vicinity. And yet, hunting and study were naught but pretexts behind which he cloaked his long, bitter reveries.

This conical island is split at its base and conceals in its openings deep gorges through which pour crystalline, roiling waters. One of these gorges is called Bernica. It is a picturesque spot, a sort of steep, narrow valley hidden between two rocky cliffs whose faces are strewn with clumps of saxatile shrubs and tufts of ferns.

A stream flows through the trough formed by the two sides. At the point where the sides meet, the stream plunges to a great depth and forms, where it falls, a pool hemmed with reeds and veiled with a damp mist. Around its banks and along the edges of the thin stream running from this basin rise orange, litchi, and banana trees which make a rich, dark-green tapestry against the walls of the gorge. There Ralph fled heat and fellow creatures. All his walks led to this favored spot; the cool monotone of the cascading waters lulled his melancholy. When his heart was torn by agony so long concealed, so cruelly misunderstood, it was there he spent, in unseen tears, in silent plaints, the wasted passion of his heart, the pent-up vigor of his youth. . . .

The only inhabitants of that secluded spot were the gulls, petrels, coots, and terns. Incessantly they swooped in and out, up and down, now hovering, now wheeling about the holes and clefts they had picked for their wild broods. Toward evening the sea birds would fly in restless groups, filling the gorge with their hoarse, raucous cries. Ralph liked to follow their majestic flight, to listen to their lonely cries. He had once taught his little pupil, Indiana, their names and habits. . . .

These memories crowded tumultuously into Ralph's mind, and bitterly, for times had greatly changed for that little girl who had been his faithful companion and had since ceased to be his friend, or was no longer his friend as formerly in the complete simplicity of her heart. Although she reciprocated his affection, there was one thing which prevented any confidence between them, one memory about which all their emotions revolved. Ralph felt he could not touch it; he had ventured on it once, one day of danger, but that courageous act had been futile. To attempt it again would be callous barbarity, and Ralph had persuaded himself to forgive Raymon, the man for whom he had less respect than anyone on earth, rather than to add to Indiana's sorrow by damning him as he justly deserved.

So he held his peace and even avoided Indiana. Living under the same roof, he had found a way hardly ever to see her except for meals. And yet, he watched over her like a mysterious Providence. . . .

PART FOUR

XXV

It happened that the change of government on the eighth of August 1829,† which upset so many things in France, dealt a rude blow to Raymon's well-being. He was scarcely one of those who benefit no matter who wins. He had made politics the heart of all his ideas, the basis of all his dreams of the future. He had flattered himself that the King, by adopting a policy of skillful appeasement, would maintain for a long time the stability which assured the continuance of noble families. But the rise of Prince de Polignac put an end to that hope. Raymon saw too far ahead; he was too well acquainted with the "new" society not to be on his guard against the triumphs of the moment. He understood that his fate tottered with the throne and that his fortune, perhaps his life, hung by a thread.

Thus he found himself in a delicate and embarrassing position. Honor made it his duty to consecrate himself, despite the risks of such devotion, to the royal family whose interests were until then tied to his own. In this respect, he could scarcely disregard his conscience and concern for his own family. But the new order of things, the new tendency toward absolute

† Charles X's new choice of ministers indicated an intention to re-establish absolute rule.

rule, shocked his prudence, his common sense, and—so he said—his deepest convictions. It compromised his whole existence; it did worse—it made him look ridiculous, he, a renowned public figure who had dared so many times to promise, in the name of the Crown, justice for all and fidelity to the social compact. Now all the government's acts gave the lie to the young eclectic politician's imprudent claims; all the sluggish souls who, two days before, asked nothing better than to hang onto the constitutional monarchy now began to throw themselves into the opposition and denounce as dastardly the efforts of Raymon and his peers. . . . He, in his embarrassment, attached as he was to his reputation as if it were the jewel of his life, was opportunely struck by an attack of rheumatism, which obliged him to leave Paris and go to the country with his mother.

There in his isolation Raymon truly suffered, feeling discarded like a political corpse in the midst of the ravenous activity of a society on the brink of collapse, feeling incapacitated by his embarrassment no less than his illness from rallying to the banners waving on all sides, which called the most obscure and least capable to the great conflict. The crushing pains of his illness, solitude, boredom, and fever insensibly directed his ideas onto another course. He asked himself, for the first time perhaps, whether society deserved all the pains he had undergone to please it, and he judged it adversely for its indifference to him, for its forgetfulness of his talents and *gloire*. . . .

Stretched on his bed of pain with no one at his side except men he had bought or a rare friend impatient to get back to the excitements of social life, he began to think of Indiana, and he sincerely missed her, for at that moment she would have been most useful. He remembered the devoted care she had lavished on her elderly, crabby husband, and he pictured the tenderness and thoughtfulness with which she would have enveloped her lover.

"If I had accepted her sacrifice," he thought, "she would be dishonored, but what would it matter to me now? Deserted by a frivolous, selfish society, I would not be alone; she whom everybody would have scorned would be at my feet with love; she would weep for my hurts and find a way to assuage them. Why did I send that woman away? She loved me so much that she would have found consolation for the insult of society in the little happiness she brought into my private life." . . .

It was at this time that he received the letter Indiana had written him from Bourbon. The brooding, unbent energy she had conserved, despite the blows that might well have crushed her spirit, impressed Raymon profoundly.

"I misjudged her," he thought. "She really loved me, she still loves me. She would have been capable of heroic efforts I thought beyond a woman's strength, just for me; and now one word from me probably would draw her, like a magnet, from one end of the world to another. If it didn't take six or eight months, I'd like to try it!"

He fell asleep thinking about it, but he was soon awakened by a noise in a neighboring bedroom. He rose with difficulty, put on a dressing gown and dragged himself to his mother's apartment. She was very ill.

Toward morning she found the strength to talk with him; she had no illusion as to the little time she had to live and she was concerned about her son's future.

"You are about to lose your best friend," she said to him.‡ "May heaven replace her by a companion worthy of you. But be prudent, Raymon; don't risk the peace of your whole life for an ambitious illusion. I have known only one woman, alas, whom I would have liked to have called daughter, but heaven has disposed of her. But listen to me, my son. Monsieur Delmare is old and broken. Who knows whether that long voyage didn't exhaust him completely? Respect his wife as long as he lives, but if, as I believe, he is called after me to the grave, there is still a woman in the world who loves you almost as much as your mother."

That evening, Madame de Ramière died in the arms of her son. Raymon's grief was deep and bitter; in such a great loss there could be neither forced emotion nor selfish calculations. . . . And he returned to his bed of fever and suffering, as crushed as an uncrowned king, a damned and fallen angel.

When he had almost regained his health, he took a

‡ The last words of her grandmother to George Sand.

look at the situation in France. Bad had become worse; on all sides people threatened to refuse to pay taxes. Raymon was amazed at the stupid assurance of his party, and judging it unwise to plunge into the melee at that point, he shut himself up at Cercy with the melancholy memory of his mother and Madame Delmare.

By dwelling on a notion at first lightly conceived, he accustomed himself to the thought that Indiana was not really lost to him, were he to take the trouble of recalling her. He saw many inconveniences in the idea, but even more advantages. It didn't accord with his interest to wait until she was a widow before marrying her, as his mother had counseled. . . .

Under the influence of these thoughts, he wrote Madame Delmare. His letter was what one would expect from the hand of so adroit and experienced a man. It breathed love, grief, and above all sincerity. Alas, what an easily swayed reed is truth to bend thus with every breath.

However, Raymon was clever enough not to indicate directly the object of his letter. He pretended to view Indiana's return as a joy beyond hope, but this time he spoke lightly of her duties. He repeated his mother's last words; he painted in vivid colors the despair he had been reduced to by his loss, the ennui of solitude and the dangers facing him politically. He drew a somber and terrifying picture of the revolution looming on the French horizon and, while feigning to rejoice at confronting it alone, he hinted to Indiana that the time had come for her to prove that passion-

ate loyalty, that perilous devotion, she had boasted of
to him. Raymon cursed his fate and said that virtue
had cost him dearly, that his yoke weighed very heavily, that he had held happiness in his hand, but that
he had had the strength of will to condemn himself to
eternal isolation.

"Don't tell me again that you have loved me," he
added. "I feel so weak and discouraged that I curse
my courage and hate my duties. Tell me that you are
happy, that you have forgotten me, so that I may have
the strength to resist coming and tearing you away."

In a word, he said he was miserable: that is, he told
Indiana he expected her.

XXVI

During the three months it required for Raymon's letter to reach Bourbon Island, Indiana's situation had
become almost intolerable as the result of a domestic
incident of the greatest importance to her. She had
acquired the depressing habit of jotting down, every
evening, the sorrows of the day. This journal of her
sufferings was addressed to Raymon, and though she
had no intention of sending it to him, she spoke to
him, sometimes with passion, sometimes with bitterness, of the wretchedness of her life and the sentiments she could not stifle. The pages fell into Delmare's hands—that is, he forced open the chest which
contained the journal, as well as Raymon's old letters,
and he devoured them with a furious, jealous eye. In

the first angry outburst he lost all control and went out to the veranda, heart pounding, fists clenched, to await her return from a walk. Perhaps if she had arrived a few minutes later the miserable man would have had time to recover control of himself, but the evil star that was theirs steered her directly to him. The words choking in his throat, he seized her by the hair, threw her to the floor and kicked her on the forehead with the heel of his boot.

He had hardly stamped that bloody sign of his brutality on that frail creature than he was struck with horror by his act. He fled in dismay and locked himself in his room where he put a pistol to his head; but before he could pull the trigger he saw Indiana, risen from the veranda floor, wipe the blood streaming from her face with a calm, mechanical air. At first, having believed he had killed her, he felt joy at seeing her alive; then his anger flared up again.

"It's only a scratch!" he cried. "You deserve a thousand deaths! No, I will not kill myself; you would only go and rejoice in your lover's arms. I don't want to assure the happiness of both of you; I want to make you suffer, to see you die slowly and drearily, to dishonor the infamous creature who made a fool of me!"

He was struggling against the torments of jealous rage, when Ralph entered the veranda by another door and found Indiana in the disheveled state to which that dreadful scene had reduced her. But she had not shown the slightest alarm, she hadn't uttered a cry, she had not lifted a hand for mercy. Tired of life, she had wanted, it seemed, to give Delmare time to kill her by not calling for help. It is certain that when the scene took place, Ralph was no more than fifty feet away but had not heard a sound.

"Indiana!" he cried, recoiling in fright and astonishment. "Who did this to you?"

"Need you ask?" she replied with a bitter smile. "Who else but your 'friend' has the 'right' and the desire?"

Ralph hurled his cane to the ground; he needed no other weapon but his hands to strangle Delmare. In two leaps he was at his door, which he broke open with a fist. He found Delmare stretched on the floor, his face purple, his throat swollen, shaking in the soundless convulsions of apoplexy.

He picked up the papers scattered on the floor. Recognizing Raymon's handwriting and seeing the shattered chest, he understood immediately what had happened, and, carefully gathering the accusing pages, he hastened to give them to Madame Delmare and urged her to burn them at once. Delmare had probably not taken the time to read them all.

Then he begged Indiana to go to her room while he fetched the slaves to take care of the colonel, but she would neither burn the pages nor conceal her cut forehead.

"No," she said haughtily. "I will not! That man didn't hesitate to tell Madame de Carvajal about my running away; he was in a hurry to make what he called my 'dishonor' public. Now I want to show everybody this mark of *his* dishonor which he has put on my face. It's a strange kind of justice that demands you to keep the crimes of the other secret, when that other claims as his right to scar you without mercy!"

When Ralph saw that the colonel was in a condition to listen to him, he called him to account with greater severity than one would have thought him capable of showing. Hearing him, Delmare, who was certainly not an evil man, cried like a child for what he had done, but he cried without dignity, as one does when one surrenders oneself to the sentiment of the moment, without trying to understand its cause and effect. Ever ready to jump to the opposite extreme, he wanted to call his wife and beg her pardon, but Ralph said "no" and tried to make him understand that such puerile reconciliation would compromise the authority of the one without effacing the injury done to the other. He knew well that there are injuries that one can never forgive and misfortunes which one can never forget.

From that moment on, the person who was her husband became thoroughly hateful in the eyes of Indiana. . . . And she determined to put the sea between her tyrant and herself. This resolution taken, she felt more tranquil and became almost carefree and gay. Delmare was so surprised and delighted that he indulged in this private, brutal reasoning—that it is good to make women feel the law of the stronger from time to time.

Henceforth she dreamed of flight, solitude, and independence, and in her grief-stricken mind she fancied a thousand possible plots involving resettlement in such distant places as the deserts of India or

Africa. . . . And amid these romantic dreams and extravagant plans she managed to forget her ills and to create a world apart that consoled her for the one in which she was forced to live. She accustomed herself to think less of Raymon, and he soon ceased to be part of her lonely, stoical existence. Constructing a future according to her fancy, she let the past rest, and as she felt her heart beat more freely, more courageously, she already imagined herself harvesting before their season the fruits of her hermitlike life. But Raymon's letter arrived and that chimerical structure vanished like a breath. She felt, or fancied she felt, that she loved him more than ever she had in the past. . . .

Raymon's situation, as he described it, rekindled in Indiana's heart that generous flame so necessary to her. Visualizing him alone and unhappy, she believed it her duty to forget the past and not to anticipate the future. Only the night before she had been yearning to leave her husband out of hatred and resentment; now she regretted that she did not esteem him more so that she would be making a real sacrifice for Raymon's sake. So great was her enthusiasm that she feared she was doing too little for him in fleeing an irascible master at the risk of her life and subjecting herself to the perils and pains of a four-month voyage. She would have given her life and thought it too slight for a smile from Raymon. Women are made that way.

So it was simply a matter of leaving, though it was difficult to get around Delmare's distrust and Ralph's perspicacity. But neither of these was the principal obstacle, which was to avoid giving public notice of one's departure, as, according to law, one was compelled to do via the newspapers.

Among the few ships lying at anchor in the quayless port of Bourbon was the *Eugène,* soon to set sail for Europe. For some time Indiana sought an opportunity to talk to its captain without her husband's knowledge, but whenever she indicated a desire to go down to the port, he put her in Sir Ralph's charge and with aggravating persistence followed them with his eyes. However, thanks to the scraps of information she eagerly picked up for possible use, Indiana learned that the captain of the ship headed for France had a relative in the village of Saline, which was in the interior of the island, and that often he returned on foot from the relative's house to sleep on board his craft. From that moment Indiana hardly left the rocky cliff that served her as an observation post. To avoid suspicion, she went there by circuitous paths and returned the same way at night when she failed to spot the person she wanted to see.

She had but two days left, for the offshore wind had begun to blow, endangering the ship's anchorage, and Captain Random was impatient to put off to sea.

Urgently she addressed an ardent prayer to the God of the weak and the oppressed and went to post herself on the road to Saline, braving the danger of being seen, risking the last hope. She had hardly waited an hour when Captain Random came down the road. He was a true seaman, rough and cynical, whether in good humor or bad; his visage froze Indiana's blood.

Nevertheless, she gathered all her courage and went to meet him with a determined, dignified air.

"Sir," she said, "I am placing my honor and my life in your hands. I wish to leave the colony and return to France. If you betray my secret instead of offering me your protection, I shall throw myself into the sea, because there will be nothing else left for me to do."

With an oath, the captain replied that the sea would refuse to sink such a trim little ship and that he himself would tow her to the end of the earth, since she had dropped sail of her own will in his wake.

"You consent then?" asked Madame Delmare anxiously. "In that case, here is my passage in advance." And she handed him the box of jewels given her long ago by Madame de Carvajal. They comprised the only treasures she still possessed. But the seaman had other ideas and he returned the jewel box with a remark that brought blood to her cheeks.

"How unfortunate I am, sir!" she replied, retaining the tears of wrath glistening on her long lashes. "My request has understandably led to your insulting me, but if only you knew how hateful my life has become in this land, you would have more pity for me than disrespect."

The noble, touching countenance of Indiana commanded respect in Captain Random. He recalled the hard, ugly look of the colonel and the scandal in the colony caused by his attack on his wife. . . .

"Damme!" he cried. "I have contempt only for a man who can kick such a pretty woman in the face! Delmare is a pirate and I'm damn glad to play this trick on him. But be careful, madame; remember I have my own reputation to protect. You must sneak away when the moon sets and fly like a seagull—"

"I know, sir," she interrupted, "that you cannot do me this great favor without breaking the law; you may have to pay a fine; that is why I am offering you this box of jewels, which are worth twice the passage."

The captain accepted the box with a smile. "This is not the time to settle your bill," he said. "I'm willing to take charge of your little treasure. Seeing how things are, I'm sure you won't have much luggage. On the night we sail, be among the rocks at Lataniers Cove. Between one and two in the morning you will see a boat put ashore with two sailors who will bring you to the ship."

XXVII

The day before her departure . . . Indiana locked herself in her room to prepare the few things she would take; then she hid them under her dress and carried them one by one to the rocks at Lataniers Cove, where she put them in a bark basket which she buried in the sand. . . .

Toward evening the wind fell. The *Eugène* drew closer to the port and at sunset Madame Delmare heard from her rocky hideout the echoing sound of a ship's cannon. It was the signal for departure on the following morning. . . .

The clock struck eleven. All was silent and peaceful

in the house. Madame Delmare dropped to her knees and prayed, weeping bitterly, for she was about to burden her heart with a great sin which God alone could forgive. Quietly she entered her sick husband's bedroom. He was sleeping deeply; his face was calm, his breathing steady. About to withdraw, she noticed someone asleep in an armchair in the shadows. It was Ralph, who had silently risen and come to her sick husband's bedside to watch over him.

"Poor Ralph!" thought Indiana. "What a poignant, eloquent reproach to me!"

She wanted badly to wake him, to tell him everything, to beg him to save her from herself, and then she thought of Raymon.

"One more sacrifice," she thought, "and the hardest of all—the sacrifice of my duty."

Love is a woman's virtue; it is for love that she glories in her transgressions; it is in love that she finds the heroism to defy remorse. The more the crime costs her, the more she deserves from the one she loves. It is the same passion that puts the dagger into the hands of the religious.

She took from her neck the gold watch that belonged to her mother which she always wore; gently she put it around Ralph's neck as the pledge of eternal friendship and lowered her lamp once more to assure herself that her old husband was no longer ill. He was dreaming at that moment and said in a weak, sad voice: "Beware of that man, he will cause your fall—"

Indiana shivered from head to foot and fled to her

room. She wrung her hands in wretched uncertainty; then she suddenly grasped at the idea that she was no longer acting selfishly but rather for Raymon's sake, that she was not going to him in search of happiness but to bring it to him, and that even though she were to be damned for eternity, she would be repaid if she but enhanced her lover's life. She raced from the house and ran to Lataniers Cove, not daring to turn and look back at what she left behind.

She dug up her bark basket and sat on it, trembling and silent, listening to the whistling wind, to the waves dying at her feet, to the shrill cries of the petrel among the clumps of seaweed clinging to the plunging cliffs; but all these sounds were drowned in the clamor of her heart which drummed funereally in her ears.

She waited a long while; she sounded the bell in her watch and realized the lateness of the hour. The sea was so bad and navigation about these shores so difficult in the best of times that she began to despair of the seamen coming for her, when she spied the black shadow of a pirogue trying to make shore. But the tide was too strong and the sea too rough; the frail boat constantly dipped, burying itself as if in the dark folds of a shroud spangled with silver stars. She rose and replied to their signals with cries that were carried away by the wind before they reached the oarsmen. At last, when they were near enough to hear, they rowed toward her with great difficulty, then paused for a wave. As soon as they felt it, they redoubled their efforts; then the wave broke, spilling them on the shore. . . .

The pirogue bore Indiana and her fate through the furious waves and the howling tempest to the stentorian oaths of the seamen, who loudly cursed the dangers they were undergoing for her sake. The ship, they said, should have been under way two hours before, but because of her the captain had stubbornly refused to give the order. They added a few insulting, cutting remarks, but the unhappy fugitive swallowed her shame in silence; and when one of the men told the other they might be punished for their lack of respect to the captain's "mistress," the other replied with a round oath:

"Blast! It's the sharks we have to reckon with tonight. If we ever see the captain again, damned if we find him harder to deal with than them!"

"Damme," said the first, "if one's not sniffing at us already! That face following us is not that of a Christian!"

"Idiot, that's a dog, not a sea wolf! Hey you, my four-legged passenger! We forgot you on shore! But blast my soul, there are no biscuits for you on board. We've orders for the maid, but not for a bitch!"

He raised his oar to brain the poor beast when Madame Delmare caught sight of her beautiful Ophelia, who had followed her scent to the rocks and was now swimming after her. As the sailor was about to strike the dog, the waves she was struggling against carried her away from the pirogue and her mistress heard her whimper with frenzied exhaustion. Indiana begged the oarsmen to take her into the boat and they pretended to agree, but as the faithful animal again approached them, they cracked her skull with loud shouts of laughter, and Indiana saw floating before her the lifeless body of the poor creature who had loved her as Raymon never had. . . . Then, as the shore receded, the sea became less rough and soon the skiff moved along swiftly and uneventfully to the ship. The oarsmen regained their good humor and with it second thoughts. They tried to undo what they had done, but their cajolery was more insulting for Indiana than their anger.

"Come, come, young lady," said one, "courage! You are safe now! The captain's sure to give us his best wine for the pretty package we've fished up for him."

The other affected to sympathize with her because she was soaking wet, but, he added, the captain was waiting to take care of *that*. Indiana listened to their remarks with dread; she recognized the horror of her situation and could see no way out except to throw herself into the sea. Two or three times she was on the point of so doing, then she picked up her courage, a sublime courage, with the thought: "It is for him that I suffer these insults, for Raymon! I must live for him, even if I die of shame!"

She put her hand to her heart and felt the dagger she had hidden there in the morning . . . and she went aboard the ship resolutely, saying to herself that a woman was safe so long as she could take her own life rather than submit to dishonor. She "avenged" herself only by rewarding her guides handsomely and went to her cabin to await the hour of departure.

At last dawn broke; the sea was covered with boats bringing passengers to the *Eugène*. With trepidation Indiana peered at their faces through her porthole: she dreaded seeing her husband among them, coming to claim her. Finally, the last echo of the departing gunshot died away on the island that had been her prison. The ship began to slice its way through the foaming waves and the sun, rising in the sky, shed its cheerful, rosy light on the white peaks of the Salazes Mountains as they sank into the sea.

A few leagues further on, a kind of comedy was played on board. Captain Random pretended to discover Madame Delmare on his ship; he affected surprise, interrogated the sailors, put on a show of anger, then of appeasement, and ended by noting the presence of a stowaway in his log.

Allow me to end the story of this voyage here, saying only that Captain Random . . . became Madame Delmare's friend and protector. . . .

XXVIII

Three days after sending his letter to Bourbon Island, Raymon completely forgot both the letter and its intention. He had felt in better health and ventured on a tour in the neighboring countryside. The estate of Lagny, which Delmare had left behind in payment to his creditors, had been sold to a wealthy manufacturer, a Monsieur Hubert, an able, estimable man, unlike other manufacturers and the newly rich. Raymon found the new proprietor installed in that house of so many memories. He gave free rein to his emotions as he walked through the garden where Noun's light steps seemed still imprinted and through the rooms where Indiana's gentle voice still seemed to echo; but soon the presence of the new mistress of Lagny changed the tenor of his thoughts.

In the great living room, on the very spot where Madame Delmare used to sit and embroider, a tall, slim young lady with an expression at once tender and mischievous, caressing and mocking, was sitting before an easel and amusing herself by copying the paneled figures on the wall in water colors. The copy was charming, a refined satire marked by the scoffing yet polished personality of the water-colorist. She had exaggerated the pretentious prettiness of the old frescoes; she had seized the false, *chatoyant* character of the age of Louis XV in those starchy figures. In brightening the faded colors she had revived the mannered postures, the perfumed courtliness, the boudoir finery and the shepherd's hut, all so oddly identical. Beneath the raillery she had written *pastiche.*

She lifted her long-lashed eyes slowly to Raymon's face; they revealed a mocking, attractive, and deceptive cajolery which reminded him, I know not why, of Shakespeare's Anne Page. There was neither timidity, boldness, affectation, nor lack of self-confidence in her manner. Their conversation revolved around the influence of fashion in the arts.

"Was not the moral color of the period in that bush?" she remarked, pointing to the woodwork and its pastoral cupids à la Boucher. "Those sheep don't walk, sleep, or browse like today's sheep. And that pretty landscape, as false as it is picturesque; those rose bushes in the middle of the forest; those domesticated birds which never existed; those pink satin gowns which never fade—is there not poetry, luxury, and pleasure, the sense of the sweetness of a useless but inoffensive life? But no doubt those silly fictions were as worthy as our own gloomy political pronouncements! If only I had been born then!" she added smiling. "Frivolous woman that I am, I was made to paint fans and embroider rather than read newspapers and follow debates in parliament!"

Hubert left the two young people to each other and their conversation slowly drifted to the subject of Madame Delmare.

"You were very close to our predecessors in this house," said the young woman. "It is generous of you to come and see *us*. Madame Delmare, I am told, was a remarkable woman." Her glance was probing as she said it. "She must have left memories that put us at a disadvantage in your eyes."

"She was an excellent woman," said Raymon indifferently. "Her husband was a worthy man—"

"But," she interrupted provocatively, "it seems, she was more than an excellent woman. If I remember rightly, she had a charm that deserves a more enthusiastic, a more poetic compliment. I saw her two years ago at a ball at the Spanish ambassador's. She was lovely that evening; don't you recall?"

Raymon started at the memory of that evening, when he had spoken to Indiana for the first time. He remembered at the same time that he had observed the fine features and clever eyes of the young woman he was now with, but he didn't then ask who she was.

Only after taking leave of her and congratulating Hubert on his daughter's graces did he learn her name.

"I am not fortunate enough to be her father," said the manufacturer, "but I was clever enough to adopt her. Don't you know my story?"

"Having been ill for several months," replied Raymon, "I have only heard of the good you have already done in the region."

"There are people," said Hubert with a smile, "who think the best thing I did was to adopt Mademoiselle de Nangy. But you, sir, who have a superior intelligence, will be able to judge for yourself whether I did more than delicacy demanded." . . .

Encouraged by the interest Raymon showed in listening to his story of the adoption, the excellent man, in good bourgeois fashion, gradually confided all his business affairs to him. The attentive Raymon discovered that he had a huge fortune which was managed with minute care and now simply awaited a younger spender of more elegant tastes than the worthy Hubert to come into its full flower. He felt he could be the man called to that agreeable task, and he thanked the ingenious fate which combined all his interests by

offering him by virtue of divers romantic coincidences
a woman of his rank, soon possessor of a fine bourgeois
fortune. It was a gift of destiny not to let slip, and he
exercised all his skill to seize it. Moreover, the heiress
was charming; Raymon became more favorably disposed toward his Providence.

As for Madame Delmare, he chose not to think of
her. He chased away the forebodings aroused from
time to time by his letter; he tried to persuade himself
that poor Indiana would not grasp its meaning or
would not have the courage to respond favorably; and
he finally succeeded in deceiving himself and finding
himself completely innocent, for Raymon would have
been horrified to discover how inordinately selfish he
was. . . . Man rarely tramples on his conscience as
coolly as Iago. He turns it over, presses it, pinches it,
deforms it, and when he has disfigured, abused, and
exhausted it, he carries it around with him as an in-
dulgent, accommodating tutor who bends to his passions and interests but whom he pretends always to
consult and respect.

He returned often to Lagny and his visits were
agreeable to Mr. Hubert, for, as you know, Raymon
had the art of making himself liked, and soon the rich
bourgeois's one desire was to call him son-in-law. But
he wanted his adopted daughter to decide for herself
and he gave them full liberty to know and appraise
each other.

Laure de Nangy was not in a hurry to assure Raymon's happiness; she kept him suspended between
fear and hope. Less generous than Madame Delmare

but more adroit, distant and flattering, haughty yet attentive, she was the woman to subjugate Raymon, for she was as superior to him in cleverness as he to Indiana. Fairly quickly she realized that her suitor sought her wealth more avidly than herself. Her passive imagination had expected no better homage; she had too much good sense, too great a knowledge of the world, to dream of love when two millions were involved. Calmly and philosophically, she had chosen her path and placed no blame on Raymon; she did not hate him because he was calculating and unfeeling like his period; but she knew him too well to love him. She took pride in not falling below the cold, calculating line of the time; her self-esteem would have suffered had she yielded to the silly illusions of an ignorant schoolgirl; she would have blushed at being deceived, for it would have meant looking foolish; in a word, she made heroism the act of keeping love at a distance, as Madame Delmare had made it the sacrifice of everything to it.

Mademoiselle de Nangy thus was thoroughly resolved to submit to marriage as a social necessity, but she took a malicious pleasure in exploiting the liberty still left her by imposing her authority for a time on the man who aspired to take it from her. No youth, no sweet dreams, no brilliant, illusionary future for that young woman, condemned to suffer all the miseries of wealth. For her, life was a stoic calculation, happiness a puerile illusion against which one must defend oneself as against weakness and absurdity.

As Raymon toiled at establishing his fortune, Indi-

ana was approaching the shores of France. But what
surprise and alarm were hers when she saw, on land-
ing, the blue, white, and red republican flag flying
over the walls of Bordeaux! A violent agitation still
shook the city: the prefect had been almost killed the
previous night; the people were rising everywhere; the
garrison seemed to be preparing for a bloody fight and
the fate of the 1830 revolution in Paris was still unknown.

"I have arrived too late!" The thought struck Madame Delmare like a bolt of lightning.

In her alarm she had left the little money and the
few clothes she possessed on board the ship and now
ran about the city in a frenzy. She tried to find a
coach for Paris, but all the public conveyances were
packed with people who were either fleeing or going
to share the victors' spoils. Not before evening did she
succeed in finding a seat. As she was about to mount
the coach, a motley patrol of National Guardsmen,
come to control the departure of passengers, demanded to see their papers. Indiana had none. As she
argued against the absurd suspicions of the triumphant guardsmen, she heard people say all around her
that the monarchy had fallen, that the King was in
flight, and that the ministers had been massacred
along with all their followers. This news, shouted
with laughter and stamping and cries of joy, delivered
a mortal blow to Madame Delmare. In the whole revolution only one thing interested her personally, in all
of France only one man concerned her. She fell to the

ground in a faint and came to herself in a hospital several days later.

Without money, linen, or effects, weak, trembling, and exhausted by an inflamatory brain fever which had brought her close to death several times, she found herself discharged and on the streets, alone, barely able to stand, without friends, resources, or strength. When she tried to recall what had happened and it dawned on her that she was lost and alone in that great city, she felt terror and despair at the thought that Raymon's fate had long since been decided and that there was no one about her who could put an end to her horrible uncertainty. . . . She dragged herself to the port, asked for the *Eugène* and learned from the first seaman she addressed that it was still in the harbor. She persuaded him to take her aboard by boat and there she found Random at breakfast.

"Well, well, my pretty passenger," he exclaimed, "back from Paris already? You've come at a good time; I sail tomorrow. Do you want me to take you back to Bourbon?"

He told Madame Delmare that he had ordered a search made for her everywhere so that he might return what belonged to her. But Indiana had had nothing to identify her when she had been carried to the hospital. She had been registered there and at the police station as "unknown" so the captain could learn nothing about her whereabouts.

The next day, despite her weakness and fatigue, Indiana left for Paris. Her anxiety should have been lessened when she learned how things had gone politically, but anxiety does not reason and love is fertile ground for childish fears.

The very evening of her arrival in Paris she hastened to Raymon's house and questioned his concierge apprehensively.

"Monsieur is quite well," came the reply. "He is at Lagny."

"At Lagny? You mean Cercy!"

"No, madame, at Lagny, which he owns now."

"Dear Raymon!" thought Indiana. "He has bought that place to offer me a refuge where public maliciousness cannot reach me. He knew I would come!"

Intoxicated with joy, she hurried, lighthearted and alive again, to rent a furnished apartment and there spent the night and part of the next day sleeping. . . . In the afternoon she hired a carriage and arrived toward nine in the evening at a village on the edge of Fontainebleau. She had the driver put up the horse and carriage, told him to wait for her until the next day, and went off alone, on foot, by a path through woods to the park of Lagny, fifteen minutes away. She tried to open the small gate, but found it locked. She wanted to enter unseen by the servants, in order to surprise Raymon, so she walked along the wall. It was an old wall and she remembered that there were many breaks in it. By good luck, she found one she could climb through with little trouble.

When she touched the ground which now belonged to Raymon and would soon become her refuge, her sanctuary, her fortress and homeland, she felt her heart leap with ecstasy. Buoyant, triumphant, she hurried along the winding paths she knew so well. She reached the English garden, which was dark and deserted on that side. Nothing had been changed in the planting, but the bridge she dreaded to see had disapppeared and even the course of the stream had been redirected; only the places which might have recalled Noun's death had been changed.

"He wanted to relieve me of that cruel memory," thought Indiana, "but he was wrong. I could have borne it. Was it not for my sake that he felt remorse? From now on we are equals, for I, too, have committed a crime. I have perhaps caused my husband's death. Raymon can open his arms to me, we will be innocence and virtue for each other."

She crossed the stream on boards which temporarily served as a bridge and reached the far side of the flower garden. Here she was forced to stop, for her heart was almost bursting; she lifted her eyes to the window of her former bedroom. Wonderful! A light was shining through the blue curtains; Raymon was there. What other room would he occupy! The door to the hidden staircase was open.

"He expects me at any moment," she thought. "He will be happy, but not surprised."

She paused again at the top of the staircase to catch her breath: she had less strength for the strain of joy than for sorrow. She bent to look through the keyhole. Raymon was alone, reading. It was he, it was Raymon, full of vigor and life; his troubles had not aged him, the stress of politics had not taken a hair from his head; he was there, handsome and tranquil, his forehead resting on the white hand lost in the black hair.

Impulsively Indiana pushed open the door.

"You have been expecting me!" she cried, falling to her knees and laying her tired head on Raymon's chest. "You have counted the months, the days! You knew that time had passed, but you also knew that I could not fail to come at your call. You called me, and here I am, here I am! Oh, I'm dying!"

Her brain could endure no more; for some time she knelt there, silent, breathing deeply, incapable of speech, of thought. Then she opened her eyes, recognized Raymon as if she were waking from a dream, cried out in frantic joy and pressed his lips with hers, wild, ardent, happy. He was pale, mute, motionless, as if struck by lightning. . . .

But he did not reply; his normal presence of mind had abandoned him. He was speechless with surprise, with remorse, with terror, on seeing this woman at his feet; he hid his face in his hands and wished he were dead. . . .

"I would like to cry," he said, his voice choked.

"And I, too!" she said, covering his hands with kisses. "Ah, yes, that would do good. Cry, cry on my bosom, I will wipe away your tears with my kisses; I have come to give you happiness, to be all that you wish—your companion, your servant, or your mistress." . . .

I do not know what infernal idea suddenly crossed Raymon's mind. He lifted his face from his clenched hands and regarded Indiana with a diabolical cold-bloodedness; then a terrible smile twisted his lips and made his eyes glisten, for she was still beautiful.

"First of all," he said, rising, "we must hide you."

"Why hide me here?" she asked. "Aren't you the master, free to take me in and protect me, I who have no one else on earth but you, who without you would have to beg on the public highway? Why, even society can no longer call it a crime for you to love me; it is I who have taken everything upon myself. It is I! But where are you going?" she cried, as she saw him walking toward the door.

She fastened herself to him with the terror of a child who did not want to be left alone one instant and dragged herself on her knees, following him.

He wanted to lock and bolt the door, but he was too late. The door had opened before he could reach it and Laure de Nangy entered. She appeared less surprised than shocked; she did not let one exclamation slip from her, but leaned forward to look with flickering eyes at the woman who had fallen, in a half faint, to the floor; then with a cold, derisive smile, she said:

"Madame Delmare, it seems to me you enjoy putting three people in an odd situation, but I thank you for giving me the least ridiculous role, which I will now play in this manner: be good enough to leave."

Indignation gave Indiana strength; she rose forcefully to her full height.

"Who is this woman?" she asked Raymon. "And by what right does she give me orders in your house?"

"You are in *my* house, madame," Laure intervened.

"Speak, for heaven's sake, sir, speak!" cried Indiana, furiously shaking the wretched man's arm. "Tell me whether that woman is your mistress or your wife!"

"She is my wife," replied Raymon dazedly.

"I pardon your confusion," said Madame de Ramière with a cruel smile. "If you had remained where duty required, you would have received a card inviting you to Monsieur's marriage. Come, Raymon," she added with sarcastic amiability, "I have pity for your embarrassment; you are rather young; you will know now, I hope, that prudence is more advisable in life. I leave it to you to put an end to this absurd scene. I would laugh at it, if you didn't look so miserable."

Thus delivering herself, she withdrew, fairly satisfied with the dignity she had displayed and secretly pleased because the incident had put her husband in an inferior, dependent position.

When Indiana recovered her senses, she was alone in a closed carriage, speeding rapidly toward Paris.

XXIX

The carriage stopped at a tollgate; a man whom Madame Delmare recognized as one of Raymon's servants came to the carriage and asked where Madame wished to go. Indiana mechanically gave the name and street of the hotel where she had stayed the night before. On arriving there, she slumped into a chair and didn't stir until morning, giving no thought to going to bed, wanting to die, but too crushed, too inert, to call on the strength to kill herself. She thought that it was impossible to live after such terrible suffering, that death would come on its own to find her. She remained thus all the following day, without eating, without replying to the few offers of service. . . .

They found her on the morning of the second day, stretched on the floor, stiff with cold, her teeth clenched, her lips blue, her eyes lifeless; but she was not dead. The hotelkeeper went through her things and, seeing so little of value, thought of handing this stranger over to the almshouse, since she obviously couldn't pay the costs of a long illness. However, since the hotelkeeper was a humane woman, she had Indiana put to bed and sent for a doctor to see whether the illness would last more than a few days. A doctor she hadn't sent for appeared.

Indiana, on opening her eyes, found him at her bedside. I needn't tell you his name.

"Oh, it is you, you!" she cried, throwing herself weakly into his arms. "My good angel! But you have come too late, all I can do now is to die blessing you."

"You will not die, my dear," replied Ralph with emotion. "Life may still smile upon you. . . . I have come to tell you that you are free, that you can join your fate with Monsieur de Ramière's. Delmare is no more."

As he spoke, tears rolled down Ralph's cheeks. Indiana abruptly sat up in bed and, wringing her hands desperately, exclaimed: "My husband is dead? It is I who killed him! And you talk to me of the future and of happiness, as if that were still possible for one who detests and despises herself! Be assured that God is just and I am damned. Monsieur de Ramière is married."

She fell back, utterly exhausted, into her cousin's arms. They could resume their conversation only several hours later.

"May your justly troubled conscience be at rest," said Ralph in a solemn, sad and gentle tone. "Delmare was dying when you left him; he did not wake from his sleep, he never knew of your flight. . . . When I had the strength to take my eyes and my thoughts from his dead body, I thought of you, Indiana. . . . A ship came into port that had passed the *Eugène* in the Mozambique Channel; some of its crew boarded the *Eugène*. A passenger had recognized you, and in less than three days the whole island knew of your departure. . . . I left shortly after you, but I had a terrible voyage and arrived in France only a week ago. My first thought was to go to Ramière to inquire about you, but by chance I met his servant Carle, who had just brought you here. I asked no questions except where you were staying, and I came here convinced that I would not find you alone."

"Alone, alone, disgracefully abandoned!" cried Madame Delmare. "But let us not speak of that man, let us never speak of him." . . .

Ralph sought to distract her; he took her away from everything that could remind her of Raymon. He took her to Touraine; he surrounded her with all the pleasant things of life; he consecrated all his time to making a few of her moments tolerable; and when he failed, when he had exhausted all the resources of his

art and his affection without kindling the feeblest
gleam of pleasure in that anguished, stricken face, he
deplored the impotence of his words and bitterly
blamed himself for the ineptitude of his affection.

One day he found her more crushed and despairing
than ever. He didn't dare speak to her, but sat sadly
beside her. Indiana turned to him, gently pressed his
hand and said:

"Poor Ralph! I cause you a great deal of torment!
You must have an unbelievable patience to endure the
sight of such selfish, cowardly misery as mine! Your
difficult task has long since come to an end. The most
insanely demanding woman could not ask more of
friendship than what you have done for me. Now
leave me alone with my gnawing misery; don't spoil
your pure, sainted life by contact with my accursed
one; try to find elsewhere the happiness which cannot
exist in my presence." . . .

She burst into tears. Sir Ralph took her hand.

"Listen to me, my dear Indiana," he said, "forgetfulness is beyond us. I do not accuse you! I can suffer
patiently, but to see you suffer is more than I can bear.
Besides, why should we struggle like this, we weak
creatures, against our iron fate? It is quite enough to
drag our ball and chain about; the God we worship,
you and I, did not destine man to so much misery without giving him the instinct to escape it; and what
makes man superior to the brute, in my opinion, is his
being able to prescribe the cure for his ills. That cure
is suicide; that is what I propose, that is what I coun-
sel." . . .

The idea gripped Ralph and Indiana for several days at the end of which they decided to die together. There remained only the choice of how and where they would die. . . .

"I will tell you the place," said Ralph after a moment, "where suicide appeared to me in its most noble and solemn aspect. It is on Bourbon Island, on the edge of a precipice, at the top of a plunging cascade . . ."

* * *

They sailed from France. The schooner *Nahandove*, as fast and light as a bird, carried them to their twice-abandoned homeland. Never was a passage so pleasant and swift. It seemed as if a favorable wind had been charged with conducting them to a safe harbor, those two ill-starred creatures who had been battered so long on the reefs of life. During the three months of their voyage Indiana harvested the fruit of her obedience to Ralph's advice. The sea air, so tonic and penetrating, strengthened her frail health, and peace reclaimed her tired heart. The certainty of soon ending her suffering had the effect of a doctor's reassurance to a trusting patient. Forgetting her past, she opened herself to the emotion of religious hope. Her thoughts were infused with a magical spell, a celestial perfume. Never had the sea and the sky seemed so beautiful to her. She seemed to see them for the first time, discovering rich, unknown splendors. Once again her brow became serene and one would have said a divine ray had entered her blue, gently melancholic eyes.

A no less extraordinary change took place in Ralph's soul and appearance; the same cause produced almost the same effects. His heart, so long hardened against sorrow, softened in the warmth of hope. Heaven, too, came down to settle in that hurt, bitter heart. His words were infused with his feelings, and Indiana, for the first time, discovered his true character. The sacred, filial intimacy that held them together relieved the one of his painful shyness and the other of her unfair judgments. Each day delivered Ralph of some clumsiness of his nature, Indiana of some error in her criticisms. At the same time, the poignant memory of Raymon paled and gradually faded away in the light of Ralph's discovered virtues, his sublime candor. As the one rose in her eyes, the other fell. Finally, the act of comparing the two effaced the last vestige of her blind, fatal love from her heart.

XXX

It was but last year, one evening during the perpetual summer of those climes, that two passengers from the schooner *Nahandove* walked deep into the mountains of Bourbon Island, three days after they had landed. . . .

Fate willed that it should be one of the loveliest tropical evenings upon which the moon had ever cast its light. That great orb, just risen from the dark waves, was beginning to spread a long trail of quicksilver across the sea, but its rays did not penetrate the gorge before them and the pool reflected only the glimmering light of a few stars. Even the lemon trees dotting the upper reaches of the mountain did not yet wear the pale diamonds which the moon makes of their brittle, polished leaves. The ebony trees and the tamarinds murmured in the darkness; only the tips of the great palm trees, rising a hundred feet above the ground, were silvered with a touch of green by the moon.

The sea birds were quiet in the crevices of the cliff and only a few blue pigeons, nestling in the overhangs of the mountain, lifted their sad, passionate, and distant notes. Beetles, lovely as living jewels, chirped among the branches of the coffee trees and scuttled across the waters of the pool; the rhythmical splashing of the cascade seemed in mysterious exchange with the echoes coming from the banks.

The two lonely figures climbed to the top of the gorge by way of a steep, winding path, to the place where the turbulent waters plunge in a white, foamy column down to the bottom of the precipice. There they found themselves on a small ledge ideal for their purpose. Vines hanging from the trees formed a natural cradle suspended over the cascade.

Sir Ralph, with remarkable sangfroid, cut away some of the vines which might break their fall, then took his cousin's hand and drew her to a seat beside him on a moss-covered rock from which by day the full, beautiful view was visible in its wild, stunning grandeur. But at that moment the night's darkness and the mist from the cascade obscured everything and made the gorge awesomely bottomless.

"I might say, my dear Indiana," Ralph remarked, "that the success of our undertaking requires the greatest coolness on our part. If you jump heedlessly where darkness suggests empty space, you will hit the overhanging rocks and your death will be slow and painful; but if you throw yourself toward the white line that shows where the water falls, you will plunge into the pool far below—the cascade itself will take you to it. But if you prefer waiting an hour, the moon will be high enough to light our way."

"I am willing to wait," replied Indiana, "especially since we ought to devote these last moments to religious thoughts." . . .

Ralph thereupon sat at Indiana's feet and began to pray in a voice that rose high and loud above the cascade's roar. Perhaps it was the first time since he was born that he expressed his entire thought. . . . It was the moment to be completely himself, to lay bare his whole moral being, to remove before his Judge the disguise men had imposed upon him. Thrusting aside the hair shirt in which sorrow had swathed his bones, he arose sublime and radiant as if he were already in the dwelling house of divine rewards.

Listening to him, Indiana felt no surprise; she did not ask herself if this were really Ralph who spoke thus. The Ralph she had known no longer existed and he to whom she was listening seemed to be a friend whom she had once seen in her dreams and who had at last become flesh for her at the edge of the grave.

She felt her own pure soul rise in the same flight. . . .

Sir Ralph kneeled before her and said: "Now, Indiana, you must forgive all the harm I have caused you, so that I may forgive myself."

"What can I have to forgive you, my dear Ralph?" she replied. "Should I not, on the contrary, bless you on my last day as I have, in gratitude, every miserable day of my life?"

"I don't know to what extent I have been guilty," said Ralph, "but it is impossible not to have been, despite myself, during that long, terrible battle I fought with my destiny."

"*What* battle?" asked Indiana.

"That is what I must tell you before we die; it is the secret of my life. You asked me to tell it to you on board the ship that brought us to our island, and I promised to do so here above Bernica Lake, when the moon would shine upon us for the last time."

"The moment has come, and I am listening," she said.

"Be patient then, Indiana, for I have a long story to tell, and it is my own."

"I thought I knew it, since we've hardly ever been separated."

"You do not know it," said Ralph sadly, "not a day, not an hour of it. . . . I was born to love; none of you wanted to believe it and that misjudgment decided my character. . . . Heaven, however, sent me a present, a consolation, a hope. You came into my life as if you had been created for me. Poor child! Abandoned like me, like me thrown out upon life without love and without protection, you seemed destined for me, or at least I so flattered myself. Was I too presumptuous? For ten years you belonged to me completely, without rivals, without any doubt. I didn't yet understand what jealousy was. . . .

"But already passions whose names you didn't even know were fermenting in my bosom; my fifteen years of age were ravaging my imagination and you were surprised to see me melancholy so often, sharing your games but without pleasure. You could not understand why a fruit or a bird was not a delight for me as it was for you, and I already seemed cold and strange to you. Yet you loved me as I was, for there was not a moment of my life that was not devoted to you, despite my melancholy; my sufferings made you dearer to me; I nourished the mad hope that you would change them some day into joys. . . .

"Don't be alarmed to discover that you grew up under the wing of a poor bird devoured by love; never did any impure adoration, any guilty thought, endanger the virginity of your soul; never did my mouth take from your cheeks that innocent bloom which covered them as fruit is by the morning dew. My kisses were those of a father, and when your playful, innocent lips met mine, they did not find the burning flame of virile desire. No, it was not with you, the little blue-eyed girl, that I was in love. When I held you with your candid smile and your delicate little caresses in my arms, you were simply my child or at most my little sister; but I was in love with you fifteen years when, giving way to the ardor of mine, I devoured the future with an avid eye. . . .

"How many free and peaceful days we have spent by this ravine! How many times I have bathed your feet in the waters below us! How many times I have watched you sleeping among the reeds, shaded by the parasol of a palm leaf! It was then my torments returned. It tortured me to see you so small; I would ask myself whether, with such sufferings, I would live until the day when you could understand and respond to me. I would swiftly lift your silken hair to my lips and kiss it passionately. I would compare it with the locks I had cut years before and had preserved in my wallet. I would be happy to find that each spring had darkened your hair. Then I would look at the marks on a date tree which I made every four or five years to see how much you had grown. The tree still bears those scars, Indiana; I found them when last I came here, sadly, to remember. Alas, in vain you grew taller; in vain your beauty fulfilled its early promise; in vain your hair became black as ebony; you did not grow taller for me; nor for me did you become more beautiful. The first time your heart beat faster was for another. . . .

"Yes, it was a pure love, a profound and true love that you inspired in me even then. Noun, at ten, was a head taller than you; a Creole in every sense, she was already fully developed, her melting eyes already shone with a special look, her bearing and character were those of a young woman. Well, I did not love Noun, or I loved her only because of you who played with her. I didn't dream of asking myself whether she was beautiful or whether some day she would be more beautiful. I never looked at her. In my eyes she was more of a child than you. You see, I loved you. You were all for me: you were the companion of my life, the dream of my youth.

"But I did not take account of the future. The death of my brother obliged me to marry his fiancée. I won't say anything to you about that period of my life; it was not the worst, Indiana, and yet I was the husband of a woman who hated me and for whom I had no love. I was a father and lost my son; I became a widower and discovered that you were married!

"Those days of exile in England, that period of pain, I will not describe to you. If I did wrong to any-one, it was not to you; and if anyone did wrong to me, I prefer not to complain. There I became more egotistical, that is to say, more depressed and distrustful than ever. By being so doubtful of me, people forced me to become proud and self-sufficient. Thus, in those trials, I had only the company of my own heart to sustain me. They said it was a crime that I did not love a woman who had married me only because she had been obliged to and who had never shown me any-thing but contempt! They later said that one of the principal characteristics of my egotism was the dislike I *seemed* to show for children. Raymon used to chaff me cruelly about that, remarking how caring for the education of children was inconsistent with the rigid habits of a confirmed bachelor. I think he did not know that I had been a father and that it was I who had been your teacher. But none of you wanted to understand that the death of my son was as painful for me, despite the years, as on the first day and that my stricken heart swelled at the sight of blond little heads which reminded me of him. When a man is miserable, people are afraid of not finding him properly guilty, because otherwise they might have to pity him. . . .

"When I returned to Bourbon, when I saw the man to whom they had married you—forgive me, Indiana, that's when I was really selfish; there must always be selfishness in love, since there was some even in mine—I felt a cruel joy at the thought that that legal mockery would give you a master and not a husband. You were surprised at the kind of affection I showed him, but that was because I did not see him as a rival. I knew that elderly man could not inspire or even feel love and that your heart would emerge virginal from that marriage. I was grateful to him for your coldness and your sadness. If he had stayed here, I might have become very guilty; but departing, you left me alone and I was unable to live without you. I tried to conquer the love that came to life with redoubled force when I found you again as beautiful and melancholic as I had dreamed you in your childhood. But solitude only intensified my torment and I surrendered to the need of being with you, of living under the same roof, of breathing the same air, of drinking in the sound of your voice. You know the obstacles I had to meet, the suspicions I had to overcome; I realized then what obligations I had undertaken; I could not join my life to yours without reassuring your husband with a solemn vow, and I have never known what it was to break my word. So I swore with heart and soul never to forget my role of brother; and now tell me, Indiana, have I ever betrayed my vow? . . .

"I felt that I must erect a triple wall of ice around me, in order to keep your interest in me at a distance, to deprive myself of the compassion which would have ruined me . . . and I resigned myself to living under the weight of that terrible accusation of being selfish and hard of heart . . .

"Besides you, the person who showed me the most indulgence was Delmare. You accused me of preferring him to you, of sacrificing your well-being to my own in refusing to intervene in your domestic quarrels. Unjust, blind woman! You didn't see that I was serving you as well as was possible, you did not understand that I could not raise my voice in your defense without betraying myself. What would have become of you if Delmare had expelled me from his house? Who would have protected you, patiently and silently, but with the persevering firmness of an imperishable love? It would not have been Raymon. Besides, I liked him out of gratitude, I admit, that rough, vulgar creature who could have torn my sole remaining joy from me and who did not; that man whose misfortune was not to be loved by you, so that his fate was bound by a secret sympathy to mine! I liked him, too, because he never caused me jealousy.

"But now I have come to the most wretched hour of my life, to that fatal time when your love, which I had dreamed of so long, belonged to another. It was then I finally realized the kind of emotion I had suppressed so many years. It was then that hatred filled my breast and jealousy consumed my strength. . . . However, your sufferings were so intense I forgot my own. I did not want to kill him, because you would have wept for him. I was tempted, heaven forgive me, twenty times to be a vile, contemptible creature, to betray Delmare and to serve my enemy. Yes, Indiana, I was so insane, so miserable at the sight of your suffering, that I was sorry I had tried to tell you the truth and would have given my life to leave Raymon my heart as a legacy! Oh, the villain! May God forgive him the wrong he has done me! But may He punish him for what he has done to you! It is for that I hate him, for I forget what my own life has been when I see what he has done to yours. It is he whom society should have marked with a sign on his forehead the day he was born; whom it should have branded and cast out as the most hardhearted and vicious of men! . . .

"Yes, yes! May God punish him, for he was a brute to you; rather, may He forgive him, for perhaps he was more fool than brute! He did not understand you, he did not appreciate the happiness he might have known. Oh, you loved him so much; he could have made your life so beautiful! In his place I would not have been virtuous; I would have fled with you deep into the mountains, I would have stolen you from society to have you for myself, and I would have feared only that you were not sufficiently damned and abandoned so that I might be everything for you." . . .

Ralph wept like a child. It was in truth the first
time that stoical soul had let himself give way to self-
pity; and yet there was more sorrow in his tears for
the sad fate of Indiana than for his own.

"Do not cry for me," he said, seeing that she too
wept. "Do not pity me. Your pity effaces the entire
past, and the present no longer holds any bitterness.
Why should I suffer now? You no longer love him."

"If I had only really known you, Ralph, I would
never have loved him!" cried Madame Delmare. "It
was your self-sacrifice that was my loss!" . . .

"Then my love arouses no disgust, no anger in you,
Indiana! Oh my God, I thank Thee! I shall die happy!
. . . This is why I asked you to dress in white; it is a
wedding gown and that rock below, projecting into
the basin, is the altar that awaits us."

He rose, broke off a flowering spray from a nearby
orange tree, and placed in on Indiana's black hair; he
then knelt at her feet and said:

"Make me happy. Tell me that your heart consents
to our marriage in another world. Give me eternity; do
not oblige me to ask for oblivion." . . .

Sudden light flooded the inmost reaches of Indiana's heart; the bandage that had long been loosened
fell completely from her eyes. Awakened to truth, to
nature, she saw deep into the soul of Ralph. She also
saw his face as she had never before seen it, for his exalted state had affected him like a voltaic battery gal-
vanizing paralyzed limbs; it freed him from the pet-
rification that had walled up his eyes and voice.

Arrayed now in all his candor and virtue, he was far handsomer than Raymon, and Indiana felt that he indeed was the man she should have loved.

"Be my husband in heaven and on earth," she cried to him, "and may this kiss betroth us for all eternity!"

Their lips united; and without a doubt there is in love that comes from the heart a greater surging power than in all the ardors of ephemeral desire; for that kiss, on the threshold of another life, summed up for them all the joys of that other life.

Ralph took his betrothed in his arms and bore her to the precipice, to plunge with her into the falling waters.

> *Ralph and Indiana survived the plunge, we are told in an epilogue, and decided to live, ending their days in a thatched, Indian cottage by the great cascade.*

PREFACE TO THE 1842 EDITION OF *INDIANA*[4]

If I agreed to have the preceding pages* republished, it is not because they sum up my present belief on the right of society over individuals. It is, rather, because I regard opinions freely expressed in the past as something sacred, which we should neither change nor subdue nor censor in our own way. But now that, hav-

* This preface had immediately followed that of the 1832 edition, which was included in the 1842 edition.

ing walked through life, I see horizons opening around me, I feel bound to tell the reader what I think of my work.

I was young when I wrote *Indiana,* I was obeying sentiments full of vigor and sincerity which overflowed into a series of other novels based on the same theme: the disequilibrium of the sexes due to society. These novels were all vaguely accused by critics of endangering the institution of marriage. Despite its few insights and its naïve uncertainties, *Indiana* did not escape the indignation of so-called serious minds whose words I was then disposed to accept in all docility. However, though my reason was scarcely mature enough to write on such a serious matter, I was sufficiently adult to judge the thoughts of those who judged mine. However simple the accused might be, however learned his judge, the former has sense enough to know if the sentence of the latter is just or perverse, wise or absurd.

Journalists who pose as defenders or guardians of public morality (I know not by virtue of what mission, since I know not in the name of what faith) severely condemned the temptation of my poor tale. Presenting it as a plea against the social order, they gave it an importance and renown it would never have had on its own. They thus vested with a serious and heavy role a young writer scarcely familiar with basic social ideas, whose only literary and philosophical paraphernalia were a bit of imagination, courage, and love of truth. Sensitive to blame, almost thankful for the lessons others deigned to teach him, he examined the indictments brought before public opinion as to the morality of his thought. Thanks to this study, from which he banished pride, he slowly acquired convictions which, at the start of his career, were mere sentiments, but which have since become principles.

Throughout ten years of research, qualms, and often painful but sincere irresolution, fleeing the role of pedagogue assigned to me by those who wished to invite people to ridicule me, loathing the charges against me of vanity and outrage designed to stir up hate for me, proceeding by analysis of life before seeking its synthesis, I pursued my artistic bent and recounted facts which readers sometimes found credible and portrayed characters which were on occasion recognized to have been painted with care.

I contented myself with this work, seeking to consolidate my convictions rather than unsettle those of others, telling myself that if I were wrong, society would somehow awaken powerful voices to destroy my arguments and make up for my imprudent questions by the wisdom of their replies. Many voices were heard, indeed, warning the public against this dangerous writer; but both public and author still await the wise replies.

Long after having written the preface of *Indiana* with all due respect for established society, I still sought to solve the insoluble problem of *reconciling the happiness and dignity of individuals oppressed by this society, without changing society itself*. Bent over the victims, mingling his tears with theirs, acting as emissary between them and his readers, refusing—

prudent defender that he is—to palliate the faults of his clients, invoking the judges' clemency rather than their rigor, the novelist is the true advocate of those abstract creatures who represent our passions and our sufferings before the court of power and the jury of opinion. It is a serious task behind a cover of frivolity, difficult to fulfill, as it should be, troubled as one is by those who would have the form more serious or the matter more trivial.

I do not claim to have accomplished this task with skill. But I am certain of having tried earnestly, in the midst of internal conflicts in which my conscience, now terrified by ignorance of its rights, now stimulated by a heart enamored with truth and justice, marched steadily toward its goal without straying too far or retreating too often.

Initiating the public in this internal struggle by means of a series of prefaces and discussions would have been a puerile measure denoting the vanity of talking about oneself. I refrained from it, as from dealing too rapidly with aspects which remained obscure in my mind. Conservatives found me too bold, innovators too timid. I confess that I had respect and sympathy for both past and future, and in this battle, I found peace only the day when I understood that the one was not necessarily the destruction or desecration, but the continuation and development, of the other.

After ten years of apprenticeship, opened at last to broader ideas which I found not in myself but in the philosophical advances around me (in particular from a few brilliant minds I respectfully interrogated and in general from the spectacle of the sufferings of my fellow creatures), I finally admit that although I was right to doubt myself and withhold my judgment at that time of ignorance and inexperience during which I wrote *Indiana,* my present duty is to take pride in the boldness I have yielded to before and since. I have been reproached for these audacities, but they would have been even bolder had I known that they were legitimate, sincere, and sacred.

Before committing the first novel of my youth to the publicity which a popular edition will give it for the first time, I have now reread it with the severity and detachment I would have had for somebody else's work. Resolved not to retract (one should never retract what has been said or done in good faith) but to condemn myself had I found my youthful inclinations erroneous or dangerous, I found myself in such agreement with the sentiment that inspired *Indiana* (and which would inspire it again if I had to write this story for the first time) that I refused to change anything in it, except for a few awkward phrases and inadequate words. There are certainly many more, and I submit the literary merits of my writings entirely to the lectures of my critics: here I grant them all the competence I lack. I do not deny—I am glad to acknowledge—the undeniable mass of talent at work in the daily press. But that many moralists and philosophers are to be found in this circle of elegant writers I deny resolutely, with all due deference to those who have condemned me and will condemn me again at the first opportunity from the heights of their morality and philosophy.

I repeat, I wrote and had to write *Indiana;* I yielded to a powerful instinct for protest granted me by God, who gives existence to nothing in vain, not even the feeblest creature, and who puts forth His power in the smallest as in the greatest cause. But, then, was it that small, the cause I defended? It is that of half the human race; the suffering of the woman implicates that of the man, as that of the slave his master's; and this I tried to show in *Indiana.* It is said I was pleading an individual cause: as if—assuming I were moved by a personal sentiment—I were the only unfortunate creature of our otherwise peaceful and radiantly happy humanity! From the cries of suffering and sympathy which responded to mine, I now know exactly what to think of that utter felicity of others.

I don't recall having written anything under the influence of egocentric passion. I have never even thought of having to defend myself against it. Those who have read me without prejudice understand that I wrote *Indiana* with an unreasoned but profound and legitimate sense of the injustice and barbarity of those laws which still govern women in marriage, in the family, and in society. I've never had to write a treatise on jurisprudence, but I've had to battle against public opinion, for it is this which retards or accelerates social advancement. The war will be long and hard; but I am not the sole, nor the first, nor the last champion of such a great cause, and I will defend it as long as I live.

As for the sentiment that inspired me at the start, I developed and amplified it even as others fought it and blamed me for it. Unjust, malicious critics taught me more about it than I would have discovered had I been unattacked. In this sense I thank my blundering judges for having enlightened me. The motives behind their judgments have contributed a bright light to my thoughts and conveyed a profound security to my conscience. An open spirit draws profit from everything, and what might discourage vanity intensifies devotion to a cause.

Let no one see in the reproaches uttered to journalists from the depths of a serene and serious heart a sort of protest against the right of criticism entrusted to the French press by public morality. That critics often misuse and misunderstand their social mandate is evident to all; but that the mission itself is providential and sacred no one will deny, unless he be an atheist drunk with progress, an enemy of truth, a blasphemer of the future, or an unworthy child of France. Freedom of thought, freedom to write and speak, sacred conquest of the human mind! What are the petty sufferings and fleeting troubles provoked by your errors or abuses compared to the infinite blessings you promise for the world?

Valentine

(1832)

Six months after the appearance of Indiana,
George Sand scored a second success with Valentine, *published November 17, 1832—a writing
pace she would maintain much of her long life.*
*Valentine de Raimbault is the first of Sand's
aristocratic women who fall in love with a "man
of the people," in this case Bénédict Lhéry, who
had been raised by his uncle, a prosperous farmer
of Berry, whose daughter, Athénaïs, he was expected to marry. Instead, Bénédict falls in love
with Valentine, who is engaged to Count de Lansac. Bénédict's love is returned. However, Valentine is married by her family to Lansac, who con-
tentedly collects the dowry, pays off his debts,
and complaisantly leaves Valentine largely to herself—and Bénédict. Athénaïs marries a local
farmer, Pierre Blutty, who remains jealous of her
love for Bénédict. Count de Lansac eventually
dies in a duel; Bénédict proposes marriage to the
widowed Valentine but is killed by Pierre Blutty,*

who wrongly suspects him of secretly seeing Athénaïs. Bénédict dies in Valentine's arms.

The novel opens with a characteristic description of George Sand's corner of the Berry countryside, which she named "the Black Valley." ⚜—

The southeastern corner of Berry contains a stretch of uncommonly picturesque country. The views from the highway from Paris to Clermont which runs through it, bordered as it is by the most inhabited strips, gives the traveler no inkling of the beauty of the countryside beyond. But should he, in search of shade and quiet, venture along one of the many winding, sunken byways that lead off from the main road, he would soon see unfolding before him a cool, tranquil landscape, a gentle, pastoral scene of lush green meadows, melancholy streams, and clumps of alders and ash trees. He would look in vain for miles around for a slate-roofed, stone-walled house. A wisp of blue smoke flickering behind the foliage would barely hint at the presence of a thatched roof; and should he glimpse the spire of a little church through the walnut trees astride a hill, a step or two would bring him to a bell tower of moss-clad tiles, a dozen scattered cottages surrounded by orchards and fields of hemp, a stream with a small, joisted bridge, a cemetery of scarcely an acre enclosed by a quickset hedge, four elms *en quin-*

conce, and a ruined tower. This is what is called a *bourg* in these parts.

Nothing can equal the peace of these forgotten regions. Wealth, the arts, the mania for experiment, the hundred-tentacled monster called industry, none of these have penetrated here. Revolutions pass almost unnoticed, and the last war to leave the merest trace in the soil was that in which Huguenot opposed Catholic; and even the memory of this is so faint and pale that should you ask the inhabitants about it, they would reply that these events took place at least two thousand years ago; for the principal virtue of the peasants here is unconcern for all matters of antiquity. You may wander through their holdings, pray before their saints, and drink from their wells without ever incurring the risk of hearing the obligatory feudal chronicle or the expected tale of miracles. The grave, taciturn character of the peasant is not the least of the region's charms. Nothing surprises him, nothing attracts him. Your chance presence on his path will not even make him turn his head, and should you ask him the way to a town or a farm, his only reply would be a knowing smile, as if to show that he has not been deceived by your obviously facetious question. The peasant of Berry cannot conceive of anyone walking without knowing where he is going. His dog hardly deigns to bark at you; his children hide behind the hedge to escape your look or your query, and if the youngest among them should be unable to follow his brothers' hasty retreat, he will let himself fall in fright into the ditch, crying aloud mightily. But the most impassive figure of all will be a great white ox, ineluctable doyen of all the pastures, fixing you with his stare from the middle of a thicket and seeming to keep at a respectful distance the less serious, and less benevolent, tribe of startled bulls.

Apart from this initial coolness at the stranger's first approach, the farmer is as pleasant and hospitable as the peaceful shade and aromatic meadows of the Berry countryside.

And one corner of this land, which is bordered by two small rivers, is particularly noted for the vigor and dark hues of its vegetation, which have led to its being named "the Black Valley."

* * *

Bénédict did not find her attractive. He had created an ideal woman—dark-haired, pale, passionate, Spanish, changeable—which he did not wish to relinquish. Mademoiselle Valentine de Raimbault did not fulfill these requirements; she was fair, blonde, calm, tall, cool—in every way wonderfully lovely. She had none of the faults with which Bénédict's fevered brain was enamored, a consequence of works of art where the brush has treated ugliness so poetically as to make it more attractive than beauty itself. Moreover, Mademoiselle de Raimbault had a quiet, solid dignity which at first sight was too imposing to be really charming. The curve of her profile, the fineness of her hair, the graceful line of her neck and white shoulders stirred a thousand memories of the Sun King's court.

One felt that an entire strain of noble ancestors had been necessary to bring forth this combination of pure, aristocratic features, the most regal graces which slowly revealed themselves as those of a swan languorously and majestically gliding in the sunlight.

* * *

[Valentine to Bénédict] ". . . We receive a worthless education; we are given rudiments of everything and never permitted to study anything thoroughly. We have to be educated, but if ever we should become learned, we would be ridiculous. We are always brought up to be rich, never to be poor. The education of our grandmothers was much better, however restricted it may have been; at least they knew how to knit. The Revolution judged them to be mediocre women; they resigned themselves to living as mediocre women; they were not above making lace for their living. But we who have an imperfect knowledge of English, drawing, and music, who know how to make lacquer paintings, water-color screens, velvet flowers, and a score of other wasteful trifles which republican custom should surely spurn, what could we do? Which one of us would, with no regret, stoop to take up a mechanical trade? Not one in twenty of us has a thorough knowledge of anything. I know but one situation for which we would be suited, that of chambermaid." . . .

* * *

When Bénédict saw Valentine enter the stables, run after the young lambs, take them in her arms, hug all Madame Lhéry's favorite creatures, even feed from her own white hand the great oxen staring vacantly at her, a flattering yet cruel thought made him smile; this was that Mademoiselle de Raimbault seemed much better fitted than Athénaïs [farmer Lhéry's daughter] to be his wife; it seemed as if there had been a mistake in the allotment of roles, that Valentine, as a good, simple farmer's wife, would have known how to make him love a quiet domestic life.

"Why isn't she Madame Lhéry's daughter!" he asked himself. "I should then never have had the yearning to study. Even now I would give up all vain ambitions of playing a role in society. I would happily become a peasant; I would lead a useful, positive life. In the depth of this lovely valley with Valentine, I would be a poet and plowman: a poet to admire her, a laborer to serve her. Oh! how easily I would forget the bustling crowd of the city!"

He surrendered himself to these thoughts as he followed Valentine through the barns, where she breathed with pleasure the healthy, rural smells. Suddenly she turned to him, saying:

"I honestly believe I was born to live on a farm! Oh! how I would have loved this simple life, these daily chores! I would have made everything myself, just like Madame Lhéry. I would have bred the finest cattle of the region; I would have had lovely crested chickens and goats which I would have taken to browse in the undergrowth. If you knew how often, in the tiresome hubbub of a salon party, I have found myself dreaming that I was a shepherdess sitting at the edge of a meadow! The orchestra would fetch me back to the group, but my dream would remain with the milk jug!"

Leaning against a rack, Bénédict listened with deep emotion, for she expressed ideas in sympathy with his, saying aloud what he silently thought.

They were alone. Bénédict ventured to pursue the subject of Valentine's dream.

"But what if you had had to marry a peasant?" he asked her.

"In our time," she replied, "there are no more peasants. Do we not receive the same education in almost all social classes? Is not Athénaïs more talented than I? And is not a man like yourself much superior to a woman such as I by virtue of his knowledge?"

"Do you not have the prejudices of your high birth?" Bénédict persisted.

"I see myself as a peasant woman, so I could not possibly have them."

"That is no reason. Athénaïs was born on a farm, and *she* deplores not having been born a lady."

"Oh! how happy I should be in her place!" she said with intensity.

And she remained there, thoughtful, leaning against the crib, facing Bénédict, but with her eyes riveted on the ground, little dreaming that she had told him things for which he would gladly have paid with his blood to hear.

227

* * *

[Bénédict to Valentine's half-sister Louise] ". . . I despise those who thrive with impunity on other people's work. I can conceive of a civic sense existing in free and virtuous nations, if any such exist. But here, on French soil, where, whatever one may say, there is a lack of hands to work the land but every profession has a host of aspirants; where human beings, hideously massed together around palaces, crawl and lick the footprints of the rich; where enormous capital, accumulated—in accordance with the laws of social wealth—in a few men's hands, is the prize in a never-ending lottery of avarice, immorality, and ineptness—in this country of lewdness and misery, of vice and desolation, in this civilization, rotten to its very roots, you want me to be a loyal citizen? You want me to sacrifice my will, desires, imagination to its needs, being either its dupe or its victim, so that the penny I might toss to a beggar will end up in a millionaire's coffers? I must do my utmost to do good, only to increase the existing evil, only to make my contribution to a government which licenses informers, croupiers, and prostitutes? No, I swear that I will never do that."

* * *

Bénédict, who was ruthless and skeptical in character, whose mind was discontented and rebellious, who was so harsh on social absurdities and faults, claimed—this was probably one of his paradoxes—that there is no

more monstrous impropriety, no more disgraceful practice, than the public spectacle made of marriage.
He had never seen, without pity, some poor young
girl, her heart almost always filled with shy love, passing through a bustling crowd of wedding guests, an
object of impudent attention and impertinent looks, to
reach her husband's arms, a bride already deflowered
in each man's imagination. He also pitied the poor
young man whose love was displayed as banns on
town-hall doors and in church pews and who was
forced to subject his fiancée's virgin-white bridal dress
to the filth of town or country. He felt that in removing love's veil of mystery love itself was degraded. . . .

"How," he would ask, "can you hope to have
women of pure moral character when you publicly vi-
olate their modesty? When, as virgins, you bring them
in front of a gathered crowd, and, taking this crowd to
witness, you tell them: 'You now belong to this man;
you are no longer a virgin.' And the crowd claps its
hands, laughs, exults, scoffs at the young couple's
blushes, and pursues them into the very secrecy of
their wedding bed with shouts and obscene songs!"

* * *

"Oh abominable violation of the most sacred rights!"
Bénédict cried to himself. "Infamous tyranny of man
over woman! Marriage, society, institutions, how I
hate you, how I wish for your death! And You, God!
You whose creative will has placed us on earth, who
afterwards refuses to intervene in our destinies—You,

who delivers the weak to so much despotism and abasement, I curse You! You rest, satisfied with Your creation, and fail to preserve it. You give us intelligence which You allow misfortune to smother! Curses on You! Cursed be the womb that bore me!"

While thus proclaiming, the wretched young man was loading his guns, lacerating his breast with his nails, and walking agitatedly about, all concern for concealment forgotten. Suddenly reason, or rather a ray of lucidity in the middle of his ravings, came to enlighten him. There was a way to save Valentine from a hateful and degrading tyranny.* There was a way to punish that heartless mother who coldly condemned her daughter to legalized disgrace, to the worst infamy that can be inflicted on woman, to rape.

"Yes, rape!" Bénédict repeated with rage (it should not be forgotten that Bénédict was of an extreme and exceptional disposition). "Every day, in the name of God and society, some boor, some coward, wins the hand of a wretched girl who has been forced by her parents, honor, or misery to smother a pure and sacred love for another in her breast. And there, before the eyes of all society, which approves and ratifies it, a modest, trembling woman who has resisted her lover's raptures ends up soiled by the kisses of a hated master! And this is the way things are supposed to be!"

And Valentine, creation's most beautiful work, sweet, simple, pure Valentine, like all others had this disgrace in store!

* To kill Count de Lansac, then himself; he changes his mind about the first act; attempts the second but survives.

* * *

Fifteen months passed in this fashion;† fifteen months
of calm and happiness in five people's lives—it seems
almost incredible. Nevertheless, it happened. Bénédict's only sorrow was to see Valentine at times
become pale and absent. He would then quickly try to
find a reason, and it always turned out to be some fear
that was troubling her pious, timorous soul. He always
succeeded in clearing away these small clouds, because
Valentine could no longer doubt either his strength or
his amenability. Monsieur de Lansac's letters gave her
further reassurance; she had decided to write to him
that Louise and her son were established at the farm
and that Monsieur Lhéry [Bénédict] was taking care
of the young boy's education, but without telling how
intimately she was living with these three people.
This was how she had explained their relationships,
pretending to consider Lansac bound by his promise
to let her see her sister. The whole tale seemed strange
and ridiculous to the count. If he had not quite
guessed the whole truth, he was at least on the way to
doing so. He had shrugged his shoulders at the
thought of the lack of taste and bad form of his wife
having an affair with a pretentious country book-
worm.

But on the whole, this state of things pleased him
better than any other. He had married with the firm

† Count de Lansac is away; Bénédict and Valentine (now
Countess de Lansac) see each other in almost daily intimacy.

intention never to be burdened by Madame de Lansac, and for the moment his relationship with a leading ballerina of the St. Petersburg theater made him
view life very philosophically. Thus he found it quite
fair that his wife, on her part, should form affections
which would bind her far from him, with no reproaches or complaints. All that he asked was that she
should act carefully, avoiding all dissolute public behavior, so that he would not be subjected to the foolish, unfair ridicule that deceived husbands attract.
So he relied upon Valentine's character to have no
worries on that score. And since it was essential for
this neglected young woman to have something, as he
put it, to occupy her heart, he preferred to see her
seek it in the seclusion of a country retreat than in the
bustle and glitter of the salons. He was careful not to
criticize or to condemn her way of life, and all his letters expressed, in the most affectionate and honorable
terms, the profound indifference with which he had
resolved to greet all Valentine's activities.

* * *

[Valentine to her husband] ". . . Yesterday you
talked to me about our several obligations, but how
are you fulfilling yours? You see me on the verge of
falling into an abyss which I abhor, and when I implore you to lend me a hand, you only push me toward
it. Well then, may my errors be on your own
head!" . . .

". . . All this is fine, my dear, but it is supremely
ridiculous. You are very young. Please accept some

friendly advice: a woman should never use her husband as her confessor; it demands more virtue of him than his situation allows. Personally I find you charming, but my life is too busy to let me undertake to cure you of a great passion. Besides, I would never be so conceited as to hope to be successful. It seems to me that I have done enough for you by closing my eyes. You force me to open them, and thus I have to go away, because the situation between us would no longer be bearable and we could no longer look at each other without laughing."

"Laughing, sir! Laughing!" she cried out with justifiable anger.

"Adieu, Valentine!" he continued. "I must admit that I am too experienced to blow out my brains over an infidelity, but I have too much common sense to be ready to act as chaperon to a hothead like you. This is also why I have no special wish to see you break off this relationship which still holds for you all the romantic beauty of a first love. The second would already be briefer, the third—"

"You are insulting me," said Valentine, downcast, "but God will protect me. Adieu, monsieur, I thank you for this cruel lesson. I shall do my best to take advantage of it."

* * *

"Oh, my dear!" said the marquise [Valentine's grandmother, dying] with an attempted smile, "it is not so easy to save a young head like yours from passion! Well! In my very last hour I can at least be honest.

Why should I be hypocritical toward you now? Shall I be able to be hypocritical when, in a few moments, I shall stand before God? Of course not! It is impossible to protect oneself from this disease while one is young. So love, my dear girl. It is the only good thing in life. But take your grandmother's last piece of advice and never forget it: never take a lover who is not of your own social rank."

* * *

Count de Lansac had just been killed in a duel.

* * *

"Oh, that is true," said Valentine, with a bitter look back on the past. "They all treated my virtue with incredible levity. I whom they were accusing, I alone understood the nobility of my duties, and I wanted to make marriage a sacred, mutual obligation. But they laughed at my ingenuousness. One would speak to me of money, another of dignity, a third of social conventions. Ambition and pleasure were all that governed their actions, that gave meaning to their precepts. They tempted me to fall short of my duty, and urged me to keep up only a virtuous appearance. My poor Bénédict, if instead of being the son of a peasant you had been a duke and their peer, they would have borne me aloft in triumph."

Lélia[1]

(1833)

George Sand's third novel emerged from the black spring of 1833, when disenchantment—not simply with lovers—led to existential despair, spiritual impotence, and a metaphysical form of expression. Lélia is the novel's hero (Sand may be the first to have created Woman as hero) on a philosophical quest for the meaning of life, particularly her own. She is thirty. Sténio, a twenty-year-old poet fatally in love with her, complains of her coldness. Trenmor, a mystical ex-convict, advises Lélia to send Sténio away. They part instead. Lélia retires to the desert to meditate, then returns to the world. She meets her sister Pulchérie, courtesan-prostitute whom she had not seen for a long time, at an elaborate costume ball where Sténio mistakes Pulchérie for Lélia, understandably. While Lélia is Sand, Pulchérie is both Marie Dorval, Sand's intimate actress-friend of the time, and Sand's double. The Lélia-Pulchérie dialogue is the heart and core of the novel. In the end, Sténio drowns himself and Lélia is strangled

by a love-maddened, improbable priest, Magnus,
who is led away to expiate his sin by Tren-
mor.

[Sténio to Lélia] "I have brought you to this deserted valley, untrodden by cattle and unsullied by the
hunter's boot. Across precipices I have brought you
here, Lélia. Fearlessly you have faced all the perils of
this journey, measuring with a tranquil glance the
crevasses that score the glaciers' flanks, crossing them
on a shaky board thrown over their bottomless depths
by our guides. You have passed over cataracts light
and agile as a white stork who settles now on one
stone, now on another, and who falls asleep, neck
bent and body balanced on a single fragile leg in a
fuming whirl of waves, above pits vomiting overbrim-
ming foam. Never once have you trembled, Lélia; and
I, how I have shuddered! How many times my blood
has turned to ice and my heart missed a beat seeing
you thus above the abyss, gazing upwards with care-
less inattention and scorning to look for a foothold for
your slender feet! You are very brave and very strong,
Lélia! When you say that your soul is unnerved, you
lie; no man has more confidence or audacity than
you."

"What is audacity," replied Lélia, "and who is not
audacious? Who, in these times, cares for life? We
call this kind of courage nonchalance when it produces some good, but when it does no more than lay

bare the working of a futile destiny, inertia is a better name for it.

"Inertia, Sténio, is our inner malady, the great curse of this age. Nowadays there are only negative virtues and we are brave because we are no longer even capable of fear. Alas! everything is worn out, even man's weaknesses and vices. We no longer have the strength which gives that force that used to make us cling to life with the coward's obstinacy. When men were still strong, they would wage war with cunning, with prudence, with calculation. Life was a perpetual battle, a struggle in which the bravest would constantly recoil from danger, for he was bravest who lived longest in the midst of perils and hatred. Ever since civilization has made life easy and calm for everybody, we all find it monotonous and insipid; it has so little worth that we risk it for a word, for a look! Duels have become accepted custom as a result of this indifference to life. The apathy of our century is evidenced by the sight of two men, calmly and politely drawing lots as to which of them will kill the other without hatred, without wrath, and to no purpose. Alas, Sténio! We are no longer anything, neither good, nor evil, not even cowards—we are inert."

* * *

"Ah, I too recognize your voice," replied Lélia. "You are Pulchérie."

"I am your sister," said the courtesan, unmasking herself, "the daughter of your father and mother. Have you no word of affection for me?"

"Oh, my still beautiful sister!" said Lélia. "Save me, save me from life, save me from despair; offer me tenderness, tell me that you love me, that you remember our happy days, that you are my family, my blood, my sole possession on earth!"

They kissed each other, both in tears. Pulchérie's joy was passionate, Lélia's sorrowful; they examined each other with moist eyes and touched with wondering hands, amazed to find each other still beautiful, still full of love and admiration for each other, and, despite the changes in them, still able to recognize each other.

Suddenly Lélia recalled that her sister was defiled. This she could have forgiven any other human creature, but seeing it in her sister, some involuntary trace of that indomitable social vanity we call honor made her blush with shame.

She withdrew her hands which she had put in Pulchérie's and stood motionless, overwhelmed by some new dejection, pale, her body bent double and her eyes fixed on the dark foliage against which the lightning's glow expired.

Pulchérie was dismayed by her gloomy mien and by the bitter, frozen smile that hovered vacuously upon her lips. Forgetting the degradation to which the world had condemned her, she felt sorry for Lélia, so quickly does pain reduce human beings to the same level.

"Then this is what you are like!" she said in the tender tones of a mother comforting a grieving child. "I have spent long years far from my sister and when

I find her again, she is cast down like a worn-out garment that nobody wants, choking back her cries with the tresses of her hair and tearing her breast with her nails. Thus you were when I came upon you, Lélia; and now you are even worse, for you used to weep, but now you seem dead; you used to live through suffering, but now you do not live through anything. This is what you are reduced to, Lélia! Oh God! What use have been all those brilliant talents of which you were so proud! Where has the road you ventured on with so much hope and confidence led you? Into what abyss of misfortune have you fallen, you who aspired to walk above us? Jerusalem, Jerusalem, did I not tell you that pride would be your downfall!"

"Pride," said Lélia, who felt herself wounded in her innermost soul. "It ill befits you to speak of pride, poor misguided creature! Which of us is the more lost in this wilderness, you or I?"

"I do not know, Lélia," said Pulchérie sadly. "I have come a long way in this life, I am still young, still good-looking. I have suffered much, but I am not weary yet, I have not yet said, 'Oh, my God, this is enough!' Whereas you, Lélia—"

"You are right," said Lélia despondently. "I have used up everything."

"Everything except pleasure!" said the courtesan with a bacchanalian laugh which transformed her suddenly from head to foot.

Lélia shuddered and took an involuntary step backward; then, hastily drawing nearer, she gripped her sister's arm.

"And you, dear sister," she cried out, "have you then tasted pleasure? And have you not exhausted it? Are you still a woman and still alive? Hurry then, tell me your secret, share with me the happiness you seem to have!"

"I have no happiness," replied Pulchérie. "I have never sought it. Unlike you, I have known no disappointments because I have never asked more of life than it could give me. My aim has been limited to knowing how to enjoy things as they are. I have made a virtue out of not despising them, and my wisdom has been not to hanker after anything more. Anacreon has written my liturgy. I have chosen antiquity as my model and naked Greek goddesses as my divinities. I can bear the evils of our present distorted civilization. And I have the religion of pleasure to keep me from despair. Oh, Lélia, how avidly you watch me and listen to me! You no longer find me repulsive! I am no longer that foolish, vile being from whom you recoiled with so much loathing."

"I have never despised you, dear sister. I pitied you; at present I am only surprised at not having to feel sorry for you. Dare I say that this makes me very glad?"

"Hypocritical spiritualists," said Pulchérie, "you never dare to approve of joys in which you have no share! Oh, but you are weeping now! You hang your head, my poor sister! There you are, bent down and crushed under the weight of this destiny which you yourself have chosen! Who is to blame? May this lesson be of use to you! Remember our quarrels, our struggles, and our separation; each of us then predicted the other's ruin!"

"Alas, Pulchérie, for you I predicted the contempt of men, abandonment, and a wretched old age. Now I see I was wrong: thank Heaven, you are still young and beautiful. But has the searing iron of shame never yet burned you? Do you not hear this rapacious, idle crowd, which at this very moment is seeking you out to appease its impudent curiosity, growling like an unclean, dangerous beast? Do you not feel its hot breath pursuing you and contaminating you? Listen, it calls for you, baying for its prey; you are a courtesan and you belong to them! Oh! if they should come now, do not reveal that you are my sister! They might think that we are two of a kind! They might dare to touch me with their miry hands! My poor Pulchérie, there is your master, there is your God and your lover —the people, that noisome, reeking rabble over there! You have found pleasure in their embraces; but you must know, my poor sister, that you are even viler than the dust under their feet!"

"Yes, I know," said the courtesan, wiping her shameless forehead as if to brush away the mist, "but defiance of shame is my virtue, my power, just as yours is the avoidance of it; I tell you that this is my wisdom which leads me to my ends, overcomes all obstacles, outlives constantly recurring anxieties, and pleasure is my reward for these struggles. This is my ray of sunlight after the storm, the enchanted island upon which the tempest throws me, and though I may be degraded, at least I am not ridiculous. To be useless, Lélia, is to be ridiculous; to be ridiculous is worse than to be infamous; to serve no purpose in the world is more despicable than to serve the most debasing one."

"That is true," said Lélia gloomily.

"Besides," continued the courtesan, "what does a truly strong soul care about shame? Do you realize, Lélia, that this public opinion in face of which the so-called honest souls are so servile, do you realize that only the weak submit to it and that one must be strong to resist? Do you make a virtue of a facile, calculated self-interest which everything encourages and rewards? Would you compare the labors, the pains, the courage of a housewife with those of a prostitute? Would you say that she who has had the fewer troubles in the struggle of life deserves the greater glory?

"But, Lélia! Do you no longer shudder at my arguments as you did before? You have nothing to say? This silence is dreadful, Lélia—have you become nothing at all? Have you vanished like the ripple of a wave or a name written in the sand? Does your noble blood no longer revolt against the heresies of debauchery, against the shamelessness of the flesh? Wake up, Lélia, try to defend virtue if you wish me to believe in the existence of such a thing!"

"Speak on, woman," replied Lélia harshly. "I am listening."

"What, then, does God ask of us here on earth?" Pulchérie continued. "To live, surely? And what does society demand of us? Not to steal. Society is so constructed that many people have no other way of making a living but by a trade which the social body sanctions, yet at the same time stigmatizes with the hateful name of vice. Do you realize of what temper of steel a poor woman must be made to live this way? With how many insults people try to make her pay for the weaknesses she has discovered and the brutalities she has satisfied? Under what burden of ignominy and injustice must she learn to sleep, to live, to be lover, mistress, and mother, three aspects of the female destiny from which no woman can escape, whether she sell herself as a prostitute or through a marriage contract? Oh, dear sister, how justified these publicly and unjustly dishonored creatures are to despise the crowds that curse them after soiling them with their love! You see, if there be a heaven and a hell, then heaven will be for those who will have suffered most and have managed, on their bed of pain, to find a few smiles of joy and blessings to bestow on God; hell will be for those who, having seized the best things of life, have failed to appreciate their worth. In the midst of the horrors of social degradation, the courtesan Zinzolina [Pulchérie] will have made a profession of faith by remaining true to sensual pleasure, while the ascetic Lélia, under a life of austerity and respectability will have repudiated God every moment by closing her eyes and her soul to the blessings of life."

"Alas, Pulchérie, you are accusing me without knowing whether I was free to choose and follow a plan in life. Do you know what my fate has been since our parting?"

"I have heard what the world has said about you," replied the courtesan. "All I know is that your life as a woman has been beset with problems. I have heard that you lived shrouded in mystery and poetic affectations, and I have smiled with pity when thinking of the hypocritical virtue which consists in deriving empty pride from impotence or fear."

"You may humiliate me," replied Lélia. "Today I have so little confidence in myself that I can offer no justification; but would you care to listen to the story of this moral life, so barren and colorless, and yet so long and bitter? Afterwards you may tell me if a remedy can be found for such long-standing griefs and so deep-rooted discouragements."

"I am listening," replied Pulchérie, resting her white, rounded arm on the foot of a simpering marble nymph half-hidden among the dark branches. "Speak, dear sister, tell me the sorrows of your destiny; but first let me tell you that I know them beforehand; already in the days when, pale and slender as a sylph, you would walk in the depth of our forests, leaning on my arm, attentive to the flight of birds and the hues of flowers, to the changing aspects of the clouds, but indifferent to the eyes of the young hunters passing by who watched us through the trees, already then I knew, Lélia, that you would waste your youth away pursuing vain dreams and scorning the really good things in life. Do you recall our endless walks on our father's estate and our long evening reveries when, leaning together on the gilt balustrade of the terrace, you would watch the stars above the brow of the hills and I the dusty horsemen coming down the path?"

"I remember it all," replied Lélia. "With attentive eyes you would follow every one of these travelers as they disappeared in the mist of the sunset. Though you could scarcely make out their clothes or their bearing, you were captivated by or contemptuous of each one of them, according to his boldness or caution in coming down the hill. You would laugh mercilessly at the careful rider who dismounted and led his hesitant, lazy horse by the bridle. You would applaud from afar the horseman who tackled the dangers of the abrupt slope at a firm and steady trot. I recall that I once reproved you harshly for waving your handkerchief in a burst of admiration and encouragement for some young madcap who dashed forward at full gallop and who two or three times just saved his horse from falling into the ravine."

"And yet he could neither hear nor see me," continued Pulchérie. "You, my shy sister, you were indignant if I showed interest in a man; you were responsive only to the elusive beauties of nature, to a sound or a color, but never to a clear or tangible figure. A distant song would make you shed tears. But as soon as the bare-legged shepherd appeared on top of the hill you would avert your eyes in disgust; you would cease to listen to his voice or to enjoy it. In all things, reality belied your own vivid perceptions and ruined your too demanding hopes. Was it not so, Lélia?"

"You are right, my dear sister, we were not alike. Wiser and happier than I, you lived only for enjoyment; I, more ambitious and perhaps less obedient to God, lived only to desire. Do you recall that sultry summer's day when we rested on the bank of a brook under the cedars of the valley, in a mysterious, dark retreat where the murmur of water falling from stone to stone mingled with the sad song of the cicadas? We lay down on the grass, and as we looked up through the trees at the burning sky above our heads we were overcome by a deep untroubled slumber. We woke up in each other's arms unaware that we had slept."

At these words Pulchérie started and squeezed her sister's hand.

"Yes, I recall this better than you, Lélia. It stands as a glowing memory in my life, and I have often thought of that day with emotion full of charm, and maybe also of shame."

"Of shame?" said Lélia, drawing back her hand.

"You have never known, you have never guessed this," said Pulchérie. "I would never have dared to tell you of it then. But now I can confess all, and you can learn all. Listen, dear sister, it was in your innocent arms, on your virgin breast, that God revealed to me for the first time the power of life. Please do not withdraw this way. Put aside your prejudices and listen to me."

"Prejudices!" exclaimed Lélia, drawing closer again. "If only I had prejudices! That at least would be some kind of belief. Speak, tell me all, dear sister."

"Well," said Pulchérie, "we were sleeping peace-

fully in the warm, moist grass. The cedars gave off
their exquisite, sweet-smelling scent and the noon
wind fanned our damp foreheads with its burning
wings. Until then, carefree and merry, I had greeted
each day of my life as a new blessing. At times sudden, deep-reaching sensations would stir my blood. A
strange ardor would seize my imagination; the colors
of nature would seem more sparkling; youth would
throb more vivaciously and more cheerfully in my
breast; and if I looked at myself in the mirror, I found
myself flushed and more beautiful at such moments. I
felt like kissing my own reflected image which inspired me with an insane love. Then I would start
laughing, and I would run, stronger and lighter, over
the grass and the flowers; for nothing was ever revealed to me through suffering. I would not, like you,
tire myself out trying to divine things; I would find
because I did not seek.

"On that day, happy and calm as I was, the hitherto impenetrable and calmly unquestioned mystery
was revealed to me through a strange, delirious, extraordinary dream. Oh, dear sister! you may deny the
heavenly influence! You may deny the sanctity of
pleasure! But had you been granted this moment of
ecstasy, you would have said that an angel from the
very bosom of God had been sent to initiate you into
the sacred mysteries of human life. As for me, I
dreamed simply of a dark-haired man bending over
me to brush my lips with his burning red mouth; and
I woke up overwhelmed, palpitating and happier than
I had ever imagined I could possibly be. I looked

around me: the sun was glinting on the depths of the wood; the air was good and sweet and the cedars were lifting their majestic, spreading branches like immense arms and long hands stretching up towards heaven. Then I looked at you. Oh, my dear sister, how beautiful you were! I had never considered you as such before that day. In my complacent girlish conceit I preferred myself to you. I thought that my glowing cheeks, my rounded shoulders, my golden hair made me the more beautiful. But at that moment the meaning of beauty was revealed to me in another creature. I no longer loved only myself: I felt the need to find an object of admiration and love outside myself. Gently I raised myself and I gazed at you with strange curiosity and unusual pleasure. Your thick black hair was sticking to your forehead, its tight curls twisting and intertwining, clinging as if endowed with life to your neck, velvet with shade and perspiration. I ran my fingers through it: your hair seemed to tighten around them and to draw me toward you. Tight over your breast, your thin white shirt displayed skin tanned by the sun to an even darker shade than usual; and your long eyelids, heavy with sleep, stood out against your cheeks which were of a fuller color than they are today. Oh, how beautiful you were, Lélia! But your beauty was different from mine, and that I found strangely disturbing. Your arms, thinner than mine, were covered by an almost imperceptible dark down which has long since disappeared under the treatment that luxury imposes. Your feet, so perfect in their loveliness, were dipping in the brook, and long blue veins stood out on them. Your breast rose and fell as you breathed with a regularity that seemed to betoken calm and strength; and in all your features, in your posture, in your shape more clear-cut than mine, in the darker shade of your skin, and especially in the proud, cold expression on your sleeping face there was something so masculine and strong that I scarcely recognized you. I felt that you looked like the beautiful dark-haired child I had just been dreaming of, and trembling I kissed your arm. Then you opened your eyes and their expression filled me with an unknown shame; I turned away as if I had done something shameful. And yet, Lélia, no impure thought had even crossed my mind. How did this happen? I was then totally ignorant. I was receiving from nature and from God, my creator and my master, my first lesson in love, my first sensation of desire. Your eyes were mocking and severe as they had always been. But never before had they intimidated me as they did at that instant. Do you not recall my confusion and the way I blushed?"

"I even recall a remark that I could not explain," replied Lélia. "You made me bend over the water and said: 'Look at yourself, dear sister; do you not think that you are beautiful?' I answered that I was less so than you. 'Oh, no! much more so,' you continued. 'You look like a man.'"

"And that made you shrug your shoulders contemptuously," Pulchérie went on.

"And I did not guess," replied Lélia, "that destiny

had just been achieved for you, while for me no destiny would ever be accomplished."

"Begin your story," said Pulchérie. "The sounds of the festivities have moved away; I can hear the orchestra taking up the interrupted tune; they have forgotten you; they have given up looking for me; we are free for a little while. Please speak."

* * *

[Lélia to Pulchérie] ". . . This unbridled desire for happiness, which I sought through him [an unnamed lover] and which no human enjoyment could ever satisfy, was an everlasting and profound torture. Had not passions of the mind destroyed in me the salutary calculation of egoism, I could never have loved. But as I did not know on what to expend my intellectual force, I laid it down, fawning and clinging, at the feet of an idol created by my own creed; for he was a man like other men, and when I tired of prostrating myself, I smashed the pedestal and I saw him reduced to his true dimensions. . . ."

* * *

[Pulchérie to Lélia] ". . . I have often regretted my inability to damp down the ardor of my blood and to temper the impetuousness of my desire so as to contemplate a happy man in my arms. I would have liked to combine the purified pleasures of the spirit with the feverish joys of the body, but why is it that they seem to be incompatible or that they mutually smother each other?"

"Because we know how to distinguish between them," said Lélia. "How well I have known the generous pleasures of the soul disunited from the flesh, but they were not enough for me, for human egoism is ferocious, intractable, constantly rising anew, secretly gnawing at us, or waking suddenly to tear us apart. You are right to deride the colossal ambition of platonic love. In vain does the spirit try to rise; suffering always brings it back to earth. Oh, how well I remember! During those feverish nights spent beside a man, I learned how pride revolts against the vanities of abnegation; I felt that one could at the same time love somebody else to the extent of submitting entirely to him and love oneself to the extent of feeling hatred for the one to whom one has submitted."

"And then," said Pulchérie, softening her earlier sarcastic tone and seizing Lélia's hand with a gesture of sympathetic agreement, "there is the fact that men are vulgar. You see, dear sister, in our life of intrigue and change, similar things happen to us. Sometimes we are covered with riches by one, and we share them with another. Most of the time we hate anyone who loves us enough to pay us, and we give to the one who loves us casually enough to accept our money. But man is a brute and does not know where a woman's love begins or where it ends. He does not realize that it is folly to accept the gifts of a loving heart under the eyes of a subtle mind; she offers all without restraint, she gives joyfully; then she stops, astonished, despising the man who, though the stronger and more powerful, has taken without shame. Man is stupid and woman is fickle. These two beings, so similar and so different, are made in such a way that there will always be hatred between them, even in the love they feel for each other. The first emotion that follows their embraces is disgust or sadness; this is a higher law against which revolt is vain. In the designs of Providence the union of a man and a woman must be seen as transitory, and change must be considered inherent in their nature."

"Cruellest for me," Lélia rejoined, "was the fact that he failed to appreciate the scale of my sacrifices. He always dismissed the troublesome idea of my resignation as if acknowledgment of it would have made him blush. He pretended to believe I was deluded by a feeling of hypocritical modesty. He affected to take for expressions of rapture my moans of pain and impatience. He laughed unkindly at my tears.* Sometimes his unspeakable egoism would even feed on them with pride; and when he had crushed me under his fierce embrace, he would fall asleep at my side with brutal unconcern, while I stifled my sobs to avoid awakening him. Oh, the wretched plight and subjection of woman! You are so strongly implanted in nature, at least society could have tried to soften you!

"And yet I loved him passionately, this master of my own choice whom I accepted as a fatal necessity,

---

* As did Prosper Mérimée, according to a letter from George Sand to Sainte-Beuve, July 24(?), 1833.

whom I revered with a secret self-satisfaction, since I had chosen him myself. I loved him madly. The more he made me feel his domination, the more I would cherish it, the more pride I took in bearing my fetters. But the moment that through his neglect or indolence, I had a taste of freedom, I began again to curse my servitude. I made a religion of my love, or at least a virtue; but I wanted him to be grateful to me, he who followed only some instinctive choice. I was wrong. He could only despise such heroic weakness, whereas I cherished his cowardly hold over me.

"Why did I love him for so long (long enough to burn out my soul)? Undoubtedly because of the feverish irritation produced in me by the absence of any personal satisfaction. Near him I felt a sort of peculiar, delirious longing which originated in the most refined, exquisite forces of my intelligence and thus could not be appeased by any carnal embrace. I felt my breast consumed by an unquenchable fire and his kisses brought me no relief. I would clasp him in my arms with superhuman strength and then fall exhausted beside him, disheartened by my total incapacity to convey my yearnings to him. For me, desire was an ardor of the soul which paralyzed the power of my senses before they had even been aroused; it was a savage fury which seized my brain and concentrated there exclusively. My blood would freeze, impotent and thin, before this immense upsurging of my will. Then would have been the moment to die. But selfishly he would never agree to suffocate me, pressing me against his chest; yet therein lay my only hope for sensual pleasure. I hoped at last to know the languors and delights of love while falling asleep in the arms of death.

"When he had dozed off, satisfied and sated, I would lie motionless and dismayed at his side. Thus I passed many hours watching him sleep. I found him so beautiful, this man! There was such strength and nobility on his peaceful brow! My heart would throb violently next to him; the burning tide of my restless blood would rush to my face; then unbearable tremors would race through my limbs. I seemed to feel again the excitation of physical love and the mounting confusion of carnal desire. I was strongly tempted to awaken him, to fold him in my arms and ask for those caresses I had earlier been unable to enjoy. But I resisted these deceptive solicitations of my suffering, for I well knew that he had not the power to calm them: God alone could have done so by deigning to subdue the morbid vigor of my soul. Then I fought this demon of hope which stayed awake in me. I would flee that voluptuous yet wretched bed, that sanctuary of love which became the coffin in which all my strength and illusions were buried. I would pace the cold marble floor of my rooms and cool my burning temples in the night air; then I would fall to my knees and pray God to regenerate me. If someone had promised to renew the impoverished blood in my veins, I would willingly have let myself be stabbed like Aeson and cut into pieces.

"Sometimes in my sleep, prey to those rich ecstasies which assail the ascetic mind, I felt myself carried away with him on balmy breezes high above the clouds. I seemed to float on waves of inexpressible voluptuousness, and slipping my languid arms around his neck, I would fall on his breast murmuring some muffled words. But he would wake and my happiness would be at an end. Instead of this airy sprite, this angel who had rocked me in the wind with his wings, I found a man as brutal and voracious as a wild beast, and I would flee in horror. But he would pursue me, declaring he would not have his sleep disturbed in vain, and he would take his grim pleasure on the bosom of a fainting, half-dead woman.

"One day I felt so worn out with loving that I suddenly ceased. There were no other dramas in my passion. When I saw how easily this tie could be broken, I was amazed that I had so long believed it to be everlasting.

"I wanted to surrender myself without reservation to this lackluster state of exhausted indifference. I retired into seclusion [in] a vast, abandoned monastery . . ."

* * *

[Lélia to Pulchérie] "In me, this contempt for natural duties, this burning aspiration toward an impossible existence, led to a kind of intellectual depravity. As I did not feel myself bound to any man by the specific, voluntary consecration of physical love, I let my restless, passionate imagination travel the universe, seizing on anything it met on the way. To find happiness became my only thought, and, to confess how far I had sunk below my own standards, my only rule of conduct, the only aim of my will. First I would, unconsciously, let my desires drift toward the shadows passing around me; then I would run after them in my dreams, grasp them in flight, impetuously demanding of them if not happiness, then at least a few days' emotion. And as this invisible dissoluteness of my thoughts was in no way incompatible with my austerity of habit, I would indulge in it without remorse. In imagination I was unfaithful, not only to the man I loved, but each new day saw me unfaithful to the one I had loved the night before. Soon one love of this kind was not sufficient to fill my always hungry, insatiable soul, and I would embrace several phantoms at the same time. I would on the same day and at the same instant love both the eager musician who played upon my nerve fibers with his bow and a musing philosopher who made me a part of his meditations. I loved at the same time the actor who reduced me to tears and the poet who had put in his mouth the words which touched my heart. I would even love the painter and the sculptor whose works I had seen, but whose own features were unknown to me. I would fall in love with a tone of voice, a lock of hair, a garment, and even with a portrait, the portrait of a man who had been dead for centuries. The more I gave myself over to these whimsical admirations, the more frequent, short-lived and empty they became. God is my witness that they were not betrayed by any outward sign! But I must admit with shame and dread that I have wasted my soul away by devoting my higher faculties to these frivolous occupations. I remember a great expenditure of moral energy, and I no longer recall the names of those who, all unknowingly, frittered away bit by bit the treasury of my love.

"Squandered in this way, my heart finally died; I became capable only of sudden crazes; and as these feelings would fade away the moment the slightest light was projected on the objects of my illusions, I was forced to change idols as soon as a new one appeared.

"And so I now exist, the captive of the latest caprice that crosses my sick mind, though these caprices, once so frequent and impetuous have now become rare and tepid. For my enthusiasm has also grown cold, and only after long days of torpor and disgust do I, at times, recapture brief hours of youth and activity. Ennui desolates my life, Pulchérie, ennui is killing me. Everything has dried up for me or vanished. I have seen almost every facet of life, all the aspects of society, all the splendors of nature. From now on what is left for me to see? When I have succeeded in filling the gulf of one day, I ask myself in terror with what I shall fill the next? At times there still seem to exist beings worthy of interest and things capable of interesting me. But out of dejection and weariness I give them up before I even know them. I feel that I have no longer the sensitivity to appreciate men or sufficient intelligence to understand things. I withdraw within myself with a quiet, somber desperation and no one knows what I suffer. The brutes who make up society wonder what I lack, I who am rich enough to enjoy all the pleasures, to fulfill all the ambitions that beauty and luxury have placed within my reach. Yet not one of these men has the breadth of intelligence to understand the abysmal misery of being incapable of attachment or of desire."

* * *

[Lélia to Sténio] "The longer I live, the more I am forced to admit that the ideas of youth concerning love's exclusive ardor and its claim for total possession and eternal rights are wrong or at least harmful. All theories should be allowed and I would concede that of conjugal fidelity to certain exceptional people. Most of us have other needs, other powers. For some, mutual freedom and tolerance, abjuration of all jealous egoism. For others, mystical ardors, passions long smoldering in silence, a long and voluptuous holding back. For others again a heavenly peacefulness, brotherly chastity, and eternal virginity. Are all people alike? Do all men have the same faculties? Are not some born for the austerity of religious faith, some for the languors of sensual pleasure; others for the labors and struggles of passion, others again for the hazy reveries of poetry? Nothing is more arbitrary than the meaning of *true love*. All loves are true, whether they be passionate or peaceful, sensual or ascetic, lasting or fleeting, whether they lead men to suicide or to pleasure. Loves of the *mind* bring about as many great actions as loves of the *heart*. They have the same violence, the same power if not the same duration.

To Marie d'Agoult and Franz Liszt, 1836

Sensual love can be ennobled and sanctified through struggle and sacrifice. How many veiled virgins have not, unconsciously, obeyed the impulse of nature when kissing the feet of Christ and shedding burning tears on the marble hands of their heavenly spouse! Believe me, Sténio, this deification of proprietary and possessive egoism, this law of moral marriage in love, is as insane, as incapable of restraining desires, as laughable in the eyes of God, as the law of social marriage is in the eyes of men."

July 10, 1836

To Marie d'Agoult and Franz Liszt†:

Have you, to use Obermann's words, seen the moon rise over the Vélan? How fortunate you are, dear children, to have Switzerland at your feet and to be able to study all the wonders of nature! That is what I could do with to help me write two or three chapters of *Lélia,* since, as I may have told you, I am rewriting *Lélia.* The poison which made me sick has now be-

---

† Extract of a letter to the pair of famous lovers who had become close friends of George Sand (their daughter Cosima would marry Richard Wagner). The passage reveals Sand's rewriting *Lélia* as a result of the violent critical reaction to it which touched her personally (she was called Lélia the Impotent). The revised version would be published in 1839, with much of what we have quoted changed or excised.

come a remedy. This book which plunged me into skepticism is now rescuing me from it; as you know, the disease produces the book, the book aggravates the disease, and the same goes for healing. To transform this angry work into one of meekness while maintaining its form does not at first seem an easy task. And yet considering the characters (if you still recall them) you will see that wisdom exudes from Trenmor, and heavenly love from Lélia. The narrow-minded, fanatical priest, the courtesan and the weak, proud young man will all be sacrificed.

The Journeyman-Carpenter, or
The Companion of the Tour of France

(Le Compagnon du Tour de France, 1840)

The Journeyman-Carpenter, or Joiner, *as it was
translated in the mid-nineteenth century and re-
viewed by Walt Whitman in the Brooklyn* Daily
Eagle, *may be called George Sand's first proletarian novel. Her social commitment and Christian Socialism was a sensitive response to the historical movements of her period and the
sharpening political conflict which would result
in the Revolution of 1848. It did not begin with
her reading Agricol Perdiguier's* Le Livre du
Compagnonnage *(The Book of the Compan-
ionship), about the Masonic trade unions of
France, but her carpenter-hero, Pierre Huguenin,
was modeled upon Perdiguier and had similarly
undertaken a tour of France among its secret
worker societies before the novel proper begins.
The plot involves social statement and a love
affair between the commoner Pierre Huguenin
and Yseult de Villepreux, a young noblewoman.
The novel ends with the likelihood that "in one*

year or ten" they will come together again, marry, and, rejecting Yseult's inheritance, live happily ever after.

In a dialogue with Balzac which George Sand recorded in the Preface to the 1852 edition of The Journeyman-Carpenter, *she indicates her penchant for depicting "man" as she thought "he ought to be." In the Preface to a popular edition of her collected works (1842), she had this to say of her critics: "In a novel titled* The Companion of the Tour of France *I asked what was the right of society and what was human right; what justice was being practiced in our day and what arguments we must use to persuade workers that the present inequality of rights and the means of development was the last word of our social structure, of the wisdom of our laws. The reply to this was that I wished to know too much, that I courted the masses, that I was the follower of a certain Jesus Christ and of several other very wicked thinkers whom the justice of all ages and the interest of all governments had condemned to death."* ❧—

FROM THE PREFACE (1852 EDITION)

. . . Since when must the novel necessarily portray things as they are—the hard, cold reality of contemporary men and events? I know that it may be so: Balzac, a master whose talent I have always respected, has written *The Human Comedy*. But, although I was bound in friendship to this illustrious man, I saw human facts under a quite different light and I recall having said to him, approximately at the time I was writing *The Journeyman-Carpenter:* "You are writing *The Human Comedy*. The title is too modest. You could just as well call it *The Human Tragedy* or *The Human Drama.*"

"Yes," he replied, "and you, you are writing *The Human Saga.*"

"This time," I answered, "the title would be too pretentious. But I would like to write *The Human Ecologue, The Human Poem,* or *The Human Romance*. In short, you wish to, and know how to, depict man as you see him. Very well! As for me, I feel inclined to depict him as I wish he should be, as I think he ought to be." And as it was not a matter of competition between us, we soon acknowledged our mutual right to go our own ways. . . .

[Pierre Huguenin, journeyman-carpenter, to himself] "A tireless worker, from dawn to dark I must water with the sweat of my brow a soil that will grow green and flower for other eyes than mine. If I should lose one hour a day by feeling alive in my heart or mind, I will want for bread in my old age: worry about the future forbids my enjoying the present. If I pause one instant too long under the shade of this tree, I shall compromise my honor-bound contract to expend my strength unceasingly and to renounce all life of thought. But I must be off. Even these thoughts are forbidden."

* * *

[Huguenin to a rich bourgeois] "The rough daily dress of the worker, his hideous sores, his horrible illnesses and his vermin; his soul-deep indignation when poverty grinds him down, his justified threats when he sees himself stepped upon and cast aside; his frightful delirium when the regret of yesterday and the fear of tomorrow drive him to 'drink the cup of forgetfulness of sorrow,' as one of your poets has called it; the rage, the disarray, the forgetfulness of *self* in the terrible fact of poverty—of all this you wash your hands. You know nothing about it; you would be ashamed to justify it. You say, 'They, the poor, are the enemy, too; they are the dregs and disgrace of society!' But they are also people!

"Remove their grime, cure their afflictions, and you will plainly see that this foul herd came from the bowels of God like yourselves. In vain you make distinctions and categories: there are not two people, there is only one. Those who work in your homes—smiling, quiet, well clothed—are the same as those who are howling at your doors—joyless, angry, and clothed in rags. The only difference is that to the first you have given work and bread, to the second—nothing." . . .

Consuelo and The Countess de Rudolstadt
(1842–44)

Among George Sand's most ambitious, imaginative, and important novels, Consuelo, *and its sequel,* La Comtesse de Rudolstadt, *were originally published in thirteen volumes and frequently compared to Goethe's* Wilhelm Meister. *Too complicated for summary, the story takes Consuelo, a singer modeled in part upon Pauline Viardot, on a long, free-spirited, trip through Europe in search of herself ("life is a journey with life as its goal"). The influence of Pierre Leroux, a contemporary messianic philosopher, utopian socialist, and encyclopedist, is strongly felt, but* Consuelo's *influence in turn is still to be completely measured.[1] The extracts below are the merest samplings.* ⊱⋅⋅

As the first chords from the orchestra summoned Consuelo back to her place, she slowly rose to her feet. Her mantilla fell to her shoulders and at last the anxious and impatient spectators in the nearby gallery saw her face. But a miraculous transformation had now taken place in this young woman just before so deadly pale and so downcast, so overcome by weariness and fear! As if her brow were bathed in some heavenly fluid, a soft languor suffused the gentle, noble angles of her serene, gracious face. Her calm eyes revealed none of those petty passions which search and covet ordinary success. In her was something grave, mysterious, and profound which commanded respect and compassion. . . .

A divine glow rose to her cheeks and the sacred flame shone forth from her large black eyes as her peerless voice filled the vault with that pure, triumphant, noble sound which only a great intelligence combined with a great heart can produce.

* * *

[Trismégiste to Spartacus] ". . . Yes, you are right to try to lead your action within society. You are obeying your destiny, that is to say, your inspiration. Now I understand. What I have felt while listening to you, what you have managed to convey to me of your hopes, is clear proof of your mission's reality. Go forward then, act and work. Heaven has made you an instrument of destruction: to destroy, to dissolve—this is your task. One must have faith to demolish as well as to build. I myself had voluntarily withdrawn from the paths along which you are venturing: I had judged them to be the wrong ones. Probably they were wrong, but only incidentally. If true servants of the cause feel called to engage upon them again, they must once more be serviceable. I believed that nothing more could be expected from established society and that it could not be reformed from the inside. Thus I set myself outside it and, giving up all hope of seeing salvation come down to the people from this summit of corruption, I dedicated my last years of effort to working directly with the people. I have spoken to the poor, the weak, the oppressed, offering them my teachings in the form of art and poetry which they understand because they love them. Perhaps I have been too distrustful of the generous instincts that still dwell in the hearts of scientists and men of power. I am no longer familiar with them, since, wearied of their skepticism and their even more ungodly superstitions, I withdrew from them, disgusted, to seek out the simple of heart. In all probability they have changed, mended their ways, and educated themselves. What am I saying? It is certain that the world has progressed, been purified, and become greater during the last fifteen years; all things human gravitate constantly toward the light, and everything joins, both good and evil, in the march toward the heavenly ideal. You want to appeal to the world of the learned, the patricians, the rich; you want to achieve equality by persuasion: you seek to seduce even kings, princes, and prelates with the charm of truth. You are bubbling over with a confidence and a strength that can overcome all obstacles and breathe new life into all that is old and worn. Obey then, obey the promptings of your mind! Continue and enlarge our work; gather up our weapons scattered on battlefields of earlier defeats." . . .

"Yes," said Spartacus, "I feel that I have a mission. I have seen something of those who govern the world, and I was struck by their stupidity, their ignorance and their hardness of heart. Oh! how beautiful is life, how beautiful is nature, how beautiful is humanity! But what do they do to life, to nature, and to humanity! . . . Long have I wept to see myself, my fellow men, and God's whole creation the slaves of such scoundrels! . . . But after lamenting for an age like a feeble woman, I asked myself: 'What is there to prevent me from throwing off their chains and living free?' . . . But after a time of solitary stoicism, I understood that to be free alone is not to be free. Man cannot live alone. The object of man is man; he cannot live without his necessary object. And I said to myself: 'I am still a slave; my brothers must be delivered.' . . . And I have met noble hearts who have joined me in my cause . . . and my friends call me Spartacus."

"Did I not tell you that all you would achieve would be to destroy?" replied the old man. "Spartacus was a rebel slave. But once again, it does not matter. Organize to destroy. At your summons, let a secret society be created to destroy the inequities of today. But if you want it to be strong, efficient, powerful, then imbue this society, destined to destroy, with as many true and eternal principles as you can—first, so that it can destroy (because to destroy one must *be*; all life is positive), and then, so that out of this work of destruction will one day emerge those things which must be reborn."

* * *

[From final passages of *The Countess de Rudol-stadt*] Trismégiste did not bid us farewell: he seemed to have forgotten our presence. His wife implored us not to distract him. He walked down the hill with a firm step. His face was calm and with a kind of blissful gaiety, he was helping his eldest daughter to jump over bushes and rocks. . . .

And we, too, are on our way, advancing. Life is a journey with life as its goal, not death, as is sometimes said in a material, vulgar sense. We have comforted the villagers as best we could, and we have left the old Zdenko waiting for his tomorrow: we have rejoined our brothers at Pilsen from where I have written you this account, and we are about to leave again on other quests. And you, too, my friend, be prepared for a journey without rest, for unflinching action: we are heading for triumph or for martyrdom!

The Devil's Pool

(La Mare au Diable, 1846)

Written in four days of October 1845, The Devil's Pool is one of Sand's small, enduring pastoral idylls. Widower Germain, "the skilled plowman" of the story, in search of a wife, falls in love with little sixteen-year-old Marie during a long night's journey and sojourn in the Berry countryside with its haunted mare au diable. It's as simple and charming as that. An introductory chapter is extracted here intact for its irresistible combination of Sandian philosophy and berrichon farm land and farmers as Sand inimitably described them. ❧

I had just taken a long and melancholy look at Holbein's plowman,* and I was walking through the countryside dreaming of rural life and the destiny of

---

* A print of Hans Holbein the Younger's depicting Death as the plowman's helper, whipping a team of four horses to greater effort.

the husbandman. It must be miserable spending one's strength and one's days cleaving the surface of the earth, so jealous of the fruits of its fecundity that they must be torn from it, with a slice of the blackest, coarsest bread at the day's end as the sole reward and profit for such arduous toil. This wealth covering the land, these harvests, these fruits, these splendid animals fattening on the tall grass, all these are the property of the few and the instruments of the weariness and enslavement of the many. The gentleman of leisure does not usually love for themselves the fields, the meadows, the sight of nature, or the superb creatures which are all to be transformed into gold for his use. The gentleman of leisure comes to the countryside in search of a little fresh air and health and then returns to the city, there to spend the fruits of his vassals' labor.

For his part, the man who toils is too overburdened, too wretched, and too fearful for the future to enjoy the beauties of the countryside and the charms of rural life. He, too, sees the golden fields, the lovely meadows, the splendid animals, as representing bags of gold of which his share will be small and inadequate to his needs; and yet these cursed bags must be filled each year to satisfy the master and to buy the right to live on his lands in wretched poverty.

And yet nature remains forever young, beautiful, and generous. She pours out her poetry and beauty on all creatures and plants which are allowed to develop freely. Nature possesses the secret of happiness and nobody has been able to rob her of it. Happiest among men would be he who, knowing his trade, working with his hands, and experiencing well-being and liberty in exercising his intellectual powers, still had the time to live fully with heart and mind, to appreciate his own work and to love God's creation. The artist knows such delights in the contemplation and reproduction of the beauties of nature. But when he sees the sufferings of men in this earthly paradise, the artist's just and humane heart is troubled in the midst of these delights. Happiness is to be found when mind, heart, and hands, working in unison under the eyes of Providence, create a sacred harmony between the munificence of God and the raptures of the human soul. Then, instead of [Holbein's] wretched, hideous figure of Death dogging the laborer's footsteps with whip in hand, the painter of allegories could place at his side a radiant angel, sowing with generous hand the blessed wheat seed in the freshly turned furrow.

The ideal of a peaceful, free, poetic, hard-working, and simple life for the countryman is not so difficult to imagine that one should dismiss it as a chimera. Virgil's sad, sweet words—"Happy the man of the fields, if only he knew his good fortune!"—express regret, but are, like all other regrets, also a prediction. A day will come when the laborer will also be artist enough, if not to express (which then will matter little), at least to appreciate beauty. Is it possible to believe that this mysterious poetic intuition is not already within him as an instinct, as a vague yearning? In those already cushioned today by some modest resources, in whom all moral and intellectual development is not stifled by excessive wretchedness, pure deep-felt happiness does exist in an elementary state. Besides, if the voices of poets have risen from the depths of pain and weariness, why should manual work be said to exclude all mental activity? Such exclusion is undoubtedly the result of excessive toil and extreme misery. But let it never be said that when men work moderately and usefully, there will only be bad workers and bad poets. He who draws true delight from a feeling of poetry is a true poet, even if he never sets down a line in his whole life.

This was the course my thoughts had taken, and I had not realized that my confidence in the education of man was being strengthened by exterior influences. I was walking on the edge of a field that some peasants were preparing for the coming sowing. The scene was as vast as Holbein's picture. The countryside, too, was vast and framed with great lines of greenery tinted with the reds of autumn. In some of the furrows scoring the wide field of rich brown earth, the recent rains had left lines of water that glistened in the sun like thin threads of silver. The day was clear and warm and the newly plowed earth gave off a slight vapor. At the end of the field an old man, whose broad back and gaunt face recalled Holbein's plowman, but whose clothes gave no indication of poverty, was solemnly driving his old-fashioned plow. It was pulled by a pair of quiet, pale yellow oxen, true patriarchs of the meadow, tall, somewhat lean, with long drooping horns—old workers that habit had made "brothers," as our peasants call them, and who, if separated, refuse to work with any other and let themselves die of sorrow. Those who do not know the country say that the friendship of an ox for his team companion is a myth. They should see, in the corner of a stable, some poor, thin, worn-out animal, restlessly beating its emaciated sides with its tail, snorting with terror and scorn at any food offered to it, its eyes fixed on the door, pawing the empty space at its side, sniffing the yoke and chains of its former companion, constantly calling it with pitiable bellowings. The herdsman will tell you: "The team of oxen is finished: his brother is dead and he will never work again. We should fatten him for slaughter, but he refuses to eat and will soon die of hunger."

The old plowman was working slowly, silently, without any superfluous effort. His docile team was in no greater hurry than he; but through the ceaseless, concentrated rhythm of his work and the application of well-tried, unflagging strength, his furrow was as rapidly cut as that of his son who, some distance away, drove four less vigorous oxen over a more difficult and stony piece of land.

But next, a truly beautiful sight caught my eye, a noble subject for a painter. At the other end of the field a good-looking young man was driving a magnificent team: four pairs of young animals whose dark, tawny hides seemed to sparkle with fire. Their short, curly heads betrayed the wild bull still within them, their large, fierce eyes, their sudden movements and their jerky, spasmodic manner of pulling betokened continuing resistance to both yoke and goad.

They trembled with rage as they submitted to this newly imposed domination. They were what was called "newly yoked oxen." The man driving them had to clear a piece of land formerly abandoned to pasture and deep with age-old roots—an enormous task to which his youth, his energy, and his eight almost untamed animals were hardly equal.

A six- or seven-year-old child, beautiful as an angel, the shoulders of his blouse covered by a lambskin that made him look like the young St. John the Baptist of Renaissance painters, walked in the furrow next to the plow pricking the flanks of the oxen with a long, light pole tipped with a blunt goad. The proud beasts quivered under the child's tiny hand, making the yokes and straps tied to their heads creak as they jerked the shaft violently. When the plowshare came to a halt against a root, the plowman cried out with a powerful voice, naming each animal, but to calm them rather than to spur them on. For, angered by this sudden resistance, the oxen would surge forward, tearing up the earth with their large, cloven hoofs, and would have run aside carrying the plow across the field if, by voice and goad, the young man had not held back the first four, while the child took care of the four others. The little one would shout, too, with a voice that he wished fearsome, but which remained as gentle as his angelic face. All was beauty, grace, and strength: the countryside, the man, the child, the bullocks under the yoke. And in spite of this powerful struggle wherein the earth was vanquished, a deep, sweet quiet seemed to brood over everything. Once the obstacle was overcome and the team resumed its steady, solemn progress, the plowman, whose feigned violence was but a show of vigor and an expenditure of energy, immediately regained the serenity of the simple, throwing a glance of fatherly pride at his child who had turned to smile at him. Then the young father's manly voice broke into the solemn, melancholy song, handed down by ancient tradition in this region, not indiscriminately to all plowmen but to those most skilled in the art of spurring and sustaining the ardor of working oxen. This song—thought to be perhaps sacred in origin and to which mysterious powers must have been attributed in former times—is still thought today to have the power to sustain the energy of these animals, to calm their disquiet, and to lighten their laborious task. It is not enough to know how to drive them to make a perfectly straight furrow or to ease their labor by lifting or dropping the plowshare into the earth: no one is the complete plowman unless he knows how to sing to his oxen. This is a science in itself, demanding a special taste and capacity.

The song is, in fact, no more than a kind of recitative, broken off and taken up at will. Its irregular form and false notes, according to the laws of music, make it untransposable. Nevertheless, the song is beautiful and so well adapted to the nature of the work it accompanies, to the pace of the oxen, to these quiet rural parts, to the simplicity of the singers, that no one unfamiliar with working the soil could have invented it and no singer but a skilled plowman from this district could repeat it. At the time of the year when plowing is the only work and movement in the countryside, this gentle, powerful song rises as though it were the voice of the breeze, to which its special tonality has a certain likeness. The final tone of each phrase, a sustained tremolo, demands incredible breath control and rises systematically a quarter tone above tune. The effect is primitive but charming beyond words, and once one has become accustomed to hearing it, one can not imagine hearing any other song that would not disturb the peace of these moments and these places.

Thus I had before my eyes a tableau contrasting with that of Holbein, although the scenes were similar. Instead of a tired old man, someone young and healthy; instead of a team of weary, lean-flanked horses, two four-abreast teams of strong, fiery oxen; instead of Death, a beautiful child; instead of an image of despair and destruction, a scene of vitality and an aura of happiness.

Then the old French quatrain "By the sweat of your brow, etc.," and Virgil's *O fortunatos agricolas* came together to my mind, and seeing this beautiful couple, man and child, in such a poetic setting and with such united grace and strength, accomplishing a labor of such solemn grandeur, I felt a deep pity mingled with involuntary respect. Happy the laborer! Happy, too, should I surely be, were I suddenly endowed with a strong arm and powerful chest, able thus to praise and fecundate nature, while yet retaining the power to see with my eyes and understand with my mind the harmony of these colors and sounds, the delicacy of these tones, and the grace of these outlines—in short, the mysterious beauty of all things!—and above all without losing that communion of the heart with the divine love that watches over immortal, sublime creation.

But, alas! This man has never understood the mystery of beauty, and this child never will! God forbid that I should believe them to be no more than the animals they control or that they do not at times have some sort of ecstatic revelation to soothe their weariness and to calm their worries! On their noble foreheads, I see the seal of the Lord, for they, much more than those who possess it through right of purchase, are born kings of the earth. And they feel this, as is proved by the fact that they cannot be exiled with impunity, for they love this land they have watered with their sweat and a true peasant dies of homesickness in the accouterments of a soldier, far from the fields where he was born. But this man lacks something that I have, those immaterial delights which ought to be his, this laborer in that huge temple which only the sky is vast enough to cover. He lacks awareness of his feeling. Those who have sentenced him to servitude from the womb but incapable of robbing him of his dreams have deprived him of the power of reflection.

Well! As he is, incomplete and condemned to eternal infancy, he is still more noble than those in whom knowledge has smothered feeling. Do not try to rank yourselves above him, you who believe yourself invested with the inalienable and legitimate right to subject him to your commands, for the terrible error of your ways proves that your mind has killed your heart and that you are the most incomplete and blind of men! I prefer by far the simplicity of his soul to the false brilliance of yours; and were I called upon to tell the story of his life, I would have greater joy in stressing its sweet, touching aspects than you would have merit in depicting the abject condition to which the harsh contempt of your social precepts may bring him.

I knew this young man and this beautiful child, I knew their story, for they had a story; indeed, every man has a story, the tale of his life in which he could interest us all, if only he had understood it himself. Although a peasant and simple plowman, Germain was conscious of his obligations and affections. He had told me of them, naïvely, clearly, and I had listened with interest. When I had watched him plowing for quite some time, I asked myself why his story should not be written, although it was a story as simple, as straight, as unadorned, as the furrow he opened with his plow.

Next year this furrow will be filled and covered by a new furrow. Thus are most men's traces drawn and obliterated in the field of humanity. A little earth covers them and the furrows that we have dug succeed each other like tombs in a graveyard. Is the trace of the plowman not equal to that of an idle person who may have a name, a name that will remain, if by some quirk or absurdity he has made a small stir in the world?

Well, then! Let us, if we can, rescue from oblivion the trace of Germain, the skilled plowman. He will know nothing of this, nor will he care very much, but I shall have had some pleasure in trying.

ITEMS FROM
A
LONG LIFE

Except for the initial entries, in which George Sand meditates on her forebears and the past, this section is essentially chronological. Thus selections from the same work do not always appear together. The aim has been rather to string together comments and reflections on an uncommonly long and rich life.

*Much of the material may be found in His-*toire de Ma Vie (*Story of My Life*), *published in 1854–55, but that is only half the story. Sand's letters are the best source by far. Extracts from them have been taken from three principal collections: through 1848, from George Sand,* Correspondance, *edited by Georges Lubin; beginning with the letter to Gustave Flaubert of September 21, 1866, from two less satisfactory and often faulty compilations which will have to do until Lubin's edition is complete—George Sand,* Correspondance, *edited by her son Maurice Sand, and* Gustave Flaubert, Correspondance Entre George Sand et Gustave Flaubert; *see p. 451.*

The other sources, which have been collated

283

and collected in George Sand's autobiographical writings, Oeuvres Autobiographiques, *follow in the order in which they appear:*

Sketches and Hints (*the original title was in English*) *is a miscellany of notes and moody essays first published, with other works, in a volume called* Journal Intime, *in 1926.* Lettres d'un Voyageur (*Letters of a Traveler*) *is a series of twelve popular, open letters, usually addressed to people unnamed or pseudonymous, first collected and published in 1837. The* Journal Intime *proper was posthumously published in 1926 by George Sand's granddaughter Aurore Sand in the volume of that same title.* Entretiens Journaliers avec le Très Docte et Très Habile Docteur Piffoël (*Daily Dialogues with the Very Learned and Very Cunning Dr. Piffoël*) *constitutes Sand's imaginary dialogues with a Dr. Piffoël (Dr. Bignosed), who is herself, first published in its entirety, but not without errors, in* Journal Intime. Un Hiver à Majorque (*A Winter in Majorca*) *was, as indicated in the Chronology, first published in book form in 1842 and serially in* Revue des Deux Mondes *the year previous.*

Except for a few scattered entries which have appeared in various biographies and revues, George Sand's Diary exists only in manuscript in long, slim annual ledgers preserved in Paris's Bibliothèque Nationale. "Réponse à un Ami" (*Reply to a Friend [Flaubert]*) *first appeared in the newspaper* Le Temps *during August 1871*

From *Histoire de Ma Vie*

and was published soon after in the Sand collection Impressions et Souvenirs *(1873).* ⌘—

To *Pierre-Jules Hetzel, friend:*

Nohant, February 1, 1848

We are one with the dead I am absolutely convinced. There is a mysterious bond that nourishes our lives with theirs.*

From *Histoire de Ma Vie*

All existences are linked, one to the other, and the human being who portrays his or her life as isolated, as unattached from that of fellow creatures offers naught but an enigma to be unraveled. Interdependence is even more obvious when immediate, as with the ties that link parent and child, friend and friend, past and present. As for me (as for all of you) my thoughts, my beliefs, and my revulsions, my instincts and my feelings would be a mystery in my own eyes, and I could only ascribe them to chance, which

---

* An extract, as is the case of almost all the passages quoted from Sand's letters, many of which are dozens of pages long. The items which follow in this section are also, almost always, extracts.

has never provided an explanation of anything, had I not reread the pages preceding those treating of my individuality in the great universal book. My individuality in itself is neither significant nor important. It only takes on some sense when it becomes a fragment of life in general, fusing with the individuality of each of my fellow creatures, and thus becoming part of history.

* * *

Frederick Augustus, Elector of Saxony and King of Poland,† was the most extraordinarily debauched man of his time. To have a few drops of his blood in one's veins is not an uncommon honor, for he is said to have had several hundred bastards. He begot a son with the beautiful Aurora von Koenigsmark, famous, witty coquette, before whom even Charles XII [of Sweden] retreated and who could thus deem herself more formidable than an army—a son who would outdo him by far in nobleness, although he became only a marshal of France. This was Maurice, Count of Saxony, victor of Fontenoy, honest and brave like his father but no less debauched, more knowledgeable in the art of war but also more fortunate and better seconded.

† George Sand's great-great-grandfather.

To Charles Poncy, proletarian poet:

Paris, December 23, 1843

I who was born, it appears, into the ranks of the aristocracy am of the people by blood as much as by
heart. My mother was more lowly placed than yours
in our bizarre, hard society. She did not belong to the
hard-working, conscientious class which gives you a
title of nobility among the people. She was of that
degraded, vagabond race—the Bohemians of the world.
She was a dancer, no, less than a dancer, a bit player
in one of the lowest theaters of Paris, and rich men removed her from this degradation only to subject her to
worse. My father met her when she was already thirty
and living in the midst of who-knows-what debauch-
eries. But he had a generous heart. He realized that
this beautiful creature could still love, and he married
her against the wishes, and almost under the curse, of
his family. For a long time he knew poverty with her
and he even loved the children she had had before
she knew him.‡ I was born in their garret flat [in
Paris] and started life in poverty, in the harsh, vagabond life of military camps, a disorderly existence full
of wild adventure, strange enthusiasms and miseries. I
recall following the 1808 campaign in Spain in a cart,
covered with scabies. After this my grandmother, who
was an angel at heart, forgave and forgot all and took
in her arms her son, his wife, and children. I was

‡ Particularly Caroline, born in 1799.

287

turned into a young lady and an heiress. But I never forgot that the blood of the people ran in my veins and those who have made up charming biographies about me, freely dubbing me countess and marquise and mentioning my great-grandfather, the marshal of France, and my great-great-grandfather, the King of Poland, have always omitted to mention my mother, the bit player, and my grandfather, the bird seller.

From *Histoire de Ma Vie*

As I analyze and study the emotions and thoughts of my father when he was yet a child, I am at times under a strange illusion. I imagine that instead of being his daughter, I am his mother, that he confides to me his troubles and thoughts and that I explain them to him to soothe his worries, to strengthen his resolution, and finally to prove to him that there is more strength, reason, virtue, and religion in the world than he realizes. It may also be that the name Maurice which I gave to my son, their identity of age, the one beside me, the other living before my eyes through his letters, and even the fortuitous likeness of their handwriting, all contribute to plunge me into this kind of delusion.

Well, then, my young father, my friend, my child . . .*

* This line and the entire preceding paragraph was omitted in the printed version of *Histoire de Ma Vie* but is preserved in the manuscript now in the Sand collection of the Bibliothèque Spoelberch de Lovenjoul, in Chantilly, France.

From *Histoire de Ma Vie*

* * *

[*July 1, 1804*]

One evening my parents had a dancing party for some friends. My mother wore a pretty dress the color of roses. My father played a quadrille of his own composition on his Cremona violin (I still have this old instrument, to whose music I first saw the light of day). My mother, slightly indisposed, left the dance and went to her bedroom. Since her expression had not changed and she had left so quietly, the dancing continued. As it was ending, my aunt Lucie went to my mother's bedroom and was almost immediately heard to cry:

"Come, come quickly, Maurice, you have a daughter!"

"She shall be named Aurore after my mother, who is not here to bless her, but who will be some day," said my father, taking me in his arms.

This was on the fifth of July, 1804,† the last year of the Republic, the first year of the Empire.

"She was born to the sound of music and in the color of roses," said my aunt. "She will know happiness."

* * *

Whether by education, inspiration, or predisposition, I was seized by a passion for romances even before I had learned to read. . . .

† In reality it was July 1, 1804.

I remember that I was still so small that I had to climb onto the foot warmer to indulge my pastime. . . . I would compose aloud interminable stories which my mother called my "novels." I have no memory of these pleasant compositions. My mother has spoken to me about them a thousand times and long before I ever thought of writing. She found them extremely boring because of their length and my digressions. I have kept this weakness, I am told, for I must admit that I am little aware of what I am doing, and today, as at the age of four, I have an invincible unrestraint in this kind of creation.

It seems my stories when I was a child were a sort of *pastiche* of everything I had heard. They were invariably in the form of a fairy tale, with a good fairy, a virtuous prince, and a beautiful princess. There were few wicked people and no great misfortunes. . . . Most curious was their length, for I continued a story where I had left off the day before. . . . My aunt also remembers my stories and recalls them gaily. She remembers saying to me more than once, "*Eh bien,* Aurore, hasn't your prince gotten out of the forest yet? Will your princess ever finish putting on her gown and her golden crown?"

"Let her be," my mother would say, "I cannot settle down to work until she begins her novels between the four chairs."‡

* * *

‡ They formed Aurore's "playpen."

From *Histoire de Ma Vie*

I recall clearly my eagerness at games simulating real actions. To begin with, I was rather sulky. When my sister and the oldest daughter of the glazier came to invite me to the usual games of *pied de boeuf* or *main chaude,* I found none to my liking or I was quickly bored. But with my cousin Clotilde or other children of my age, I went straight into games of more fantasy. We would simulate battles and flights through the woods, which have always played such an important part in my imagination. Then one of us would pretend to be lost and the others to search for her. We would find her asleep under a tree, that is to say, under the sofa, and would come to her rescue. One of us played mother to the others, or Napoleon, for the military world outside penetrated even our little nest, and more than once I played the Emperor and commanded on the battlefield. We would tear dolls, soldiers, dolls' houses to pieces, and my father's imagination must have been as youthful as ours, for he could not bear this miniature representation of the horrors he had seen in the war. He would say to my mother: "Please sweep away these battlefields. I may be mad, but it hurts to see these arms and legs and bloody rags scattered on the ground."

* * *

[*Madrid, 1808*]

Every time I appeared before [Marshal Murat], I had to put on my uniform. It was a pure marvel and remained with us a long time after I had become too big to wear it. So I can recall it perfectly. It was a white cashmere dolman, buttoned and braided with gold, a matching pelisse lined with black fur, thrown back over my shoulder, and reddish purple cashmere pantaloons with gilded embroidery and embellishments in the Hungarian style. I also had red morocco boots with gilded spurs, a saber, a swordbelt of plaited crimson silk with little canons and a shoulder knot of enameled gold, a saber scabbard adorned with an eagle embroidered in tiny pearls. Nothing had been omitted! Seeing me dressed exactly as my father [Murat's aide-de-camp], either because he took me for a boy or because it pleased him to pretend to, Murat laughingly introduced me to his visitors as his aide-de-camp and admitted us to his intimate circle.

* * *

[*Nohant, 1808*]

This was not the first time I had seen my grandmother, but before that day I had no recollection of her. She seemed very tall, although she was little over five feet,* and her pink and white face, her imposing air, her unvarying costume of a long brown silk dress with low waist and straight sleeves, which she refused to change despite the new Empire fashion, her blond wig with its crimped bangs on her forehead, her little round bonnet with its cockade of lace in the center

* As was George Sand.

made her an extraordinary being who looked like nothing I had ever seen before.

* * *

[1808–9]

Every day my grandmother grew more devoted to me, probably not because of my disposition, which was already fairly capricious, but because of my striking likeness to my father. My voice, my looks, my ways, my tastes, everything about me reminded her of her son as a child, to the extent that at times, when she watched me play, she was confused and often called me "Maurice." And when she spoke of me, she would say "my son."

* * *

At about the same time my grandmother began to teach me music. In spite of her half-paralyzed fingers and her cracked voice she could still sing admirably well, and the few chords she could strike as accompaniment were of such a splendid harmony that when she locked herself up in her bedroom to play airs from some old opera and she allowed me to stay with her, I was genuinely ecstatic. I would sit on the floor under the old harpsichord, where her favorite dog, Brilliant, would let me share a corner of the carpet, and I could have remained there the rest of my life, so fascinated was I by her tremulous voice and the piercing sound of the spinet.

* * *

I must tell how my mother and my grandmother lived together. These two women were as different by disposition as by education and behavior. They were truly two extremes of our sex: my grandmother—fair, blond, serious, calm, and dignified, a veritable Saxon of noble blood with the ease and poise of her birth and the largesse of her class; my mother—dark-haired, pale, hot-blooded, gauche and shy in company but ever ready to explode when storms raged too strongly in her, Spanish by nature, jealous, passionate, quick-tempered and weak, cruel and at the same time kind. It was not without a deadly reluctance that these two women, so different by nature and social rank, had accepted each other, and during my father's lifetime† they had quarreled too much over his affection not to hate each other a little.

* * *

The people around my two mothers repeated everything to them and further envenomed their disagreements. My poor child's heart began to be buffeted by the rivalry of my two mothers. As the object of their perpetual jealousies and struggles, I could not possibly avoid being the prey of their prejudices, just as I was the victim of the sorrows that I caused.

* * *

† Sand's father, Maurice Dupin, died in a fall from a horse in 1808, when Sand was four.

From *Histoire de Ma Vie*

The family arrangements were finally done with; my mother signed a formal agreement to leave me in the custody of my grandmother, who wanted to take absolute charge of my education. I had shown such strong aversion to this agreement that from the moment it was decided upon, no one mentioned it to me. They determined slowly to detach me from my mother without my being aware of it, and, to begin with, she departed alone for Paris, since she was eager to see Caroline [who had been left in Paris when the Dupins went to Madrid].

* * *

[*Nohant, 1812*]

I recall with some certainty that my mother spent that summer with me and that I was grieved because, until then, I had slept in her bedroom whenever she stayed at Nohant and now, for the first time, this favor was denied me. My grandmother said I was too big to sleep on the divan in her bedroom, and indeed the little couch which I had used before was truly becoming too short. But the large yellow bed in which my father had been born and which my mother used at Nohant (I still use it today) was six feet wide, and being allowed to sleep in it with her was a special treat for me. I was like a small bird nestling against its mother's breast; I seemed to sleep better there and to have more beautiful dreams, too.

295

Despite my grandmother's forbidding it, I waited patiently two or three nights until eleven o'clock, when my mother retired to her bedroom. Then I would rise noiselessly and tiptoe barefooted from my room to snuggle deep in my mother's arms. She did not have the heart to send me away, and she herself was happy to fall asleep with my head on her shoulder. However, my grandmother became suspicious or was informed by [her personal maid] Mademoiselle Julie, her *lieutenant de police*. She came up the stairs and surprised me just as I was leaving my room. Rose [Aurore's maid] was severely scolded for having let me escape. Hearing the noise, my mother emerged from her room. Sharp words were exchanged. My grandmother claimed that it was neither healthy nor chaste for a girl of nine to sleep with her mother. . . .

I cried all that night. I felt physically and morally bound to my mother by a diamond chain which my grandmother vainly tried to break, but only managed to tighten all the more around my chest so that I gasped for breath.

* * *

[1812]

[My mother] took me on her lap and tried to make me understand the situation. "Your grandmother," she said, "would reduce my allowance to fifteen hundred francs if I carried you off with me to Paris."

"Fifteen hundred francs!" I cried. "But that's a lot of money! It is enough for the three of us!"

"No," she said, "it would not even be enough for Caroline and me. Her *pension* and upkeep consume half my allowance already, and I can hardly live and dress on what is left. . . . If I take you with me, we will be so poor you will never be able to endure it. You will ask me to take you back to Nohant and your fifteen thousand francs a year."

"Never, never!" I cried. "We will be poor, but we will be together. . . . We will be happy!"

"I am not thinking of myself," she said, "but of you. I am afraid that one day you would reproach me for having deprived you of a good education, a good marriage, and a fine fortune."

"Ha!" I cried. "A good education! They want to make a wooden doll out of me. A good marriage! With a man who would be ashamed of my mother. And a fortune that would cost me my happiness! . . . I would rather be poor with you!"

"Listen to me, my child," she said, "you do not know what being poor means for a young girl. I do, and I do not want you and Caroline to undergo what I went through—a poor orphan at fourteen. Suppose I were to die and leave you orphans? Your grandmother might take *you* back, but never your [half-]sister. What would become of *her?*"

* * *

[Nohant, 1816(?)]

One night, during my dreams, a shape and a name came to me. The name had no meaning so far as I

297

know; it was a fortuitous combination of syllables as sometimes occurs in dreams. My phantom was called "Corambé," and this name remained for him. He became the title of my childhood novel and the God of my religion. . . .

Corambé took form all on his own in my brain. He was as pure and charitable as Christ, as radiant and beautiful as Gabriel. But I supplied a needed nymphlike grace and a touch of Orpheus' poetry. Thus he was less austere than the Christians' God and his sensibility more spiritual than Homer's. And then I completed him by dressing him sometimes as a woman, for what I had loved and understood most until then was a woman—my mother. So he would often appear to me with the features of a woman. In short, he had no sex; he assumed all different forms.

* * *

[1817]

As I kneeled beside [my grandmother's] bed and took her hands to kiss them, she said in a bitter vibrant voice that I could not recognize: "Stay on your knees and pay close attention, for what I am about to tell you, you have never heard before and will never hear again from my lips. They are things that are said only once in a lifetime, because they are never forgotten. But when they unfortunately do exist, unless they are known, you can lose your life, your very soul."

After this preamble, which made me shiver, she began to tell me about her own life and the life of my father . . . and then about the life of my mother, as she knew it, or thought she knew it. Here she was without pity and I dare say without understanding, for there are temptations, misfortunes, and a fatality in the life of the poor which the rich can never understand, any more than a blind man can conceive colors.

Everything she told me was factually true and based on events which did not allow the slightest doubt. But this terrible story could have been disclosed to me without taking away all my love and respect for my mother. Besides, the story told that way would have been more credible—and more true. All should have been mentioned: the reasons for my mother's misfortunes—her isolation and misery at the age of fourteen, the corruption of the rich, who lie in wait for hunger to corrupt the innocent, the merciless rigor of public opinion which allows no redemption or return to society. She should also have told me how my mother had truly redeemed her past, how faithfully she had loved my father, how modestly and retiringly she had lived since his death. This I knew, or thought I knew. But I was led to believe that if I was told everything about my mother's past, at least I was spared the truth about her present, that there was some new secret in my mother's life that I was not to be told, but which would make me tremble for my own future if I insisted upon living with her.‡ Finally my poor grandmother, exhausted from her long re-

‡ Sand's mother may have been living at this time in Paris with Louis Perret, a kindly younger man whom she had known since Sand's infancy.

cital, her voice choked, her eyes moist and burning, let fall the terrible, hideous accusation: my mother was a fallen woman and I was a blind child seeking to throw itself into the abyss!

It came to me like a nightmare, seizing me by the throat. Each word brought death. I felt the sweat on my forehead. I wanted to stop her, to jump to my feet, to fly away, to reject with loathing this appalling secret. But I could not. I was nailed to the floor on my knees, my head bent and racked by this voice hovering over me, drying me out like a burning wind. My ice-cold hands no longer held my grandmother's burning ones. I think I had mechanically pushed them away from my lips with horror.

Finally I rose without a word, without imploring a departing embrace, without caring about being excused. I went up to my room. . . . My tears brought no relief. I have always heard that weeping eases affliction, but I have always experienced the contrary. I do not know how to cry.

*   *   *

[*Paris convent, 1818–20*]

Life in common is the ideal of happiness for people who love each other. I felt it at the convent; I have never forgotten it. But every thinking being must have some hours of solitude and self-communion. It is only thus one can savor the sweetness of communality.

To Émilie de Wismes, 1821

* * *

[*Nohant, 1820–21*]

If destiny had had me go directly from the domination of my grandmother to that of a husband or a convent, it is possible that I, always subject to given influences, should never have been myself. . . . But fate had decided that from the age of seventeen there would be an interlude between the two exterior forces, that I would entirely belong to myself for almost a year, to become, for better or worse, essentially what I would be the rest of my life.

To Émilie de Wismes, convent friend:

Nohant, July 1821

As we are very isolated here, I dress for hunting and riding in a man's clothes, (a redingote, as we did at times at the convent); my grandmother allows me to go riding with a servant following me, also on horseback. You must not be shocked by this way of carrying on. It might be out of place in the vicinity of Angers, but here in deepest Berry the few other young ladies do exactly as I do, save that I pretend to be a gentleman and this gives rise to some rather pleasant mistakes. One day, three leagues from here in a village where nobody knows me, I had as usual sent my servant and the horses off to eat at the nearest farm while I sketched an old Gothic castle. This behavior greatly puzzled its inhabitants, who had no understanding of drawing. Soon a lady emerged from the castle and offered to buy my sketch; then came a damsel who made deep curtsies and called me "sir." Little used to seeing dandies in these parts, the young one blushed and cast meaningful sidelong glances at me, while I, with a gallant air, bowed extravagantly to her, and she was much impressed.

To her mother:

Nohant, November 18, 1821

You seem to want me to take the arm of my chambermaid or a charwoman when I go walking. Apparently this would be to keep me from falling, and indeed leading strings were necessary when I was an infant and you were caring for me; but now I am seventeen and I can walk by myself.

It is folly, you say, my dear mother, to learn Latin. I do not know who told you that I was taking up this study, but anyhow you have been deceived, for I neither know nor study this language. But I am extremely surprised, dear mother, to think that should I do so you would find it a bad thing for me to improve my mind. You probably think that for a woman there are occupations more useful and more related to the domestic cares which form the duties of her sex. I think so, too, dear mother, and if ever I become a wife and mother, I believe that my days will be dedicated to household cares rather than to studies. But for the present, although I run my grandmother's house, I still have so many hours of leisure that you yourself, I am quite convinced, would scold me for wasting them. Why must a woman be ignorant? Can she not be well-read without being presumptuous and pedantic? Suppose I should one day have sons and that I had drawn sufficient profit from my studies to teach them myself, do you not think that the lessons of a mother are equal to those of a tutor? But to come to that point, one must be married, and you say that I shall only find a giant or a weakling. In that case, it could very well be that I shall not marry, because I no longer believe in giants and do not like weaklings. A man marrying me out of fear would be a fool and I a fool to accept him. I would never look for a man who could be his wife's slave, for he would be an idiot. But I do not believe that an intelligent man could find it right for his wife to feign shyness or fear when she feels neither. I would find this hardly excusable in a woman who is really afraid, for she is giving in to a weakness, but I could find no excuse whatsoever for a woman who feels no fear but pretends to it out of affectation. This would be the case with me were I to play the coward, and any husband who approved of my making myself ridiculous to that extent would be extremely ridiculous to me.

From *Histoire de Ma Vie*

[*Paris, 1822*]

One evening, as we were having ices at Tortoni's after the theater, Angèle du Plessis said to her husband: "Look, there is Casimir!"* A slim, rather elegant young man with a lively face and military bearing came over to shake hands and reply to eager questions about his father, Colonel Dudevant, much loved and respected by the Du Plessis. He sat down next to Madame Angèle and asked her in a low voice who I was. "She is my daughter," she replied loudly. "Well then," he continued in a low voice, "so she is my wife? Do you remember that you promised me your first-born daughter's hand? I thought it would be Winephride, but this one seems of an age closer to mine, so I accept her, if you will let me have her." Madame Angèle burst into laughter, but the joke was prophetic.

* * *

[*1822*]

We were married in September 1822. After the wedding visits and return calls, after lingering a few days with our friends, the Du Plessis, we left in the com-

---

* Seventeen-year-old Aurore and her hosts, James and Angèle du Plessis, whom she called "Father" and "Mother," were visiting Paris's famous Café Tortoni.

pany of my [half-]brother† for Nohant, where we were joyfully received by the good Deschartres.‡

To Émilie de Wismes:

Nohant, January 30, 1823

Your letters are so kind, dear Émilie, that I cannot possibly be lax in replying. I shall not sermonize to you to induce a taste for marriage, for this will come to you as to any other and besides, your situation is so agreeable and happy that I fail to see why you should be in a hurry to surrender it. I will only reassure you concerning the interest you show for the discomforts of my condition. I can assure you, dear friend, that these discomforts are not very important and, on the contrary, there are no sweeter sufferings than those announcing a baby. I admit that afterward the worries and griefs it may cause you are very real, but physical pain I count for nothing, and should even the doctor, the nurse, the apothecary, evils of all kinds, etc., terrify me as much as they do you, I believe that the tiny kisses of the newborn child will make you forget them all. Meanwhile, you can't imagine the pleasure it is to feel your child stirring in your womb and how many tender plans you make for its future.

† Hippolyte Chatiron (1799–1866), Sand's older half-brother, illegitimate child of her father and a young working-class woman of La Châtre.
‡ Sand's childhood tutor.

The second point of your letter is truer. I admit that conflicts born of different tastes and personalities are only too real for most couples. It must also be fully accepted that it is totally impossible to meet someone whose temperament and tastes are exactly the same as our own, since it can be said of each one of us what Father Magnani said so aptly of you:

*Natura la fè e ruppa la stampa**

This was very justified praise, but whether nature has worked for good or for evil, the fact remains that it never uses the same mold for two people. So each time one or the other of the spouses wishes to maintain all his or her personal ideas and never give in, he or she is bound to be unhappy. I believe that in marrying, one of the two must renounce all thought of self, sacrificing not only will but opinion, accepting to see through the eyes of the other, to love what the other loves, etc. What torture and bitterness when you marry somebody you hate! What sad uncertainty, what a bleak future when you marry a stranger! But also what an inexhaustible source of happiness when one obeys the one one loves! Every privation becomes a new pleasure. One sacrifices to both God and married love, and one does one's duty while building one's happiness. It remains only to be asked whether man or woman should remake himself or herself on the model of the other. And since "the bearded one is the all-powerful" and men are incapable of such attach-

* Loosely quoted from Ariosto's *Orlando Furioso*: "Nature made him and then broke the mold."

ment, then we are necessarily the ones who must bend in obedience. I am drawing a picture which must seem very gloomy to the eyes of an outsider and which will probably not reconcile you to marriage. But I am incapable of deception, and I would be ill put to it to present you the condition of the newly-wed bride as one of unclouded happiness. One must love one's husband and love him enormously to accept this fate and to make the honeymoon last forever. Like you, I had a low opinion of marriage until the moment I grew fond of Casimir, and if my opinion has changed now, it is in relation to myself alone; I would not dare express an opinion about the happiness others might find in marriage.

Consumed by a gnawing ennui brought on by a growing sense of Casimir's insufficiency, Aurore left Nohant on July 5, 1825, for a vacation at the spa of Cauterets in the Pyrenees, accompanied by husband, child, nurse, and valet. There she met Zoé Leroy and above all Aurélien de Sèze, a young magistrate of twenty-five from Bordeaux. Casimir went hunting; Aurore and Aurélien went walking, fell in love, and flirted platonically (Aurélien, according to Sand, did the pursuing). Casimir hurriedly took Aurore and ménage to Guillery, his father's place in Gascony, where they were supposed to spend the winter. However, they accepted an invitation to Zoé Leroy's country house and traveled to Bordeaux to meet her. By no accident, Aurore also met Aurélien again. Casimir found them with her head on his shoulder; Aurore flung herself at Casimir's feet, pleaded innocence, and effectively fainted. All three together with Zoé went on to Zoé's country place. Aurore exulted in the friendship of her husband and her platonic lover and dreamed of a kind of ménage à trois (which would be limited to an exchange of letters until some years later). Aurore and Casimir returned to Guillery, where, from October 11 to November 16, 1825, Aurore wrote Aurélien almost daily letters, to be sent later. Casimir discovered them. His reaction went from anger and outrage to humiliation and a sense of failure and finally to contriteness. He would change, he promised Aurore from Nohant, where he had gone to inspect their estate. He was even reading Pascal's Pensées, he wrote. Meanwhile Aurore had written him an extraordinary "confessional" letter of twenty-one pages of fine script, dated November 15, 1825, awaiting him on his return to Guillery. The letter ended with a proposal for amiable coexistence that was almost like a modern marriage contract. Casimir said neither yes nor no to it, but Aurore had become the dominant one of the couple and went on, as we have noted, to Stéphane de Grandsagne and Jules Sandeau (see Chronology). ⊁⋯

From *Histoire de Ma Vie*

[*Cauterets, 1825*]

Monsieur hunts with passion. He kills chamois and eagles. He rises at two in the morning and returns at night. His wife complains. He does not seem to foresee that a time may come when she will rejoice.

To Aurélien de Sèze, friend:

Guillery, October 24, 1825

You know how much I love riding—I had great fun on this outing. The horse given me jumped very well and this thrills me. In my days of dejection I have been bored and disgusted with everything. I have spent years without touching a pencil, months without going near a piano, days without opening a book, but I have always felt in the mood to go riding or regretted my inability to do so. On horseback one seems to be reborn, one recovers one's love for life. Then one can truly behold and see nature, for on foot, constantly concerned about not falling, constantly looking at the ground, one cannot keep one's eyes fixed on the horizon. Have you never on days of melancholy found an indefinable charm in letting your imagination race beyond the limits of what you can see? While watch-

ing a distant prospect, have you never dreamed of
woods, rivers, enchanted sites amid hazy, blue-gray
vistas which the eye can see but cannot distinguish?
Your eyes have followed the swift, soaring flight of
the kite or the vulture. You have longed, borne on
their wings, to cover in a trice distances that in
thought can be envisaged only with terror. Oh yes!
you must have felt all this! We understand each other
so well that the experiences of our souls must be the
same. It is on horseback, at a walk, that one dominates
the landscape and it seems most beautiful. At a gallop
all thoughts leave their ordinary course, so to say,
changing place. Cleaving the air in a gallop one no
longer suffers or thinks. One breathes. One's mind is
in suspense as if intoxicated by the body's *brio*. And if
difficulty or danger looms, alas for him who fears to
brave it. He reins back his horse, thwarting and hin-
dering it, loses his balance, and deprives himself of
one of the most intense sensations one can experience
—to encounter and flirt with death and then laughingly escape its arms. But if you encourage the proud
animal with rein and word, if you place your faith in
its courage and pride, then it will jump over ravine
and gate, cross marshes, battle the current of a river,
trample underfoot the reeds and roots that impede its
progress, get out of its depth, swim and climb the
bank in a single jump. Then look behind you—as
Madame de Staël says, you have just reconquered life
and you like it better than ever, because you have
taken it into your own hands. Those who have never
known and have never loved danger have no idea of
the value of life.

To Casimir Dudevant, husband:

Guillery, November 15, 1825

You know how our mutual friends gave us the idea of getting married. Of the suitors suggested to me, I could not bear Prosper, Garinet was hateful, several others were richer than you. But you were good and this was the only valid attribute for me. Seeing you every day I came to know you better and better, appreciated all your fine qualities, and nobody has cherished you more tenderly than I.

And yet I took no care to discover if you liked studying, reading, or if your opinions, your tastes, your disposition were in harmony with mine. I was too busy with my affairs to pursue my usual interests, and you knew nothing of them. I had given up all the things I liked and never spoke about them. Our conversations always turned on our affairs and projects, and these were too opposed, too contradictory; our plans were thwarted by too much agitation and disagreement; we were surrounded by too many vexations to allow us to think of anything else. After much discussion we were finally married and untroubled, we could start to become better acquainted. I saw that you did not like music, so I stopped practicing, because the sound of the piano drove you away. You used to read to please me, but after a few pages, bored and drowsy, you would let the book fall from your hands. Above all, when we talked about literature, poetry, or ethics, either you did not know the authors I spoke about or you called my ideas crazy, exalted, romantic sentiment. So I ceased to speak of them. I started to be truly grieved to think that there could never be any concert in our tastes. I was careful to hide these bitter reflections. I was disgusted with everything. Frightened at the thought of living alone, I decided to adopt your tastes, but I failed, for living like you, doing nothing, bored me to death, and you did not even notice. Tired of everything and almost regretting that I had spent my youth acquiring skills and knowledge that my husband in no way appreciated, not stirring from Nohant became unbearable for me. I wanted to go to Paris. There I sought amusements, and you gave them all to me. I had fun, but I was not happy. I became an ardent theatergoer. You made every sacrifice rather than deprive me of a single performance. I was grateful. But, again, I was not happy. We had no home life, none of those quiet chats by the fireside which give such delightful hours. We did not agree. I could not stay at home an hour on end. I was restless, unconsciously oppressed by a terrible vacuum. I did not want to seek out the cause of my malaise. It never entered my mind to hold you responsible for it. You were so good and considerate! It would have been harsh and unjust to reproach you because your parents had neglected to broaden your mind and increase your knowledge. Then my son was born. I nursed him joyfully. But in spite of this gentle occupation, my sorrows remained. I looked after my son. I did my utmost to forget them. But as soon as

Maurice was weaned I was overcome by an inconceivable ennui. My malaise had, so to say, been lying
dormant in my heart. Now it awoke and I did not
know what would become of me. I wanted a good
piano. Although we were out of funds, you immediately ordered it, but I soon lost interest. At the age of
sixteen I spent years alone at Nohant, with a bad
piano, books, and with only my dogs and horses for
company during my grandmother's paralysis. Then, I
did not know boredom. I used to spend days and
nights working in my bedroom or at her bedside. But
at nineteen, freed from worry and sorrow, married to
an excellent man, mother of a beautiful child, surrounded by all that could gratify my tastes, I was
bored with life. Oh, this state of mind is easily explained! There comes a time when one needs to love
exclusively. All one's activities must be related to the
loved one. For him alone does one wish to have grace
and talent. You did not notice mine. My knowledge
was wasted; you did not share it. I did not tell myself
all these things. I felt them; I clasped you in my arms.
You loved me; yet something I could not express was
lacking in my happiness. . . .

Finally, in my unjust chagrin I completely failed to
appreciate you and felt within me an overwhelming
desire to be loved as I myself felt capable of loving. . . . I noticed Monsieur [Aurélien] de S[èze]
the first time I saw him. It was not his face that made
me pay attention to him; I am not so frivolous as to let
myself be caught by outward appearances. I was
struck by his mind, his conversation. At first I only
found him amiable and witty; I liked to laugh with

him. In the twist he gave to his jests, I felt I don't know what rapport between us, as if I might have expressed my thoughts in the very same terms. . . . Each day his conversation pleased me more. Was I being coquettish? Was he being deliberately seductive? I leave it to you to decide. . . .

When you went hunting I often found myself alone with him for hours. . . .

Your embraces would hurt me. I feared to be insincere if I returned them, and you believed me to be cold. . . .

How happy I would have been if every night I could have written down my day, then have you read what I had written, and so have you share all my most intimate feelings. I did this with Aurélien. I needed a *friend;* you forced me to it, but you did not see things from my point of view. Now you will understand me, as did Aurélien. I shall become as confident in you as I was in him, I shall be as happy with you as I was with him, if, after reading this letter, I see you with me, pleased, satisfied, happy. . . .

So now, Casimir, answer me—can you say to me in good faith: "I esteem Aurélien; I do not blame you for the *friendship* you feel for him and I believe it will not hurt your affection for me?" If you tell me this, I'll take heart, and here is the plan I have worked out. I submit it to you. *Judge it,* change it according to your wishes, and I shall follow it just as you want it.

Article 1—We will not go to Bordeaux this winter. The wounds are too fresh and I feel it would be too much of a burden on your confidence. . . .

Article 2—I promise, I swear, never to write Aurélien in secret. But you will allow me to write to him once a month, or less often if you wish. You will see all my letters and all his replies. I pledge before God not to conceal a line from you.

Article 3—If we go to Paris, we shall take lessons in languages together. You want to instruct yourself and to share my interests. That will give me the utmost pleasure. While I sketch or work, you will read to me and our days will pass deliciously in this manner. N.B.: I do not insist on your liking music. I will bore you as little as possible, by playing the piano while you are out walking.

Article 4—You will allow me to write often to Zoé, but I solemnly pledge to let you see all my letters and all her replies. . . .

Article 5—If it is at Nohant that we spend the winter, we shall read many of the useful works in your library which you are unacquainted with. You will give me an accounting of them. We shall talk about them afterward together. You will tell me your thoughts, and I mine. All our thoughts and pleasures will be shared in common.

Article 6—There must be no quarrels, no outbursts on your part, no annoyances on mine. . . . When we speak of the past, it will be without bitterness, without sharpness, without distrust. . . . Has not what has happened brought us closer together, and made you more dear to me than ever? Without it, I would not have known your worth, and you would not have learned how to make me happy.

Article 7—At last, having banished all regrets, all bitterness, we shall be happy and at peace. . . . You will permit me to speak to you at times of Aurélien and Zoé. . . . You will permit me to send him your regards in my letters. It will make him so happy!

Last Article—Some other year we shall spend the winter in Bordeaux,† if our affairs permit. . . . If not, we shall postpone it, but you will let me count on it for some time or other.

To Jules Boucoiran, younger friend and her son's future tutor:

Nohant, October 27, 1830

Those who do not like me very much say I "love" Sandot [Sandeau‡]—and you know what they mean by "love." Those who do not like me at all say I "love" Sandot and Fleury at the same time. Those who detest me say that adding your name and that of Duvernet would not displease me. So, I have four lovers simultaneously. That is not too many for a woman such as I, with such devouring passions. Ah, the wicked fools! How I pity their being alive! Good night, my child. Write me. And by the way, Sandot specially charges me to send you his regards.

† And thus see Aurélien.
‡ See Chronology, 1830–31, pp. xxx–xxxi. Alphonse Fleury and Charles Duvernet are friends at nearby La Châtre.

To Jules Boucoiran:

> *Nohant, December 1 or 3, 1830*

I just happened to come across a packet, addressed to me, when searching for something in my husband's desk. . . . Good God! What a testament! Nothing but maledictions! He had gathered into it all his ill feelings and anger against me, all his broodings about my perversity, all his sentiments of contempt for my character, and he wanted to leave me this as the last token of his affection! . . .

My decision was immediately and, I dare say, irrevocably taken. As you know this is a strong word for me. I use it rarely. Without waiting another day, still weak and ill, I announced my decision, spelling out my reasons with such aplomb and coolness that he was petrified. He hardly expected a creature like me to stand up tall against him. He scolded, argued, pleaded, but I remained firm. "I want an allowance, I am leaving forever for Paris and my children* will stay at Nohant." This was the outcome of our first argument. I remained inflexible on all points. As you can imagine, it was pure bluff. I have no desire to give up my children entirely, but I let myself be accused of heartlessness, I declared that I was ready for anything. I wanted to persuade him that nothing could make me waver. Once convinced, he became meek as a lamb, and today he is crying. He has come to tell me that he

---

* Maurice is seven, Solange two.

will lease Nohant and close the house, that he cannot live alone, that he will take Maurice to Paris and put him in a boarding school. I do not want this yet. The child is too young and too delicate. Besides, I do not wish to see my house vacated by my servants, who have always known me and whom I love almost as friends. I agree to reducing our way of life, because the allowance I require to live independently will make this saving necessary. I wish to keep on Vincent and André and their wives, and Pierre. Two horses and two cows will be sufficient, etc.—I shall spare you the details. This way I will be supposed to live on my own. But in fact I expect to spend part of the year, at least six months, at Nohant with my children, or even with my husband. The lesson will make him more cautious and besides, my position will make me independent of him. Until now, he has treated me as if he found me odious. Now that I know this to be so, I am leaving. Today he is mourning for me; so much the worse for him! I am proving to him that I won't be tolerated as a burden, but must be sought after and appealed to as a free companion, who will only remain with him so long as he is worthy of my company.

From *Histoire de Ma Vie*

[1830]

Once the resolution to try my luck had ripened—that is, having the personal income of a thousand crowns I had always dreamed of—expressing and pursuing it was a matter of three days. My husband owed me a fifteen-hundred-franc allowance. I asked him for my daughter and permission to stay in Paris for three months twice a year, with two hundred and fifty francs per month of absence. This presented no difficulties. He thought it a mere caprice of which I would soon tire.

My brother [Hippolyte], thinking the same, said: "How can you dream of living in Paris with a child on two hundred and fifty francs a month! It is too ridiculous. Why, you don't even know the price of a chicken! You will be back in a fortnight without a sou, for your husband is quite determined to remain deaf to all demands for further subsidy!" "That may be," I replied, "but I am going to try. Lend me your apartment in Paris for a week, and keep Solange until I find lodgings. I agree to be back soon."

My brother was the only one to oppose my resolution. He felt a little guilty about the loathing my household inspired in me. He would not admit it to himself, but he did to me unknowingly. His wife understood better and showed her approval. She had faith in my courage and my destiny. She felt I was choosing the only way to avoid, or put off, a more painful decision.

* * *

[*Paris, 1831*]

I was eager to become deprovincialized and acquainted with all the ideas and arts of my time. I felt it necessary and I was full of curiosity. Except for outstanding works, I knew nothing about the contemporary arts. Above all, I was thirsting for theater.

I knew well the impossibility for a poor woman to indulge in these fancies. Balzac has said: "It is impossible to be a woman in Paris without a private income of twenty-five thousand francs." And this witty remark became truth for the woman who would be an artist.

And yet I saw my young friends from Berry, my childhood companions, living in Paris with as little as I and keeping up with everything of interest to bright young men. Literary and political events, the excitements of the theater and museum, clubs, and streets—they saw everything and went everywhere. My legs were as good as theirs, those steady little country legs which had learned to walk on rutted roads, balancing on heavy wooden shoes. But on the Parisian pavement I was like a ship on ice. My thin shoes cracked every second day, my sagging stockings tripped me; I did not know how to lift my skirts. I was dirty, tired, sick with cold, and I saw shoes and clothes, not to mention tiny velvet hats, soaked by dripping gutters, ruined with frightening speed.

I had experienced this before I thought of settling in Paris and had asked my mother, who was living there elegantly and comfortably on three thousand five hundred francs: "How can you cope with even the most modest clothes in this awful climate, unless you stay locked up in your room six days a week?" She replied: "At my age, and with my habits, it is very easy. But when I was young and your father lacked for money, he had thought of dressing me up as a boy.

My sister did the same, and we went on foot with our husbands, to theaters and everywhere. That meant a saving of half our household costs."

The idea at first seemed amusing and then very ingenious. Having dressed as a boy during my childhood, having later hunted in smock and gaiters with [my tutor] Deschartres, I felt no surprise whatsoever at putting on again a familiar costume. At that time, fashion was especially favorable to my disguise. Men were wearing long, square redingotes, *à la propriétaire*, falling straight to the heels and so loose at the waist that my brother once laughingly said, when getting into his at Nohant: "Isn't this jolly? It's the fashion and it's not too tight. The tailor takes his measure on a sentry and the coat can fit an entire regiment!"

So I had myself made a "sentry redingote" of strong gray cloth, with trousers and waistcoat to match. A gray hat and a large woolen cravat completed my outfit as a perfect little first-year student. I cannot possibly express the pleasure my boots gave me: I would gladly have slept with them on, as did my brother as a boy, when he put on his first pair. My little iron-tipped heels kept me solid on the sidewalk. I would fly from one end of Paris to the other. I felt as if I could have gone around the world. My clothes risked nothing. I was out in all kinds of weather, I came home at all hours, I sat in the pit at the theater. Nobody paid attention to me or guessed at my disguise. . . .

I had an idea lodged in some recess of my brain, and only a few days of total freedom were needed to make it flower. I would bring it with me onto the

street, feet solid on the slippery ice, shoulders pow-
dered with snow, hands deep in my pockets, my stomach a bit empty at times, but my head all the more
filled with dreams, melodies, colors, forms, gleams,
and phantoms. I was no longer "lady," nor "gentleman." People pushed me about on the sidewalk as a
nuisance to those hurrying somewhere. Little did I
care, I who had no special business. I was unknown,
unnoticed, unreproached; I was an atom lost in that
immense crowd. No one said, as at La Châtre:
"There goes Madame Aurore; she still wears the same
hat and the same dress," or as at Nohant: "There goes
our ladyship riding on her big horse; she must be out
of her mind to ride that way." In Paris no one thought
about me, no one looked at me. I had no need to
hurry away to avoid small talk. I could make up a
whole novel walking from one end of town to another
without meeting anybody who asked me: "What the
devil can you be thinking about?" It was better than a
monk's cell, and I could say with [Chateaubriand's]
René, although with as much satisfaction as he with
sadness, that I was walking in the desert of men.

* * *

[*1831*]

Monsieur de Kératry† followed me into the waiting
room and detained me there a few minutes to ex-

† Auguste de Kératry, a fairly popular, conventional author
and politician to whom Sand brought her first writings for
comment. He was, incidentally, an old man with a young wife.

pound his theories concerning the inferiority of women and the impossibility for even the most intelligent among them to write a good book (his *Le Dernier des Beaumanoir,* obviously); and as I was leaving, without arguing or giving any biting reply, he ended his harangue with a Napoleonic stroke, aimed at crushing me completely. "Believe me," he said solemnly, as I opened the last door of his sanctuary, "don't make books, make babies." "Upon my word, sir," I replied, bubbling with laughter and closing the door in his face, "you should follow your own advice, if you can."

* * *

[1831]

As for Baroness Dudevant [Casimir's mother] . . . she asked me why I stayed so long in Paris without my husband. I replied that my husband did not object.

"But is it true that you have the intention of having books *published?*"

"Yes, madame."

"Té!" she exclaimed. (This was a Gascon expression meaning *tiens!,* which she was in the habit of using.) "What a droll idea!"

"Yes, madame."

"That is all very fine, but I hope you have no intention of putting the name *I* carry on the covers of *published books!*"

"Oh, certainly not, madame! There is no danger of that."

To Jules Boucoiran, now her son's tutor:

Paris, March 4, 1831

I am more than ever determined to follow a literary career, despite the fact that at times it disgusts me, despite the days of laxness and weariness which punctuate my work, despite the more than modest life I live here, for I feel that my existence is henceforth fulfilled. I have a goal, a task, and, let's say it, a passion. The writer's trade is a violent, almost indestructible passion. Once it has entered a poor head, nothing can stop it. I have not been successful. My manuscript‡ has been judged improbable by the people whose advice I have sought. They have told me, in good faith, that it was too full of ethics and virtue to be acceptable to the public. They are right; the poor public must be served according to its tastes and I am going to do as fashion demands. It will be bad, but of that I wash my hands. An article has been accepted in the *Revue de Paris,* but they keep me waiting. Famous names have to come before mine. This is only fair, so I must be patient. I am busily trying to become accepted at *La Mode* and *L'Artiste,* two papers in the same style as *La Revue.* It will be too bad if I do not succeed with one of them. Meanwhile I have to live, so I practice the vilest of trades: I write

‡ *Aimée,* shortly to be burned by its author, probably the manuscript read by Kératry.

324

articles for *Le Figaro!* Ooh! If you only knew! But editor [Henri] de Latouche pays seven francs a column, and that is enough to permit me to drink, to eat, and even to go to the theater, following certain advice you gave me. This is my opportunity to observe the most useful and amusing things. When one wishes to write, everything must be seen, known, laughed at. Well, long live the artist's life! Our motto is freedom.

To Émile Regnault, Paris friend:

Nohant, May 25, 1831

I have a mother, an aunt, a sister, a brother, etc., who will certainly come and bother me.* . . . With only one room, I run the risk of being unable to avoid them, of being caught *en flagrant délit* embracing *le petit* Jules [Sandeau]. I should like to have a second door for him to use at any moment, because my husband might suddenly drop in, not from the blue sky, but from a diligence [stagecoach], at four in the morning, and not having a place to stay, do me the honor of disembarking *chez moi*. Imagine my state if I heard him ring and knew the charming gentleman was at the other side of the door! He might even break it down before I opened it.

* In this letter, Sand is asking Regnault to find a suitable place in Paris for Sandeau and herself.

To her mother:

Nohant, May 31, 1831

You have been told that I wear the trousers; well, you have been deceived, as you would soon realize if you spent a day here. On the other hand, I do not want my husband to wear my skirts. Each to his dress, each to his freedom. I have failings, so has my husband his, and if I told you that ours is a model household, that there has never been the slightest cloud between us, you would not believe me. There is good and bad in my situation, as there is in everybody's. In fact, my husband does what he wants—he has mistresses or not as he desires, he drinks muscatel or plain water according to his thirst, he accumulates or spends according to his taste, he builds, buys, changes, rules over his possessions and his house as he wishes. All this is no concern of mine and I find everything perfect, for I know that he is orderly, that he is thrifty rather than lavish, that he loves his children and in all his projects has only their interests in mind. You see that I value and trust him, and since I have given him complete control over our wealth, I do not think that I can be suspected of wanting to dominate him. As for myself, I need very little. The same allowance, the same ease as you. A thousand crowns a year make me wealthy enough, in view of the fact that I like writing and my pen already furnishes me a small income. Besides, it is also just that the freedom my husband enjoys should be mutual. Otherwise he would be hateful and despicable to me and to all others, and this he does not want to be. Thus I am entirely independent. I go to bed when he rises, I go to La Châtre or Rome, I come home at midnight or six o'clock in the morning; it is entirely my business.

To Charles Duvernet, friend:

Paris, July 19, 1831

To live! How sweet, how wonderful! Despite husbands, and troubles, and debts and relatives and gossip, despite poignant despairs and wearisome pinpricks! To live is intoxication, to love and be loved is happiness, heaven itself!

To Émile Regnault:

Nohant, September 20, 1831

Dear Émile, I am absolutely mad, but very happy! . . . In three days I have lived three years. . . . What will you think of it all? You won't scold me. That is impossible. You love me too much to reproach me such happiness. Gustave [Papet]† did not scold. Not he! He is devoted. He plunged up to

† Another La Châtre friend.

his neck in our madness. He bivouacked in a ditch in my garden all the time that Jules [Sandeau] was in my bedroom, because he came to me last night!— under the very nose of [my dog] Brave, my husband, my brother, my children, my maid, everybody.‡ . . . I had foreseen and planned everything. The only risk Jules really ran was being salted with gunshot while he climbed to my window, which is only six feet above the ground, a risk no greater than being overturned in a diligence or breaking your leg dancing. . . . And last night he was here!—in my bedroom, in my arms, happy, beaten, kissed, bitten, scolding, crying, laughing. Never, I believe, have we experienced such wild joy. . . . Tonight, I hope, he will come again. Twice is not too much. More would not be wise. My husband cannot fail to learn that Jules is staying only three gunshots from Nohant. So far he knows nothing. He is busy with the wine harvest. At night he sleeps like a porker.

I am an idiot—a mass of bites and bruises! I can hardly stand on my feet. I'm in a state of ecstatic joy. If you were here, I would bite you until the blood ran, so you could participate a bit in our mad happiness.

But admire me! Lower your flag in salute! In the midst of all this delirium, these torments of impatience, these burning palpitations, the work goes on. Yesterday evening I made enormous changes in the second volume!*

‡ Sleeping elsewhere in the house!
* Of *Rose et Blanche,* a novel written in collaboration with Jules Sandeau and published later the same year, signed "J. Sand."

To Émile Regnault:

Nohant, February 27, 1832

I believe my Noëmi [eventually Indiana†] to be a typical woman, both weak and strong, overwhelmed by the weight of the air but capable of holding up the sky; timid in everyday life but courageous in battle; adroitly disentangling the threads of communal life but stupidly failing to see where her own happiness lies; laughing at the whole world but letting herself be duped by a man; taking no pride in herself because she is too full of pride in the object of her choice; disdaining the vanities of the world but letting herself be seduced by a man who epitomizes them all. This is how I see woman in general: an incredible mixture of weakness and energy, of greatness and pettiness, a being always composed of two distinct natures, at times sublime, at times wretched, skilled at deceiving but easily deceived herself.

To Marie Dorval, actress and intimate friend‡:

Paris, January 26, 1833

Do you think that you can bear with me? You do not know yet, nor do I. I am such a boor, so stupid, so

† See Chronology, 1832, p. xxxi.
‡ See Chronology, 1833, p. xxxi, as well as p. 429.

slow to speak out what I have on my mind, so gauche and so dumb when my heart is overflowing! Don't judge me by appearances. Wait a bit before you decide how much pity and affection you can give me. As for myself, I feel that I love you with a heart made young and fresh again by you. If this is a dream, as everything else I have desired in life, do not wake me from it too quickly. It does me so much good!

Good-by, great and beautiful one, no matter what, I will see you this evening!

From *Sketches and Hints*

[1833?]

It is not certain that the bitter fruits of experience can be enjoyed with impunity.* You must secretly draw nourishment from them and never tell men all you know about men, for they would stone you in revenge for no longer being able to deceive you.

And yet, those who would accuse you of failing to appreciate confidence and of resisting friendship, those who feign to believe in you in order to take away your right to put them into doubt, those men, I say, are often more contemptuous and skeptical than you. They speak of affection and perseverance, they who are capable of nothing but egoism. The hypocrites!

* Perhaps written after the critics' reception of *Lélia* ("filth and prostitution").

Learn caution, however. Accept their declarations, pretend to believe them or else they will smear you with calumnies and point at you as if you were a leper. Men do not like to be exposed or made to laugh at the mask they wear.

If you can no longer love, then lie, or draw the veil so close about you that no eye can read through it.

Do unto your heart what aging libertines do unto their bodies! Hide behind cosmetics and lies, conceal with boasts and bragging the decrepitude that has made you disbelieve and the surfeit that has made you impotent. Above all, never admit to the ripe age of your intelligence or tell anyone how old your thoughts are.

To Alfred de Musset, in Paris:†

Venice, April 15–17, 1834

Do not think, do not ever think, Alfred, that I could be happy at the thought of having lost your heart. Whether I have been mistress or mother to you, what does it matter? Whether I have inspired love or friendship in you, whether I have been happy or unhappy with you, none of this changes anything in the present state of my soul. I know that I love you, that is all. But no longer with that painful thirst for your kisses every minute, which I could not satisfy without

† See Chronology, 1834, p. xxxii.

killing you. But with a strength that is wholly **virile** and with the tenderness of a woman. Taking care of you—keeping you from all evil and vexations, surrounding you with amusements and pleasures—is what I miss and what I regret since losing you . . . Why did this sweet task, which I would have fulfilled with so much joy, slowly become bitter and then suddenly impossible? What fate transformed the remedies I offered you into poison? Why did I, who would have given all my blood to assure you a night of rest and quiet, become for you a curse, a torment, a specter? When these awful memories beset me (and when do they not?), I almost lose my mind. I drown my pillow in tears. I hear your voice calling me in the silence of the night. Who will call me now? Who will need me to watch over him? How shall I use the reserves of strength I stored up for you which now turns against me? Oh! my child, my child, how I need your affection and your forgiveness! Never speak of mine, never tell me that you did me wrong. Do I know of any wrong? I recall nothing, except that we were very unhappy and that now we are separated. But I know, I feel that in our hearts and minds we will love each other all our lives and that through a hallowed affection we shall do our utmost to cure each other of the pain we have given. Alas, no! It was not our fault, we followed our destiny, and our temperaments, more mordant and passionate than those of others, prevented us from accepting the life of ordinary lovers. But rest assured, we were born to know and love each other. If it had not been for your youth

332

and a moment of weakness induced in me one morning by your tears, we would have remained brother and sister. We knew that situation to suit us. We had foreseen the evils that would come to us. Well, after all, what does it matter? We followed a hard road, but we arrived at the hilltop where we were to rest together. We have been lovers, we know each other to the bottom of our souls; so much the better. Have we discovered anything about each other that could inspire mutual disgust? What woe would have been ours had we parted one day in wrath—without understanding, without explanation! Then one hateful word would have poisoned our whole life and we could never after have believed in anything. But could we have parted that way? Did we not vainly try several times, our hearts ablaze with pride and resentment, and did they not throb with pain and regret every time we found ourselves alone? No, such an ending could not be! We had to remain eternally bound by renouncing an impossible relationship. You are right, our embraces were incestuous, but we did not know. Innocent and sincere, we fell into each other's arms. Well, do we have a single memory of these embraces which is not chaste and holy? One day, delirious and feverish, you reproached me with never having been able to give you [all] the pleasures of physical love. I cried then, but now I am very happy that your reproach was justified. I am happy that my pleasures were more austere and veiled than those you will find elsewhere. At least you will not think of me when you are in the arms of other women. But when you are

333

alone, when you need to pray and cry, you will think of your George, your nurse, your friend, your true comrade, of something better than all that, for the feeling that binds us is made up of so many things that it can be compared to nothing else. The world will not understand. So much the better; we shall love each other and laugh at the world.

By the way, I have written you a long letter [*Lettre d'un Voyageur*‡] about my trip to the Alps, which I intend to publish in the *Revue* [*des Deux Mondes*], if you don't mind. I shall send it to you and if you have no criticisms, you can give it to [the editor François] Buloz. If you wish to change or cut anything, do I need to say that you have power of life and death over all my manuscripts, past, present, and future? Finally, if you find all unpublishable, throw it into the fire or keep it in your wallet, *ad libitum*. I am also sending you a letter from your mother which I recently received and the lines you had forgotten on my desk, which I have transcribed to make them take up less space. . . .

I am living virtually alone. [Lazzaro] Rebizzo [an Italian friend] comes to see me for half an hour in the morning. [Dr. Pietro] Pagello dines with me and leaves at eight o'clock. For the moment he is much occupied by his patients and by his former mistress who, since she thinks him unfaithful, has developed a new

‡ Extracts of this follow on pp. 335–37. The Sand-Musset love affair was indeed "all rapture and all rage and all literature" (Henry James, *Notes on Novelists*, p. 171).

and ferocious passion for him, making him very unhappy indeed. . . .

Please collect from my place a copy of *Lélia,* one of
Valentine, and one of *Indiana.* I think there are two
copies of *Lélia* left, one on vellum which I ask you
not to send me, for it might get lost in the post. Include in the parcel your *Contes d'Espagne, Le Spectacle, Rolla,* and the other issues of the *Revue [des
Deux Mondes]* containing *Marianne, Andréa, Fan-
tasio,* in short everything you have written. . . .
There is already talk here [in Italy] about translating
our works, and everyone is crying for them.

From *Lettres d'un Voyageur, No. 1*

Venice, May 1, 1834

To a Poet [Alfred de Musset]:

You felt youthful, you thought that life and pleasure
should be one. You wore yourself out enjoying everything instantly and without reflection. You dis-
regarded your splendor and gave your life over to the
impulse of passions which would use it up and burn it
out, as other men have misused that right. And you
arrogated that right to yourself, forgetting that you are
one of those who do not belong to themselves alone.
You wished to live for yourself, to suicidally destroy
your own splendor through contempt for all things
human. You threw, pell-mell into the abyss, all the

jewels of the crown that God had placed upon your forehead: strength, beauty, genius—and you wanted to trample under foot even the innocence of your years, oh, arrogant child!

What was this lust for destruction burning in you? What hatred had you for heaven to scorn in this fashion its most magnificent gifts? Were you frightened by your glorious destiny? Had the spirit of God appeared to you under too harsh a light? The Angel of Poetry radiating on His right had bent over your cradle to kiss you on the forehead. But you were probably frightened by the sight of the giant with the wings of fire so close to you. Your eyes could not bear the glow from his face and you ran away to escape him. Hardly strong enough to walk, you wanted to race through life's dangers, ardently embracing them in all their reality, imploring them for refuge and protection against the terrors of your sublime and awesome vision. Like Jacob you fought against that vision, and like him you were vanquished. In the midst of the fiery pleasures in which you vainly sought shelter, the mysterious spirit of poetry came to seize and reclaim you. You had to become a poet, and so you did, despite yourself. . . .

Suspended between heaven and earth, greedy for the one, curious about the other, disdainful of glory, frightened by nothingness, doubtful, tormented, changing, you lived alone among men. You fled solitude and found it everywhere. The power of your soul wore you down. Your thoughts were too vast, your desires too immense, your slender shoulders bent under the weight of your genius. You sought oblivion from the unattainable blessings you had glimpsed from afar in the earth's aborted pleasures. But after weariness had crushed your body, your soul would awake more alive, your thirst more burning, than before. You quit the arms of your mistresses only to stop and sigh before the virgins of Raphael. "Who," asked a gentle, pious, musing bystander, "is this young man who thus troubles the pale marble statues?"

From *Journal Intime*

Paris, November 1834

Oh my God, why have you awakened my flesh, why, since I was so resigned to my glacial couch? Why did You let me meet again this phantom of my burning nights? Angel of death, fatal love, oh my destiny in the form of a blond and delicate child!* Oh, how I still love you, assassin! May your kisses swiftly burn me alive, so that I might die consumed. Then you can scatter my ashes to the wind and from them will grow flowers for your pleasure.

What is this fire devouring me? A volcano roars within me and I am about to explode like a crater. Oh God, have pity on Your long-suffering creature! Why do others die? Why cannot I succumb under the weight of my pain? Pains are said to subside and

* Alfred de Musset.

hearts to dry up, becoming cold from bleeding. When, oh my God, shall mine no longer throb and break?

Dear, blue eyes, you will never more look down upon me! Dear, blond head, I shall never again see you bending over me in sweet languor! Small, warm, lissome body, you will no longer lie upon me, as Elisha upon the dead child, to bring me back to life. You will no longer touch my head as Jesus touched Jairus' daughter's, saying: "Rise, little girl!" Farewell fair hair, farewell white shoulders, farewell everything that I have loved, all that once was mine. Henceforth, in the burning of my nights, I shall clasp the trunks of pine trees and the rocks of the forest, crying out your name, and when I have dreamed the ultimate delight, I shall fall unconscious to the damp earth.

From *Entretiens Journaliers avec le Très Docte et Très Habile Docteur Piffoël*

Nohant, June 13, 1837†

Must one be, for one's beloved, as blind, as devoted, as tireless as a solicitous mother for her first-born? No, Piffoël, there is no need for all that, and all that is to no avail if love is lacking.

You believe, Piffoël, that one can say to the object

† Extracts of one of the imaginary dialogues with "Dr. Piffoël" (herself), published after Sand's death, indicating the bitter, disillusioned end of the affair with Michel de Bourges. See Chronology, 1835, p. xxxii.

of one's love, "You are a being like myself. I chose you from among all humans because I thought you were the greatest and the best. Today I no longer know what you are. It seems to me you have dark spots in your character like other men, for you often make me suffer and perfection is in no man. But I love your flaws, I love my sufferings, I prefer your faults to the virtues of others. I accept you. I *have* you, and you have me, for I hold nothing back." . . .

No, Piffoël, no! Doctor of psychology you may be, but you are a fool. That is not the language a man wants to hear. He completely despises devotion, because he believes it his natural right by the simple fact of having emerged from the womb of Madame, His Mother. . . . To dominate, to possess, to absorb, these are the conditions he accepts for himself—to be adored as a God. . . .

Woman has only one way of lightening her yoke, of holding on to her tyrant, when that tyrant is necessary for her. That is to flatter him basely. Her submission, her faithfulness, her devotion, her care have no value in his eyes. Without that, he tells us, he would not burden himself with a woman at all. . . .

No, my dear Piffoël, learn the scientific truth about life and, when you write your novels, try to read the human heart a little better. Never take as your ideal woman someone who is strong-minded, disinterested, courageous, and frank. The public will whistle derisively at you and call you by the odious name of "Lélia the Impotent"!

Impotent? Yes, by God! Impotent when it comes to

servility, impotent in adulation, impotent in abasement, impotent when it comes to fearing you [man]—stupid beast, who would not have the courage to kill, if there were no laws punishing murder by murder, who find your strength and vengeance only in calumny and defamation! But when you find a female who knows how to do without you, then your vain power turns to fury, and your fury is punished by a smile, a farewell, an eternal forgetfulness.

From *Un Hiver à Majorque*

[1838–39]‡

When we [Sand, Chopin, and her children] went from Barcelona to Palma on a mild, dark night, lighted only by the phosphorescence in the ship's wake, everyone on board was asleep except the helmsman, who resisted that dangerous temptation by singing all night, but with a voice soft and restrained, as if he feared to wake the watchkeepers or else was half asleep himself. We could not tire of listening, for his song was most strange. It had a rhythm and modulation unknown to us and seemed to wander at random like the ship's smoke wafted by the breeze. It was reverie more than song, a kind of indolent vocal excursion in which thought had little part, but which followed the rocking of the ship, the faint noise of the

‡ See Chronology for these years, pp. xxxiii–xxxiv.

wash, and seemed like a vague improvisation with its own sweet, single-tone form. . . .

* * *

Chopin's genius was full of the strange harmonies of nature, transposed into sublime equivalents by his musical thought and never slavishly imitated from exterior sounds. That evening his composition* was filled with the raindrops sounding on the resonant tiles of the charterhouse [of Valldemosa, on Majorca], but in his imagination and song they had been transposed into tears falling from heaven and resounding on his heart.

The genius of Chopin is the deepest and fullest vehicle of emotions and feelings ever to have existed. He has made a single instrument speak the language of infinity. Often he has condensed in ten bars that even a child could play, tone poems of incredible grandeur, dramas of unequaled intensity. . . . Only Mozart is his superior. . . .

* * *

When we returned from Majorca to Barcelona in March, the heat was suffocating, and yet we weren't able to set foot on deck. Even if we had braved the danger of having our legs devoured by some bad-tempered hog, the captain would not have allowed us to annoy the pigs on deck by our presence. They re-

---

* The Raindrop Prelude, in D-flat major?

mained very quiet during the first hours, but in the
middle of the night the helmsman thought their sleep
had taken a dark, dismal turn. So they were beaten,
punctually, every fifteen minutes, and we were awakened by such dreadful cries and uproars, on one
hand of pain and fury from the beaten pigs, on the
other from the captain's swearing at his men and the
latter swearing at the pigs, that several times we
thought the whole pack was eating up the crew.

To Agricol Perdiguier, writer:

Paris, August 20, 1840

I was very happy to receive your letter. I am deeply
touched by everything you tell me about your successful tour and I have no doubt about its favorable outcome.† The future of the world resides in the people,
especially the working class. You believe this and I
too, so we will always agree on everything that you
undertake to hasten the delivery of truth and justice,
twin deities gestating in the saintly womb of the common people. I have no illusions about the obstacles,
the efforts, and the dangers of our venture, but libera-
tors have finally arisen and already there is no lack of

† Perdiguier, a trade union leader, was a former car-
penter, whose *Le Livre du Compagnonnage* inspired Sand's
Journeyman-Carpenter (see pp. 261–64). The tour mentioned
in the letter was a trip he made to the secret worker societies of
France.

generous, intelligent followers. In time, the masses will emerge from the blindness and ignorance in which the so-called enlightened classes have kept them enchained for centuries. Already the powers dominating the people are obliged, to avoid hatred and ridicule, to admit and uphold the principle of civilization and progress. They do not give in willingly, but at last that principle is marking the spirit of the age. And now the people must show that they are worthy of its practical application by demonstrating wisdom and moral superiority. Stress to those who listen to you that if a great crime (keeping the people in slavery and debasement) lies heavy on the rich, then the people can also be reproached with not having always followed the right road in their struggle for liberation. The time has come for everything to be seen, felt, and understood. Once the people give the example of merging all individual interests into a single common interest, a wonderful example which has already been demonstrated in several places in France, believe me, the people will then be great and strong. They will become the masters of the world, the initiators of a new civilization, the new Messiahs.

For the sequence of events leading to the sad items which follow, see the Chronology for 1846–47 (pp. xxxv–xxxvi). Insomnia, headaches,

*son-in-law Auguste Clésinger's accidentally
striking her on the chest with his sculptor's mal-
let (he was aiming at Maurice)—all might explain Sand's bitterness and acerbity. After the
breakup with her mother, Solange sought out
Chopin in Paris where he let it be known he
took her part. He had left Nohant in 1846; he
was never to return. Sand set about to explain
and justify herself to Chopin's friends, but the
longest letter preserved of her correspondence
(seventy-one pages) went to Emmanuel Arago,
one of her closest friends; the extract from that
letter, below, quotes the last pages intact.* ⊱—

To Albert Grzymala, Chopin's close friend:

Nohant, May 12, 1847

It is all so difficult and delicate. I do not know any
way to calm and reassure a poor, sick soul [Chopin]
who is irritated even by my efforts to restore him to
health. The disease [tuberculosis] which morally and
physically is eating up the poor thing has been killing
me for ages, and I see him wasting away without
being able to do any good, since it is his worried, jealous, touchy affection for me that is the main cause of
his sadness. For seven years now I have lived the life of
a virgin with him, and with others. I have become old
before my time, and even this was no sacrifice or effort

for me, since I had tired of passion and had become disillusioned beyond remedy. If any woman on earth should have inspired him with absolute confidence, it was I. But he has never understood. I know that many people blame me, some for having exhausted him by the violence of my sensual demands, others for having driven him to despair by my fits of anger.

I think you know how things are! But he, he complains that I have half killed him by my [sexual] restraint, while I remain convinced that I should really have killed him if I had acted differently.

To Emmanuel Arago, friend:

Nohant, July 18–26, 1847

. . . What I am about to disclose to you alone and under the seal of deepest secrecy (although its hidden meaning seems clear to several people with whom I am not at all in agreement), what you are about to read, is fantastic, but fundamentally it pleases me more than it hurts me.

Chopin, who was to come here and suddenly didn't, who hardly ever writes any more and soon will not write at all; Chopin, whose health is much better, judging from his writing, or who, at least, is showing more energy, awareness, and resistance; Chopin, totally changed and transformed toward me, no longer dying of that eternal love his friends constantly reproached me for not sharing, telling me right out that I am a bad mother, that Sol[ange] is completely right, that he will not abandon her, etc. It's all suddenly obvious to me and came this very morning as an unexpected revelation. I remember this spring, on the very same day he heard of the decision about [Solange's] marriage, he was seized with a nervous attack of asthma that made him agonize for four whole days. I recall outbursts of delirious jealousy presumably directed against me, for which I was only a pretext, for he could not possibly be jealous of me because men were courting Sol[ange]. On the contrary, it should have been a reason not to be jealous. A thousand details which until now were unintelligible to me and often made me think him mad are now clear— an intimacy between them, secrets, quarrels, tender exchanges, sudden starts, shared aversions which were as much unjust as enraged. What else can I tell you? This so faithful and blindly devoted friend (so he assured me and so *people told me*), there he is siding against me, hanging on to Solange's petticoats and making compacts with my son-in-law, when he knows that that man lifted his hand against me and that he, the invalid I have been taking care of day and night for the past nine years, cannot go on seeing him now without dishonoring himself in my eyes. Well, so be it! As soon as he sees *her* [Solange], he dares anything and breaks off everything with sublime nonchalance. His soul is perfectly chaste, that I'll swear to; he is too ill for anything but platonic love. However coquettish she may be with him now, in order to have him as liv-

346

ing testimony of her victimization by me, I am convinced she does not think of him as a man and has never thought of him except as some kind of *petit papa*. But that *he*, of that great, exclusive and undying passion his friends exert themselves to convince me of and which he is in the habit of *affecting*, should make this sudden about-face, proves passion for someone else or I don't know what I'm talking about. Besides, for two years now I have been telling myself and clearly seeing that his so-called love for me was in fact hatred.

This is the only happy outcome of the whole matter for me. The result will also be fortunate for him, when, sweetly cajoled, flattered, incessantly enticed as he is, contact with Solange and her calumnies will change his feeling for me into open aversion; and he will certainly be happier than he is now in this impossible effort he is making to have me share his *sickly* prejudices and retire into total solitude. As for me, what good riddance! What a chain finally cast off! I've had to resist his narrow, despotic spirit constantly; for nine years, bursting with life, I've been bound to a corpse, chained by pity and fear of causing his death from a broken heart. I have constantly had before my eyes and hanging over my head this warning from his coterie: "Woe to you! If you do anything that distresses him, if you say a single word that upsets him, he will die, you will have killed him!" What a future, after such a past of suffering, deadly ennui, and often deep down indignation, for I have seen nothing so insulting as his absurd jealousy! And yet for each stir of revolt and pride on my part, I was reproached by his friends as if it were a bludgeon blow against his poor life.

Well, for the past two years all this was nothing but hatred on his part, though I tiredly and desolately saw it as obstinate passion. But today he quarrels openly with me with such naïveté that I have begun to understand and even feel comforted. Thank God, I shall not be the one to cause his death and can start living again, I whom *he* has been killing with petty annoyances for nine years. Oh, how I shall work and run about and sleep! and fully enjoy speaking and thinking without being afraid that my slightest word might mean assassinating him! Perhaps he will be very happy with the chimera now feeding him. I always told him that a clever coquette would suit him better than a sincere, loyal, devoted friend. He has found what he wants. She will give him what he asks for—what in his present state he can only obtain at the cost of his last breath.

But she will smother him in chains; both will speak badly of everybody else; she will pretend to love music, she will drag him after her like a doll, a *toy Cupid*. He won't ask for anything better. Yet she has hated, mocked, and debased him more than anybody; however, this last year things changed, as he discovered.

Adieu, my friend. I am putting a stamp on this letter; it would not be deliverable otherwise. Read it well and keep it for me.

We are approaching August, so you will soon be

coming, won't you? I count on it and thank you in advance. I have told you everything so that from now on we can forget this whole sad chapter. I have been sick, deprived of sleep, completely broken for the past fifteen days, unable to work or breathe. It has been like a physical separation, as if death had taken my daughter. But it may be even worse, I fear. Death leaves sweeter regrets than treason. I have begun to regain some self-control, especially since this morning, and so I have finally been able to finish this letter.

To Louis Blanc, leading socialist:

> *Nohant, early November* 1847‡

For me you are like a son, full of strength and promise, before whom my age-worn soul is not afraid to reveal its anguish. Go forward, ever forward! Do not fear to beat down and destroy, and strike hard! You know what a life of struggle brings. But, just for that, fight all the harder, fight much better than I did. Leave behind you those who fall. Breach the trench— that is what you have to do. After victory it will be time enough to bury the dead.

‡ On the eve of the February 1848 revolution, which brought down the monarchy and established a republic.

To Charles Poncy, proletarian poet:

Nohant, March 8, 1848

Vive la république! What wonder, what enthusiasm, and at the same time what restraint and order in Paris! I have just come back from the city. I went everywhere, I saw the last barricades come down at my feet. I saw the people—great, sublime, naïve, generous —the French people, united in the very heart of France, in the heart of the world, the most wonderful people of the universe! I spent nights without sleep and days without rest. We are mad, we are drunk, we are overjoyed to have fallen asleep in the gutter and awakened in Paradise. May all around you show courage and trust. The Republic is won, secured, and we will all perish rather than let it fail. The Provisional Government is composed of excellent men, all of them somewhat inadequate for a task demanding the genius of Napoleon and the heart of Jesus. But, united, these men of soul, talent, and will shall be equal to the situation. They want what is good, they seek it, they test it. They are genuinely moved by a principle that raises them above their individual capacity—the general will, the rights of the people. The people of Paris are so good, so trustful and confident in their cause, so *strong,* that they will sustain their government. The social ideal would be for this situation to last, and this must be encouraged. From one end of France to the other, everyone must help the Republic and preserve it from its enemies. The desire, the principle, the fervent wish of members of the Provisional Government is to see the National Assembly filled with men representative of the people, with as many as possible of them coming from their ranks.

So, *mon ami*, your friends must think of this and turn their eyes toward you for the National Assembly. I am very sorry that I do not know the influential people of our opinion in your town [Toulon]. I would beg them to choose you, and I would command you, in the name of my maternal friendship, to accept without hesitation. You must *take action*; it is no longer enough to *let things happen*. The question is no longer one of vanity or ambition, as we once understood them. Now each must help to run the ship and give all his or her time, devotion, intelligence, and strength to the Republic. Poets, as Lamartine* proves, can be great citizens. The workers must now tell us their needs, give us their inspiration.

To Charlotte Marliani, Paris friend:

Nohant, mid-July 1848

Thank you, dear friend. I should have worried about you if you had not written, for in the midst of general disaster one fears the addition of some private sorrow. One fears for all the people one loves. I do not need

---

* Alphonse de Lamartine (1790–1869), French poet, novelist, and statesman, headed the Provisional Government following the February 1848 revolution; friend of George Sand.

to tell you that I am dreadfully sorry. I no longer believe in a republic which begins by killing its
workers.† . . .

I should like to come and embrace you and your
husband. But for some time, apart from the fact that I
might be unable to behave prudently in Paris, I must
keep in check by my presence [here] a sizable band of
imbeciles from La Châtre, who daily talk of coming
and burning down my house. They have neither
physical nor moral courage, and when they come
prowling around here, I go to meet them and they lift
their hats to me. But when they have passed by, they
venture to shout: "Down with the communisks [*sic*]!"
They hope to scare me, but finally realize they fail.
But one never knows what they can be incited to do
by a dozen bourgeois reactionaries, who tell them the
most ridiculous stories about me. Thus, during the
Paris events, they claimed that I had hidden in my
house [ex-Minister of Interior Alexandre] Ledru-
Rollin along with two hundred communists and four
hundred rifles.

Others, better disposed but quite as silly, came running in the middle of the night to tell me that my
house was encircled by bandits. They were so convinced that they brought along the gendarmerie.
Luckily, all the gendarmes are our friends and not
given to the kind of stupidity that might lead to my

† The June crushing of barricaded workers by the troops of
General Louis Cavaignac, Minister of War in the government
formed after the electoral victory of the conservatives in April
1848.

being unceremoniously arrested one of these days. The authorities are also on our side. But if they are replaced, which is likely, we shall perhaps be somewhat persecuted. All my friends have left the district, wrongly in my opinion. We must outface these little storms, which are simply the unavoidable offshoots of the general calamity.

Good night, my friend. What days of tears and wrath! Today I am ashamed of being French, I who used to be so proud of it. Whatever may happen, I remain your

George

To Jérôme-Pierre Gilland, imprisoned republican:

Nohant, July 22, 1848

I see a terrible social upheaval taking place, as though in accordance with some blind law of fate. I see a struggle starting over the question of bread, over whether the poor have a right to work while the rich have a right to be idle. All our lives we shall see this struggle continue, just as I have seen it being prepared over the last forty years. And it is very likely we shall not see the end of the struggle.

To Charles Poncy:

Nohant, August 1, 1848

There are two kinds of property, just as there are two kinds of lives. There is private property, as there is private and individual life. And there is common, public property, as there is a common, public life— that is to say, social life, the life of human relations. All societies have always recognized common, public property and sanctified it in their laws. No society is possible without such property.

It has been characteristic of private property, of its abuse and exaggeration, to give rise to extreme inequalities of condition. However good and legitimate it may be in itself, it has to find its remedy in the wide and wise enlargement of common property. Common property, of course, includes highways, railroads, canals, mines, revenues—everything that cannot be monopolized by private individuals without an unwarranted encroachment upon the wealth of all. Such encroachment nevertheless took place during the reign of speculation and unrestrained individualism. The riches of all became the object of speculation of the privileged class and today this class claims more loudly than ever to be proprietor of the property of the state. . . .

Thus, there must be two kinds of communism.‡ I

‡ See Sand's essay "Socialism," pp. 379–97.

have drawn your attention to the errors and excesses of one, which I have never had nor could I ever have any part in defending. And there is social communism, which only demands fundamental common rights and the progressive extension, suitably adapted to circumstances, of these rights. No reasonable creature can reject *this* communism, although the word, perverted by blindly progressive sects and by blind enemies of progress, has become a badge one can wear when one wishes to be attacked by the unintelligent, the profligate, the swindlers and fools of all kinds.

Because of their instinctive understanding of this communism but because they promoted it piecemeal, without clarity or commitment, the government of the period from February to May [1848] failed. By rejecting it with bias, prejudice, and self-interest, the majority of the Assembly brought on the June disasters. The June insurrectionists probably did not know what they were fighting for. The force of circumstance, physical and spiritual unrest, led them inevitably to be roused by leaders with no social ideas, so far as I know, and who are even suspected of having been the agents of foreign powers, of royal pretenders, and of extreme bourgeois reactionaries.

From *Diary*

Palaiseau, August 1865*

August 18: He [Alexandre Manceau] coughs all night and all day. Forty-eight hours! It's agonizing to hear him, and yet he is definitely calmer than he has been.

August 19: Diarrhea again. . . . What a fight!

August 20: Alas! Everything that I have written, *he has been reading,* and sometimes I was afraid to irritate him by making light of his illness, sometimes I was afraid he might realize how hopeless it was. It is more than a month since I have known; what a struggle to keep it from him! Now he is at his worst. He is sleeping, worn out by the fever, hardly able to breathe; he is no longer coughing. Is this the last sleep?

August 21: Poor, dear friend! *Dead* this morning at six o'clock, after a night of complete calm—or so it seemed. On waking, he spoke a little, his voice already dead, his words wandering as if in a dream. A few efforts to breathe, then pallor, and then—*nothing!* He wasn't conscious, I hope. At midnight he had spoken lucidly to me by force of will. He had talked of going to Nohant! I have changed his clothes and arranged him on his bed. I have closed his eyes. I have laid

* For the intervening years, see Chronology, 1848–65, pp. xxxvi–xli. The diary, largely unpublished, was kept jointly by Manceau and Sand, wherefore her concern about his reading previous entries as he lay dying from tuberculosis.

flowers on his body. He is handsome and looks quite young. Oh my God! I shall never watch over him again. . . .

August 22: I spent the night alone, beside this eternal sleep! He lies on his bed. He has found peace. There is nothing ugly or frightening. No bad odor. I have laid fresh roses on him. . . . [Our friends, Charles] Marchal, La Rounat, Borie, Dumas, and Fromentin came to see me. . . . Marchal dined with me. . . . Alone now, and he [Manceau] is there, beside me, in this little bedroom. No longer will I listen for his breathing, and tomorrow night, nothing more, still more lonely! Now and forever. . . .

* * *

August 1866

August 28: Arrived at Rouen at one. Found [Gustave] Flaubert at the station with a carriage. He took me on a tour of the city, its fine monuments, cathedral, town hall, St. Maclou, St. Patrice. It's marvelous. An old charnel house and ancient streets; all very odd. We arrive at Croisset at 3:30. Flaubert's mother is an old, charming woman [of seventy-three]. The location of the house [on the banks of the Seine estuary] is delicious—the house comfortable, handsome, and well-arranged; good service, spotless housekeeping, all wants *anticipated,* everything one could wish. I am living like a fighting cock—completely spoiled. This evening Flaubert read to me from his *Temptation of St. Anthony.* Superb. We talk in his study until two in the morning.

August 29: We leave at eleven on the river steamboat with Madame Flaubert, her niece [Caroline, married two years before], her friend Madame Waas and the latter's daughter, Madame de la Chausée. We go to La Bouille. Wretched weather: wind and rain. But I stay on deck, looking at the water, superb in the rain. . . . We spend ten minutes at La Bouille and return on the tidal bore, or flood, or sweep—a veritable tidal wave. We get back by one. A fire is lighted, we dry ourselves, we drink tea. I go out again with Flaubert to walk around his estate: the garden, terraces, orchard, vegetable patch, farm, and the *citadel*—a very curious old wooden house that serves him for storage. La Sente de Moïse [a path leading to the upper slope]. View of the Seine [and Rouen's spires]. The orchard—beautifully sheltered way up high. Soil dry, with whitish topsoil. Everything charming, very poetic. I dress for dinner. Dinner very good. Play cards with the two old ladies [Sand herself is sixty-two]. Talk late with Flaubert and go to bed at two in the morning. Excellent bed; slept well, but my cough came back. My cold is discontented with me. Too bad for my cold.

August 30: Departure from Croisset at noon with Flaubert and his niece. We dropped her off at Rouen. We revisited the city, the bridge—vast and superb. Beautiful baptistery belonging to a Jesuit church. Flaubert packs me off [for Paris].

To Gustave Flaubert:

> *Paris, September 21, 1866*

Although he likes you, Sainte-Beuve† makes out that you are frightfully vicious. But perhaps he observes you with rather soiled eyes, like the learned botanist who described germander as being of a dirty yellow color. His observation was so wrong that I could not resist writing in the margin of his book: "You are one who has dirty eyes."

Personally, I assume that men of intelligence can be widely curious. I have not been so myself for lack of courage. I preferred to leave my mind incomplete. That is my affair, and each of us is free to embark on a large, four-masted vessel or on a fishing boat. The artist is an explorer whom nothing should stay, who does neither good nor bad in going left or right: his goal justifies everything. It is for him to choose, after a little experimentation, the conditions necessary for the health of his soul.

To Gustave Flaubert:

> *Palaiseau, November 22, 1866*

Here I am, all alone in my little house. The gardener

† Charles-Augustin Sainte-Beuve (1804–69), leading literary critic of his age.

and his family live in a lodge on the grounds, and our house is the last one in the lower part of the village, quite isolated in the countryside—a delightful oasis. Meadows, woods, apple trees as in [your] Normandy, no large river with steamer whistles and infernal booms; a brooklet runs quietly under the willows, and silence—ah! we seem to be deep in a virgin forest: not a sound but the whisper of the little fountain, incessantly piling up diamonds in the moonlight. The heat of my fire wakes the flies asleep in the corners of my bedroom. They had settled down to die, now they come close to the lamp, possessed by an insane gaiety. They buzz, they jump, they laugh, they even seem inclined to make love. But the time of death has come, and poof! in the middle of their dance they drop dead. And it is all over. Good-by to fun.

But the place nevertheless makes me sad. This complete solitude, which has even been vacation and recreation for me, is shared now by one who ended his days here, like a lamp that has gone out, but is still here.‡ I do not believe he is unhappy in the region he now inhabits, but the image he has left behind is but a pale shadow, which always seems to be complaining that it cannot speak to me.

Never mind! There is nothing unhealthy about sadness; it keeps us from becoming hard. And you, my friend, what are you doing at this hour? Are you plugging away, alone too, since your mother is probably in Rouen? Nighttime must also be beautiful in your

‡ Alexandre Manceau.

parts. Do you think sometimes of the "old troubadour
in the tavern clock who sings, and always will sing, of
perfect love"?* Well, yes, of course you do! Your
Highness, I know, is not one for chastity, but that is
your affair. I say: there is some good in it.

And with this, a big loving hug. I'm off to put
words, if I can find them, into the mouths of people
who love in the old-fashioned way.

You do not have to write to me when you are not in
the mood to do so. There is no true friendship without
total freedom.

I'll be in Paris next week, then again at Palaiseau,
then at Nohant.

To Gustave Flaubert:

Paris, November 30, 1866

Nature, our sovereign, has established a balance in
our instincts that rapidly determines the limits of our
appetites. Great temperaments are not the most robust.
A logical education does not develop us evenly in
every direction. We are all of us cramped and we put
out our roots and branches where and how we can.
Great artists are often infirm, and several have been
impotent. Others, too potent in their desires, have
quickly burned themselves out. . . .

---

* Sand often addressed Flaubert as "my troubadour." The
"old troubadour" seems to have been a figure in a tavern clock
they had seen together.

For myself, I do not believe in Don Juans who are at the same time Byrons. Don Juan did not write poetry and Byron, it is said, made love very badly. There must have been times—never many in any lifetime—when he knew the complete ecstasy of heart, mind, and senses. He experienced it sufficiently to be one of the poets of love. We need no more to set our talent vibrating. The constant wind of petty appetites would wreck our fragile instruments.

To Gustave Flaubert:

Nohant, December 31, 1867

I believe completely the contrary.† . . . I believe that the artist should, as much as is possible, live true to his nature. For the one who likes combat, war; for the one who likes women, love; for the old, like myself, who like nature, voyages, flowers, rocks, great landscapes, children and family, too. . . .

I believe that art needs a palette brimming over with both violent and delicate colors to be used as the subject requires; that the artist is an instrument whose every chord must be played before he plays any other.

† Flaubert had just espoused in a letter his monkish devotion to writing, comparing it to the Amazons, who "cut off a breast the better to draw their bows." For Sand, wholeness was all.

From *"Réponse à un Ami"*

To Gustave Flaubert:

Nohant, July 26, 1870‡

I hate this unspeakable [Franco-Prussian] war and find the *Marseillaise,* as sung by the Empire, a sacrilege.

From *"Réponse à un Ami"**

August 1871

Well now, do you want me to stop loving? Do you want me to say that I have been mistaken all my life, that humanity is despicable and detestable, always has been and always will be?† And you blame me for my grief as if it were for a weakness, a childish regret for a lost illusion? You declare that the people have always been brutal, priests hypocritical, the bourgeoisie cowards, soldiers ruffians, and peasants fools. You say that you have known all this since your youth and you are glad never to have had any doubts, for thus maturity has brought you no disappointment. Then you have never been young! Oh, we do indeed differ, for I have never ceased being young, if to be young is to love. . . .

‡ See Chronology, 1870–71, p. xlii.
* See p. 284.
† The Franco-Prussian War and the excesses of the Paris Commune that followed (from March 18 to May 28, 1871) had confirmed Flaubert's misanthropy.

No, no, we cannot isolate ourselves, we cannot break the ties of blood, we cannot curse and despise our own species. "Humanity" is not an empty word. Our life is made of love, and to cease loving is to cease living.

The people, you say! You and I *are* the people and it would be vain to deny it. . . .

[*To her critics on the left*‡:]

Read what I write in its entirety. Do not judge me by isolated fragments. . . . By my feeling and reason I am more than ever opposed to fictitious differences, to the inequality of life's condition which is imposed as an inherited right for some and a deserved fate for others. More than ever I feel the need to lift up those who are down and raise those who have fallen. . . . If today it is the people who are underfoot, I will extend them my hand. If tomorrow they are the oppressors and executioners, I will tell them they are cowardly, odious brutes. . . .

I do not need to ask where my friends are and where my enemies. They are there where the storm has flung them. . . . The unthinking accusation of those who have broken with me does not make me think of them as my enemies. . . . The heart . . . knows how to await the return of justice and affection. . . .

I love, therefore I live; let us live, let us love!

‡ Sand's opposition to the Paris Commune had evoked criticism from former friends.

To Alfred Gabrié, young poet:

Nohant, October 21, 1871

I hate bloodshed and will have no more of the argument that advocates doing evil to bring about good and killing to create. No, no! My years protest against the tolerance of my youth. All the manifold recent events should impel us to take a great step forward. We must rid ourselves of the theories [of the Reign of Terror] of 1793.* They have been our downfall. Terror and St. Bartholomew's Day represent the same path. You are young, are you not? In any case, you are a poet. You should love what is true, beautiful, and just. So you must curse all those who build charnel houses. No life ever comes out of them. We must learn to break away from such historical errors. Evil breeds only evil. Let us learn to be stubborn, patient revolutionaries, but never terrorists. We shall not be listened to for a long time, but what does it matter. The poet should live on a height above his contemporaries, beyond his own life. Humanity will only progress when it starts to despise the lie in men and to respect mankind despite the lie.

* Sand implies that such were the theories of the Paris Commune of 1871, and such indeed were the theories *attributed* to it by the opposition press she was reading exclusively at this time in Nohant. See pp. 371–72 for a description of the evolution of Sand's political thinking.

To Gustave Flaubert:

Nohant, November 1874

I confess I do not see clearly into that great tempest.†
I can only approve or disapprove certain events taken
by themselves. The whole affair seems like a terrible
case of fever which, to an extent, makes everyone innocent. I can ascertain no real "party" or "school." I
perceive nothing but anguish as each blindly plunged
on, not knowing what he was doing, not caring about
political rights, or civil rights, or human rights, alas. Is
it in delirium that one can ever consider grave problems?

To Gustave Flaubert:

Nohant, July 8, 1874

You say you do not want to be a man of nature. Too
bad for you! Because you then attach too much importance to petty details of human affairs and you forget
to appreciate the natural force in yourself which defies
the ifs and buts of idle social chatter. We are of nature, in nature, by nature, and for nature. Talent,
will, and genius are natural phenomena, like vol-
canoes, lakes, mountains, winds, stars, clouds. What
man dabbles in is ugly or nice, ingenious or foolish.

† The Paris Commune and the death of twenty to twenty-five
thousand *communards* in its suppression at the end of May 1871.

366

To Dr. Henri Favre, 1876

What he receives from nature is good or bad, but it *is*, it exists and endures. . . .

Enough now. I can no longer hold my pen. I love you. Do not have any more black thoughts. Resign yourself to boredom if the air there [in Switzerland] is good for you.

To Gustave Flaubert:

Nohant, March 25, 1876

I trust that your niece is still well. I, too, am better now after atrocious, persistent stomach cramps, enough to drain one of life. Bodily suffering is a good lesson when it leaves the mind free. One learns to endure and even to overcome it. Of course, there are moments of discouragement when one throws oneself into bed. But personally I always think of what my old priest used to say when attacked by gout: "It will pass, or I will." And then he would laugh, pleased with his wit.

To Dr. Henri Favre, physician friend:

Nohant, May 28, 1876

My legs are fine, my eyesight far better than for the last twenty years, my sleep is quiet, my hands as steady and adroit as in my youth. When I do not suffer from these cruel pains, a strange phenomenon, probably characteristic of this localized disease, occurs: I feel stronger and freer than perhaps ever before. I used to be slightly asthmatic, but not any more. I climb the stairs as nimbly as my dog.

However, with one part of my vital functions almost completely suppressed [an intestinal occlusion had led to a complete blockage], I wonder what is going to happen to me, and whether I should not be prepared for a sudden departure one of these days.

From *Diary*

Nohant, May 29, 1876

Delicious weather. Not suffering very much. Took a nice walk in the garden. Gave [granddaughter] Lolo her lesson. Reread a play by Maurice. After dinner, Lina went to the theater in La Châtre. Played *bésig* with Sagnier [a young visitor from Nîmes]. Sketched. Lina returned at midnight.

These were the last lines that George Sand wrote. She died on June 8. She would have been seventy-two on July 1.

POLITICAL
WRITINGS

*George Sand was a republican when that meant
being a revolutionary, for her Europe was almost
exclusively ruled by absolute monarchs. She
called herself a "socialist" when the term itself
had scarcely become current (Robert Owen used
it in England in 1822, Pierre Leroux ten years
later in France) and accepted being called a
"communist" when it was the vaguest of epithets
(her neighbors in Berry muttered about the
"communisks" in the reactionary aftermath of the
Revolution of 1848).*

*Descendant of a Polish king and a Paris bird
seller, Sand spoke often of her "mixed blood" but
unadulterated sympathy for the common people.
Herself a baroness, she was one of the Romantics
then born, like Alfred de Musset, who rejected
their aristocratic past as well as the Balzacian
bourgeoisie clawing its way to great fortunes of
accumulated capital.[1] The oppressed and exploited in this social and historical process appealed to Sand's egalitarian sensibility, sentiment,
and impulse, which peaked in the Revolution of*

371

1848, when she effectively became Minister of Propaganda of the new Republic and wrote its official, widely diffused Bulletins, some of which are excerpted here.

That period marks Sand's sharpest political thinking and writing and her closest approach to an emerging Marxist socialism. Then the violence of the counterrevolution led her to reject all violence and class struggle and to place hope in a utopian embracing of all classes in a common humanity. This belief was reinforced by withdrawal and long absence from the Paris political scene and her militant friends, especially during the Franco-Prussian War and the Paris Commune of 1871, which she opposed. However, as can be observed in her correspondence with Flaubert and others, Sand's powerful sympathy for the oppressed endured to the end, and she remained, in principle, a socialist. ❧—

"Letter to the Rich" [2]
("Aux Riches," March 12, 1848)

The great fear—or pretext—of the aristocracy at this
hour is communism.* If it were possible to laugh at
such a serious moment, we would find this fear really
amusing. By the word "communism," they really
mean the people, their needs, their hopes. Let us not
be confused: the people are the people, communism is
the calumniated, misunderstood future of the people.

The ruse is useless: it is the people who upset and
worry you, the Republic whose development you fear,
and the idea of rights for all that you cannot bear
without discomfort or resentment. . . .

This phantom which you dare not even face you
have chosen to call "communism." You are terrified by
an idea because there are groups who believe in this
idea, because this belief will one day spread and, little
by little, change the whole social structure. Supposing
its triumph to be near, do you not realize that,
whether you reveal your fear and aversion, whether

* The *Communist Manifesto* of Karl Marx and Friedrich
Engels had just been published in German. A few copies had
reached France, but it is almost certain George Sand had not
read even its opening, strikingly coincidental, line: "A specter
is haunting Europe, the specter of Communism."

you cover your eyes with your hands so as not to see it, or whether, summoning your courage, you succeed in provoking blind hatred against it, you are only going to give this idea an importance, a cohesion, and a luster it does not yet pretend to have? You are still yesterday's men, you still believe that you can defend your viewpoint by bitter, hostile struggle. You are making an unthinkable error. Can you not understand that the equality to which you, as well as the people, are entitled can only be achieved through liberty? I should also invoke fraternity, if I could believe that there was among you a heart so hard as not to understand that this word carries within itself its own definition—health of the soul. . . .

Alas, no! The people are not communist. And yet France is destined to become communist within a century. Among the people communism has reached an infinitely small minority. Now, you know that if majorities represent the truths of the present, then minorities represent those of the future. Therefore we should show regard and respect for minorities and give them freedom. Refused these things, they become hostile; they may even become dangerous; we are reduced to controlling them by force; and they either suffer martyrdom or seek revenge.

Martyrdom morally kills those who inflict it, just as revenge physically kills those who suffer it. So allow communism to live in peace, for it will develop more rapidly in war, and you can only inspire its followers with wisdom, restraint, and patience by allowing them freedom to present their theories. If these are crazy and unjust, do not worry; the people will discard them with cheerful common sense, just as the monarchy was discarded. If they are worthy and can be gradually applied, you yourself will be obliged to recognize them, since, instead of threatening existing property rights, they insure their continuation for as long as is necessary.

But there are communists, people say, who want, at this moment, to put property and the family to fire and sword. Where are they? I who am a communist have never met a single one. So they are either very few or else their theories are incompatible with those of the majority of communists. But if there is a handful of poor fanatics who subscribe neither to Pierre Leroux's unfinished and essentially pacific plan nor to [Étienne] Cabet's romantic and no less peaceful utopia,† are there not also among you fanatics of wealth, inflammatory monarchists who would have approved a general massacre of the people on February 24? We forgive these madmen. We do not seek them out. We take no notice of them. We do not hold you responsible for their culpable madness. We do not calumniate you, although you and they are both called "conservatives." We do not even think of them. Above all, we are not afraid of them.

So stop worrying! Communism does not threaten you. It has just given signal proof of its lawful submission to the established order by proclaiming its adher-

† Étienne Cabet (1788–1856), French socialist and reformer, described an ideal society in his utopian novel *Voyage en Icarie* (1840).

ence to the young Republic. Communism has many voices, since most adepts of the communist idea view it as an inspiration. Some are even to be found among the rich. They come from every nation, every level of learning, and every grade of the social hierarchy. Some are neither enrolled under an organizational banner nor belong to any group, because they have not found a satisfactory formula and thus prefer to maintain in their hearts a pure ideal rather than submit it to fruitless experiments. These, too, are unwavering in their faith, and were they to live a further hundred years under a Louis Philippe, they would die with their convictions unchanged. For communism is true Christianity, and a religion of fraternity threatens nobody's money or life.

Well then, among all the voices of the communist creed, can you quote a single one which has challenged the laws that govern legitimate property rights or the sanctity of the family?

What have they done to terrify you so? Nothing! These are nightmare fears.

As for the people, you slander them when you say that they yearn for instant communism. Wiser and braver than you, the people would not take alarm at a few reprehensible demonstrations; they would simply repress them. Rather than lose faith in the future, the people would learn from such excesses a nobler patience and a firmer justice.

Bulletins of the Republic
(Bulletins de la République, 1848)

No. 3, March 17, 1848

. . . O people, you shall rule! Rule as brothers with your equals from all classes, for the Republic, holy ark of alliance, amidst whose ruins we must all perish rather than forsake, the Republic, supreme example of the stable society, calls on the whole universe to bear witness that it proclaims and enshrines the equality of rights of all men.

No. 12, April 6, 1848

Women have of necessity been the principal victims of the wretchedness that overwhelmingly oppresses body and soul. . . . The privileged classes have always mocked and disdained women's courage and self-sacrifice. The working-class man well knows that if he falls in battle, his wife and children will remain on the barricade until his death has been avenged.

. . . The new society that is soon to be built will hear with deep emotion the simple, touching petitions that may be formulated in the name of our whole sex and aimed at eradicating the lack of instruction, the neglect, deprivation, and misery which generally bear down even more heavily upon women than upon men.

We do not fear to say that the strivings of the Saint-Simonists toward the liberation of women were aristocratic in character.[3] So long as man was not free, how could woman reasonably aim at being freer than he? Today the question must be changed. Man is throwing off the yoke of misery and ignorance. It is no longer a matter of opening a temple for the chosen few of an ill-concealed theocracy, but of opening a world to all human beings, be they men or women, setting them free from the slavery of misery and ignorance.

Now, if ever, is the time for educated women who claim to be good citizens, to forget their individuality. They can prove their worth by sacrificing themselves and caring for the unfortunate women and daughters of the masses.

No. 16, April 15, 1848

Citizens,
We could not transform a regime of corruption to a regime of law in one day or one hour. One hour of inspiration and heroism sufficed for the people to establish the principle of truth. But eighteen years of falsehood have raised barriers to the reign of truth which a single blow cannot dispel. If the elections do not en-

sure the triumph of social truth, if they are only the expression of the interests of a caste, torn from a trusting people, then these elections, which should be the salvation of the Republic, will undoubtedly be its end. In that event, the only road to salvation for the people who raised the barricades would lie in their expressing their will a second time and setting aside the decisions of a body unrepresentative of the nation.

Does France wish to force Paris to this extreme, this deplorable remedy? Please God, no! . . .

Let us save the Republic at all costs. We still have it in our power to save it without schism and upheaval.

"Socialism"[4]

("Socialisme," April 1848)

I

SOVEREIGNTY OF THE PEOPLE MEANS EQUALITY

. . . You [the bourgeoisie] are vainly trying to confuse the meaning of the word equality with that of identity. All men are not identical. Their diversity of strength, instincts, faculties, appearance, and influence is infinite. There is not the slightest sameness between one man and another. But these infinite diversities are the consecration, not the negation, of equality. There

are men more skillful, more intelligent, more generous, more robust, more virtuous than others. But no
man, because of a natural superiority, has been
created to destroy the freedom of another or to betray
the ties of brotherhood that bind the weakest and the
strongest, the most narrow-minded and the most intelligent. A man who receives from God the sacred gift
of a great intelligence has larger obligations to teach
and improve others. But his rights are no larger than
theirs, and as the reward of merit is not money and as
the intelligent man has the same physical needs as
other men, no reason exists to make such a man the
oppressor, the master, and therefore the enemy of his
fellow creatures.

The Gospel ethic has always been true, even before
Christianity put it into words and spread it throughout the world. Gospel ethic remains true today and
presides over all great actions in the histories of peoples, over all revolutions aiming at progress. This doctrine is truly one of equality, and so excellent that
those who repudiate it in their hearts profess it aloud,
for they know that any resistance to it could not possibly avoid offending the human conscience. The true
law of nature, the real heavenly law, is thus equality.

Materialists have a strange understanding of the
state of nature of man. They see this state as being the
same for men and animals. The wolf devours its prey,
they say; sparrows are overcome and torn to pieces by
vultures. Everywhere the stronger rules the weaker.
At times, they even compare us to inanimate objects.
They say that the storm topples the oak, the waves

erode the foot of the cliff, and from this they conclude
that the stronger man must oppress the weaker, the
clever man must deceive the simple man, that this has
always been and always will be, for man is no more
than a wolf, a stone, or a plant. Thus, they say, the
state of nature is one of blind force, of cruel chance,
of heedless, mute fatalism. Equality is but a dream
against which nature cries out.

They are to be pitied who reason this way and see
man as mere matter. Such a doctrine allows all crimes
and sanctions all tyrannies.

In the state of nature, man, even if we imagine him
wandering alone on the earth, is still a man. He is a
thinking, understanding being who invents, endeavors, and progresses. When he meets a fellow man,
his instinct does not impel him to destroy the other,
only to find himself lost anew in fearful solitude. The
hare in its warren is afraid but not troubled; whereas
man in the desert knows both fear and restlessness.
Hunger alone does not drive him from the cavern in
which he has taken refuge, but also the need to see
the sky. Once he has contemplated its vastness, he is
no longer satisfied, like animals, to feel the air and the
heat reviving his limbs; he also needs to admire, to
dream, to meditate, and to seek out the secret of this
beauty of things which themselves offer no explanation. Then primitive man feels the dim need to share
his emotion with another man. His interrogation of
this vast, solemn, mysterious nature is painful. He
finds the grandeur that bewitched him overwhelming
and oppressive.

He calls out for his fellow creature even before he knows if his fellow creature exists. He somehow feels that his fellow creature would not be dumb like the rest of creation and would help him resolve the problem of his existence. And so, as soon as he meets his fellow creature, he joins with him to ward off, by their combined strengths and intelligences, the hostile forces of nature, to share the benefits of this association, and to seek—two or more together, in their moments of rest and contemplation—the secret of God and the laws of nature. This is how societies were formed and the only way they could have been formed. To imagine the first society arising out of an initial combat is a sinister nightmare which in no way corresponds to man's nature. Struggle, division, oppression, and inequality can only have emerged from a primary civilization already sufficiently advanced to become corrupt. . . .

II

THE EXERCISE OF SOVEREIGNTY MEANS THE
APPLICATION OF EQUALITY

. . . If the overwhelming victory of the principle "All for one and one for all" were, as some claim, to make the people vain and impudent, then the difficulties which would arise when the time came to apply this principle would suffice to make us cautious and to withdraw into ourselves. But the people are not vain—they are wise, and their great conquest has not gone to their heads. What comes from God can never be harmful.

And so we have the principle "All for one and one for all." Herein lies truth, and we have at last seen it. But it is the forms of truth—its means, its work, its positive, tangible achievements—that expand or contract, that shine forth or are dimmed, according to whether humanity is well- or ill-inspired, is uplifted or laid low, is equitable or inflamed. *Veni, creator spiritus!*

We clearly see the principle of duty inseparable from the principle of rights. Its name is "equality." And we have the rights today; tomorrow we must assume our responsibilities. The deed is done; we await its consequences. The deed is the combat; its consequences lie in the reconciliation. Yesterday's enemy is today's vanquished. How shall he be treated? We want neither prisoners, nor hostages, nor slaves! Equality is our watchword, and the defeated enemy, against whom we have invoked it in vain from the beginning of time, himself invokes it against us today! Under the ancient law he would have deserved punishment. Under the new law he is pardoned. But if he abuses our generosity, if in the name of equality he seeks to reinstate inequality, then he is already betraying and slandering us, trying to drag us down into the abyss. What then shall we do? Shall we be so generous and unmindful of all personal injuries as to allow him to smother truth in his perfidious embrace?

People, let us think. Let us enter together the sanctuary of conscience. Let us consult the oracle! Let us cast off all hatred, all resentment. We shall be so much the stronger when we re-emerge from the temple.

III

THE APPLICATION OF EQUALITY MEANS FRATERNITY

It would be, thank heaven, a commonplace to declare our revolution not only political but social as well. "Socialism is the end, the Republic is the means" is the slogan of our wisest and most progressive minds.

Social reform is the *duty* of every citizen. The regime of equality must take the place of the regime of caste and co-operative associations replace the abomination of competition and monopoly, those twin scourges which in principle are distinct but which lately have become one. We must not inscribe equality as the motto of our new code of law only to have the articles of that code prevent its application.

Thus it is a new duty, a duty that has matured for more than fifty years, that the Republic of 1848 grafts on to the duty proclaimed in 1789. Our circumstances are not identical, but analogous. Our duty is higher, more noble, and better understood. The parties may have changed their names, but the selfish interests against which we must fight are basically the same, and like our forefathers we must fight with courage and perseverance.

Our duty has three parts which must be consid-

ered: the one imposed upon us by the present, that
which the past recalls, and that which we glimpse in
the future. Thus the present must take these three
phases into account, avoiding too violent a break with
the past, yet not revering the past to the extent of laying fetters on the future. Here is our problem and our
responsibility, for in us are combined past, present and
future. The solidarity between generations is indestructible. Our predecessors' misfortunes are our misfortunes, and the glory of posterity is our glory.

What rights has the past and what is our duty towards it?

The past calls out to us: "You depose me, you strip
me, you threaten my property and my life. Whether
you shed my blood or dry up the sources of my wealth
is all the same to me. Your unbridled socialism heralds
expropriation or murder and plunder. Your progress
means my death, yet you want me to accept this
calmly and without a murmur. You are demanding
the impossible."

Now, what is justified and what is unjustified in
this complaint? Certainly there is a little of both, if
the truth is that we do want to some extent to destroy
the rights of the past. The past has true rights that we
must respect, but also false rights and inequities
which we must strike from the code of humanity.

If we threaten the lives of citizens who think
differently from us and do not recognize our rights,
we would be unjust. This we shall not do, unless they
threaten our lives or come, arms in hand, to reclaim
their privileges. Then we should know what we

would have to do, and a violent struggle between past and present would begin, as in the ill-fated days of the first Revolution. We would have the painful task of breaking and crushing those whom we would call our brothers. Please God, they may never incite this impious struggle! But we have nothing to fear. One has only to look the people in the face to see that this would be madness.

To prove that we want to respect the lives of our fellow creatures, we have allowed our enemies to flee; we have abolished the death penalty and to predict that we shall bring it back is an insult to oneself and to the authors of such an idea. Our duty in this respect is as clear as day, and we have nothing to lose by following it.

With the law of an eye for an eye legally abolished, will some unfortunate event occur that will make us reinstate it in practice? No! Whether in answer to the most shameless outrages, whether goaded by justifiable indignation or unbearable suffering, O people, our duty forbids us to use violence, to shed blood, except when fighting and in legitimate self-defense. Not for one hour, not in a single corner of republican France, must one individual execute so-called justice against another. Let the law be harsh, but let men be forbearing!

So, set your minds at ease, men of the past. Duty shall find us unshakable. Not one single life is threatened under equality's sway. "What of plunder?" they ask. Plunder—that for them is a fate worse than death! Plunder, provoked by their avarice or their petty-minded hoarding; plunder that tempts the needy man when he knows that a given house holds wealth that selfish fear has condemned to lie idle! Plunder, the burning and destruction of luxury objects that awaken not men's greed, but the desire for vengeance of those provoked by wretchedness and injustice!

No plundering! To suppose us so easily tempted is to dishonor us. Have you forgotten how faithfully we guarded the diamonds and the silver at the royal Tuileries Palace even though racked by the pangs of hunger? It is enough that our duty forbids us to plunder and steal. If there be among us, concealed in the noble rags of the worker, some runaway convict, some incorrigible criminal, we shall see to it that fair and prompt justice is done. During the early days we had to shoot them down like birds of prey. Now that we have organized a Civil Guard, we arrest them with due legal procedure and hand them over to their judges. We are the guardians of property, and even though we hope for social remuneration, we consider individual wealth as future national property. The more truly socialist we are, the better we can protect those who fear us from injury.

So, what do they fear? Graduated taxation, the suppression of indirect inheritance, revolutionary measures, obligatory contributions, socialization of the means of production—in short, all our needs and misfortunes which they will have to remedy through extensive sacrifices. They fear that they in turn will become poor, for they see that we will not allow them to enjoy in peace a luxury that involves our hunger or a security that entails our own starvation.

If this is what you fear, you have some reason not to sleep peacefully, for you will certainly have to make sacrifices. You have duties as well as rights, and we have rights as well as duties. In the past you and you alone have profited. Your stubbornness and distrust have brought about the crisis we now face; the present will not perish with the future in order to let the past go on living with impunity on both their corpses.

Yes, the men of the past must expect to pay for the war that they have caused. We have to see what we can reasonably claim from them, and on this point we must, regardless of their despair or their wrath, deliberate together to define the extent and the limits of our duty.

At first sight, it seems legitimate to take everything from those who themselves took all. The lament of widow and orphan, the sight of old men and children begging at every crossroad, makes one boil with indignation. Do not the rich deserve to be reduced to the ranks of the poor?

Alas, yes! Under the ancient law, this is what they deserve. And if we were to apply the laws of the past to the men of the past, then the rich would suffer the law of an eye for an eye.

But we are the legislators of the present, the pioneers of the future. We cannot resort to the law of retaliation.

The future will do away entirely with individual

wealth, and it will create social wealth. In the future there will be no more poor, but only equals in the full meaning of the word.

Can the present eliminate outright the evils of the past? No, since this cannot be done without violence and therefore must not be done. The present has to accept a period of transition in progress.

This will be the transition: greedy, cunning men will no longer be able to amass those scandalous fortunes which, feeding on each other, ended by devouring the people's sustenance. Society must make it impossible for the men of the past once again to monopolize the future for their own profit. No more stock exchange gamblers, no more speculation based on other men's weariness, resignation, and misery, no more human sacrifices. Let us root out these barbarous practices even in their final refuges. As for existing fortunes, let them dry up by themselves, and let us impose on them the sacrifices demanded by circumstance. The situation does not require that rich people be reduced to the poverty they have made us suffer or looked upon with indifference. Once the Republic can function without claiming from them more than the sums necessary for its fundamental needs, let us no more be jealous of the rich; for that, we are much too proud! Work, freedom, air to breathe, poetry, education, honor are all we ask. If we must suffer a little while in order to surmount a crisis whose resolution holds out the promise of these blessings, we shall patiently suffer, provided we see our chosen government doing everything to shorten our lofty ordeal. Once we have secured these basic necessities of human life, we will agree to march forward step by step toward greater improvements, provided we march forward in double time, with never a backward step. We shall progress from poverty to ease and from ease to social wealth without coming into collision with those obstacles which duty commands us to circumvent.

Herein, I believe, lies our clearly defined duty to the past. The rich, who do not want to become poor, are right to fear poverty more than we. They are not used to working. They are lazy, weak, unskilled. How long would it take the cleverest stock exchange speculator to learn an honest trade? He would be reduced to begging before he learned to use his hands. And his children, so badly educated—his children, who have learned Greek and Latin in their schools but do not have the slightest idea about the story of humanity—what a bad lot we would be letting loose on our streets! Most of them could only become cutpurses or even worse. And their wives! Would they know how to wash, clean, and sew dresses or all the other little occupations demanding so much skill or strength? Their wives, lazy and vain, would be the ruin of our young men or would die of fatigue and despair. Do we wish to be the authors and witnesses of such degradations and calamities? No! Abruptly deprived of their wealth, the rich would not become our equals. They would be so overwhelmed by wretchedness that they would succumb, body and soul. Like pariahs they would be groveling beneath our feet and their shame would reflect on us. So let us pity the poor rich! Let us wait for the day when the State can educate and give them a role to play that will make them men. And until then, though inequality still appears to exist, though there are still both workers and shirkers, so long as the latter do not hinder our progress and agree to give their money instead of their labor whenever the State demands, so long as we are not dependent upon them, so long as they respect our womenfolk and do not deprave our children, so long as we are freed from misery, so long as we have work and as our children are as well educated as theirs, and finally so long as it remains an established principle that our duty toward them is a duty of generous equality and of fraternal forgiveness, we can smilingly watch their pomp and pride pass by.

Yes, brothers, here is our duty toward the past and the future. Whether it leads to stern measures softened as far as possible, whether it adopts this or that means to consecrate this principle of reconciliation and charity, the form it takes is not, for the moment, what concerns us. Our principle is that the law of retaliation is abolished and that the people initiate humanity toward a new greatness, a virtue unexampled in the past.

Under ancient legislations the initiator killed the initiated. This savage principle was accepted among all peoples. In more advanced societies, murder was replaced by slavery: the initiator oppressed the initiated. Today the principle has achieved perfection: the initiator forgives the initiated.

IV

MAJORITY AND UNANIMITY

The question "What is the true expression of popular sovereignty?" is one that is rightly much discussed. Until now, nothing better has been found than the voice of the majority.

This must be accepted in practice, for, through wanting to act only in accordance with the ideal, if that ideal is absent from reality, we end up doing nothing at all.

But, while yielding in practice to the necessities of circumstance, we must always keep in mind the ideal, that is, the supreme principle which is based on reason, justice, and feeling.

Without this ideal, we come to a halt, we renew the past, and we fumble clumsily for the future. In our desire to remain in the present, we fail to take advantage of it. The present slips through our fingers and we waste our time on petty details. The ideal expression of the sovereignty of all is not majority, but rather unanimity. A day will come when the mists that cloud our reason will be so completely dispersed and the hesitations of conscience so fully banished that not a single voice will be raised against truth in the councils of men.

But, until then, it may be asked, between the imperfect expression of the sovereignty of the people to which the present condemns us and the satisfactory expression that the future holds out for us, is there no auspicious moment at which we can, with absolute trust, evoke unanimous assent?

Yes! In every period of history there are decisive moments when Providence undertakes an experiment and sanctions the true aspiration, the electrifying assent, of the masses. There are moments when unanimity is achieved in the sight of heaven and when "majority" no longer counts in the face of it.

We have just witnessed one of these great moments when humanity awakens, rises up, and spontaneously joins together and votes as a single man. May the memory of this event, the like of which may occur only once in a century, never fade away, may its deeper meaning never be lost or be snuffed out with the torches and festivity of an evening of intoxication. May the sun that yesterday went down on our enthusiasm never rise again without reminding us that at a given moment a single thought was captured in the unison of a million voices. In the establishment of a new constitution, France will be guided by the majority voice. But nowhere will this be an expression of unanimity. Yesterday Paris signed a compact of unconditional fraternity, in one of these moments when the miracle of reason takes hold of the masses, subdues all individualities, and tears from the breast of each man, willed or not, an expression of the truth. Tomorrow, perhaps, this noble compact will be broken or transformed in the minds of the individuals who made up the masses. But in what way does this affect the truth? Will truth cease to exist just because it has become less manifest? On the fifth of May, throughout France, the various local majorities will express their will and people say that these fractioned majorities' sovereignty will be sacred.

And so it would be, if violence and threats were needed to dispute it. But in that case, it would not be sovereignty but each individual's human rights which were being violated.

But has humanity no other court of appeal than riot?

Was the February Revolution the result of a battle that would have been lost for the people's cause if the army had opposed the wishes of the people of Paris?

This is mere sophistry! The February Revolution was the result of a spontaneous expression of popular sovereignty as revealed by a unanimous outburst. You cannot say that our Republic would have been lost if the troops had been willing to take up arms against it. Our answer is that the troops could not have wanted to make use of their weapons. Weapons! What good are eighty thousand rifles, or even four hundred thousand rifles, when the mind breaks free and the heart forbids the arms to raise the weapons they hold?

So do not say: "The National Assembly will come into being, and if you do not absolutely respect its principle of total freedom, you will be forced to commit a crime against it and consequently against yourself."

This whole discussion derives from the annals of the past. The Chamber of Deputies was violated on the twenty-fourth of February in the name of the principle of the majority against the minority. If the Assembly of May 5 should happen to be the expression of an abused majority, if it is determined to represent once more the interests of a minority, this Assembly shall not rule. Unanimity will override the decrees of the majority. Do not be scared, do not pretend to faint, do not say that we are calling for civil war and that the republicans are awakening the memory of Fructidor by their hateful provocations. Warmhearted patriots, strict guardians of our liberties, we know you —listen to the end!

There will be no riots; the people want no more of them. There will be no conspiracies; the people will thwart them. There will be no bloodshed; the people abhor this. There will be no threats; the people have no need for them. Know that the people whom you insult with your fears and whom, like Louis Philippe, you are pleased to call the "kindly working class," the people who despise your hate, your calumnies, your intrigues, and your attempts to mislead them, the people will not touch a single hair of the heads of your precious representatives. They will not cry "Death to the bourgeois! String them up! all of them!"—even as you tried to make them shout "Death to the socialists! String up their ringleaders!" A misguided minority may cry out this way. If you were richer and cleverer, you might perhaps produce a simulacrum of a majority to light the fires of civil war. But civil war would not serve your ends and you would be its first victims.

But in all your learned calculations, you have forgotten the supreme law, the great power, the great voice of humanity. It will rise and all ideas of civil war will vanish like a bad dream. The unanimous voice of the people now knows and recognizes itself! It will reduce you all to silence; passing over your heads like the breath of God, it will envelop your national representation, saying: "Until now you were not sacred, but here we come with weapons adorned with flowers and we declare you inviolable. So work and function, we surround you with four hundred thousand bayonets, with the will of millions. No party, no scheming shall touch you. Concentrate your minds and act. You cannot betray us, for you know who we are and we shall show you who you are. We shall baptize you in the waters of a new life and you will not be able to withstand the miracle brought about this day by unanimity in transforming your various elements into one single thought. If you reject our appeal, we shall withdraw, leaving you alone with your enemies, with the elements of strife and impotence that you carry within you, with your vague notions, your ignorance of our thoughts, and isolation will kill you. You will work in silence and in baneful solitude. Cut off from life, you will not be able to live. You will cast about vainly in a world of chimeras, with the real world beyond your reach. You will draw up an impossible, monstrous, ridiculous constitution, and you will apply it if you can."

Meanwhile, on the Champ de Mars,[5] we will unanimously vote another constitution, and all France will vote one with us throughout the national territory, for such will be the wish and the need of the country. To this vote we will summon all humanity, and the reply will flow back like an electric current. Smilingly we shall bring you this constitution, which you will hasten to sign, happy to be delivered from the awful scourge of neglect and impotence. We will crown you with oak leaves and carry you in triumph.

To André Bontet, friend:[6]

Nohant, August 21, 1870

As for me, I am still today as red a socialist as ever. But agreement in matters of doctrine does not oblige me to comply with and adhere to a political program. Convictions must never be imposed by force. Such behavior is criminal and senseless, for everything born of violence must perish by violence.

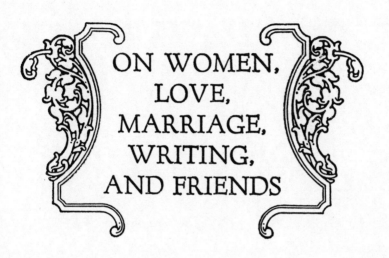

ON WOMEN,
LOVE,
MARRIAGE,
WRITING,
AND FRIENDS

One cannot say it, however often, without a certain awe. Collected, George Sand's work—novels, plays, essays, letters, sketches, short stories, prefaces, autobiographical writings—would total at least 150 volumes, and it would take another volume to contain nothing but the index of her vast range of subjects.

On women? The reader is referred simply to the index of this volume to see how that subject spreads throughout it. Similarly, on love and marriage—how many pages in Indiana alone?

George Sand examining her own writing, apologizing as she explains its faults, the pressing haste which emerges none the less as the unmatched "expressional ease" that won Henry James's admiration, captures our own. As for Marie Dorval, Delacroix, and Chopin, they were chosen for their closeness to Sand and for the occasion they provided to offer her insights on acting and the theater, music and the arts—indeed, her anticipation, in the persons of the artist and the composer, or more precisely their theories *about their work, of the Impressionists who would startle the world three decades later.*

Lettres à Marcie (*Letters to Marcie*), *from which extracts have been taken, is a series of six fictional letters to a young unmarried woman of little means named Marcie, counseling her on love, marriage, and much else called "feminine." They appeared serially (suffering some censorship) in Abbé Félicité de Lamennais's review* Le Monde *in 1837 and were published as a book much later. "Réponses à Diverses Objections" (Replies to a Few Objections) first appeared in* L'Éclaireur *of La Châtre, December 7, 1844, and was republished in the collection* Questions Politiques et Sociales *in 1879.*

The letter "To Members of the Central Committee of the Left" was an indirect reply to a proposal for Sand's candidacy in the forthcoming elections which had just appeared in La Voix des Femmes (*The Voice of Women*), *founded in March 1848 by feminist Eugénie Niboyet. The letter was never finished, for some unknown reason, or sent. The letter to Gustave Flaubert of August 20, 1872, was published in* Impressions et Souvenirs (*1873*). Lavinia *and* Jacques *are novels published in 1833 and 1834 respectively; the latter is the more enduring of the two.*

"À l'Ange Lélio" (To the Angel Lélio) is among the pages of Sand's miscellaneous journal Sketches and Hints (*1926*). *That title had been struck through and another substituted: "À*

l'Ange Sans Nom" (*To the Angel Without a Name*). *Sand further confused the possible reader as to the true identity of the "angel" (most likely Marie Dorval) by describing her prose poem as a "translation." The long extract on Marie Dorval, written in the form of an imaginary dialogue, originally appeared in the* Journal de Toulouse, *January 27, 1837, and was republished in the collection* Questions d'Art et de Littérature *(1878).*

The charming essay-short story on Eugène Delacroix and Frédéric Chopin was written in January 1841 but first published in Le Temps *of October 18, 1871 and republished in* Impressions et Souvenirs *(1873).* ⊱

On Women

From *Lettres à Marcie, No. 3*

The people are hungry. Pray, great minds, allow us to think of feeding the people before we consider building you temples. Women bewail their servitude. They must wait for men to achieve freedom, for freedom can not come out of slavery. Let the times be fulfilled and ideas reach their term. All this may not take as long as some hope and others fear. . . .

The only lot reserved for you is a life bounded by

the intellect, but the use of this intellect is just what society forbids you. You feel too full of youth and sympathy to limit yourself to the use of your mental ability. You tell yourself that at the age of twenty-five even the most gifted of men could not retire to the wilderness and devote himself to a wholly individual philosophy. Should God have bestowed greater strength upon woman than upon man? "No," you reply, "just let me lead a life of action. I feel myself to be an orator, a priest. I can and I want to fight, discuss and teach." If you can, Marcie, you are an exception, and in heroic times your name might have been Jeanne d'Arc, Madame Roland, Héloïse. But today, what is open to you? Try to find within the social hierarchy, among all the levels of government or industry, a single position which the very thought of your occupying does not seem laughable. Only the role of artist is open to you. . . .

The roles of the sexes have been laid down, their tasks allotted to them, and Providence gives each sex the tools and resources proper to it. Why should society overthrow such an admirable order and how could it eliminate the corruption that has infiltrated it by reversing the order of nature and giving women the same prerogatives as men? Society is full of abuses. Women complain of being brutally enslaved, badly educated, badly advised, badly guided, badly loved, and badly defended. Their complaints are justified, and rest assured that soon a thousand voices will be raised to demand remedy for these evils. But how could even honest judges have confidence in women who, coming forward to claim the dignity now refused them in the family home, especially the sacred authority over their children which they are denied, demand in recompense, not peace in the household or freedom for their motherly affections, but the right to take part in the political struggle, a sword and a helmet, the right to condemn to death? . . .

Please do not be bitter against me, my unlucky friend. Do not say that you defy me to follow my own advice. . . . I have told you before and I tell you again that my soul is as troubled and frightened as yours. And when I urge you to take courage, I am speaking to us both.

From *Lettres à Marcie, No. 6*

Women are given a deplorable education. This is men's greatest crime against them. Men have introduced abuses everywhere, monopolizing the advantages of the most consecrated institutions. They have played upon even the most innocent and legitimate feelings. They have succeeded in bringing about the enslavement and degradation of women, a condition which today they claim was instituted by God and is part of unchanging law.

To Abbé Lamennais:*

La Châtre (General Delivery), February 28, 1837

Without realizing it, you have drawn me onto uncertain ground. When I began these "Letters to Marcie," I had intended a less serious framework for them than the one in which I now find myself, pushed, despite myself, by the invincible *drive* of my modest reflections . . . What is most curious is that I who have written on this subject [women] all my life as a writer should hardly know what I adhere to; never having summed it up, never having come to anything but vague conclusions, I now arrive at them out of inspiration without knowing exactly where they come from, without knowing in the least whether or not I am mistaken, and without being able to stop myself from reaching them, discovering I know not what certainty in myself which is, perhaps, a voice of truth, or, perhaps, an impertinent voice of arrogant pride.

However, I am launched and now feel the desire to extend the framework of the "Letters to Marcie"

---

* Abbé Félicité de Lamennais (1782–1854) was a radical priest who had incurred the censure of the Vatican for his book *Paroles d'un Croyant* (Words of a Believer). Its Christian socialism and liberal humanitarianism had aroused George Sand's admiration and she met the author through another, younger admirer and mutual friend, Franz Liszt. When Lamennais became editor of *Le Monde,* he asked Sand for contributions. The series of *"Letters to Marcie"* resulted.

as far as I can, so as to include questions relating to women. I want to talk about all duties, marriage, maternity, etc., but I am afraid that in some instances I will be carried away by my natural irrepressibleness and go further than you might allow me should I not consult you in advance . . .

To sum up my bold proposals [for a seventh "Letter to Marcie"], they consist in calling for the right of divorce for married couples. Search as I might for the remedy to the outrageous injustices, endless miseries, often incurable passions troubling the union of the sexes, I have found no solution other than freedom to dissolve and remake marriages. I do not believe one should be able to do this lightly and for reasons less important than those now applying to legal separation, but (though for my part, I should prefer spending the rest of my life in jail to remarrying) I know affections so enduring, so imperious, that nothing in the old civil and religious law could possibly bridle them. Besides the fact that these affections become all the more powerful and worthy as the human intelligence is uplifted and refined, it is certain that in the past they could not be restrained and, as a consequence, sorely disturbed the social order. That disorder proved nothing against the law so long as it was provoked by vice and corruption. But many of sturdy soul, noble character, piety, and goodness have been dominated by passions which seem to have descended from heaven itself. What is one to say of that? And how can one write about women without discussing a question they put above all others and which occupies first place in their lives? . . .

Reply with a word. If you do not allow me to go on, I will end the "Letters to Marcie" where they are.†

From "Réponses à Diverses Objections"

1844

The pseudonym that conceals our sex is no mystery to any of those who grant our writings some attention. We do not credit the other sex with any inborn superiority, but we are forced to recognize the results of the incomplete education we have received, which does not allow us to lay claim to any kind of instruction. There is nothing in a woman's life equivalent to that basic schooling, that armed Minerva which, according to Diderot, emerges suddenly from the young graduate's brain to do battle with his first impressions and initial errors.

But that we do not possess knowledge does not imply we have no right to ask or seek for knowledge. Gone is the time when, thanks to aristocratic privilege and the fiats of Catholicism, ignorance was considered to be a life sentence and thinking to be a crime meriting the ax or the stake. We know that even now there are certain interests, certain prejudices which reject as

† Abbé Lamennais replied that he did not want a contribution advocating divorce, thus bringing the "Marcie" series to an end with the sixth letter.

a dangerous insurrection any progress of a given sex or a given class. But we have no doubt that those whom we are answering here are generous supporters of any kind of intellectual emancipation. Besides, if we did not speak up as women, we would still have the right to do so as the people. For apart from the fact that we are indissolubly linked to the people by the blood that courses through our veins, we see that there is a striking similarity between the cause of women and the cause of the people which make them interdependent. A common dependence, a common ignorance, and a common impotence bring them together. The same easily exploited enthusiasm, the same impetuous impulses free of rancor, quick to be stirred and easily won over by emotion; the same lively imagination, the same absence of forethought, the same recklessness, disregard for danger, and impatience with obstacles; the same instability, the same angers, the same resignation, the same storminess, the same disregard for the most serious personal and social interests. This similarity can be summed up in a single phrase: lack of instruction—a whole life of labor and feelings without sufficient knowledge, a whole world of dreams and yearnings without any positive certainty, without power, without initiative, without freedom.

This is not a personal plea. The sight of the sufferings of all long ago forced us to forget those who strike only at ourselves. We are not even making a special plea for the cause of women. We do not make divisions in the great, eternal cause of the poor and the ignorant to whom Jesus promised the kingdom of heaven and to whom the Church, failing to understand the words of its sublime master, has refused the kingdom of earth. But to those who with no little arrogance refer to us as a solitary voice we must humbly reply that we number in France about thirty million—proletarians, women, children, unlettered and oppressed of all kinds—who ask what must we believe and do in terms of ideas and what must we hope and call for in terms of basic education.

From a letter "To Members of the Central Committee of the Left":

Paris, mid-April 1848

I am not writing to thank you for inserting my name as a candidate on some forty lists of the Central Committee. My knowledge of myself does not allow me to believe that you wished to encourage me to come forward with an impossible candidacy, something I have never dreamed. You wished to consecrate a principle which you have evidently adopted. Allow me then to put to you some considerations on this very principle which it may now be timely to discuss and weigh seriously.

Should women participate one day in political life? Yes, one day. Here I agree with you. But is that day near? No, I do not think so. For the condition of women to be changed, society must first be changed radically.

Perhaps we already agree on these two questions. But this raises a third question. Some women ask, If society is to be changed, must not women intervene politically in public affairs from this very moment? I make so bold as to reply that they must not, because social conditions are such that women could not honorably and honestly exercise a political mandate.

As women are under the tutelage and domination of men through marriage, they cannot possibly give guarantees of political independence unless they individually, and in defiance of laws and customs, break this tutelage hallowed by custom and law.

Thus it seems senseless to me, and I ask forgiveness of those of my sex who have thought necessary to follow this line, to begin where one should end and end where one should begin. . . .

To leave no ambiguity about these considerations I am bringing forward, I shall express my whole thought concerning this famous emancipation of women, so much discussed of late.

I believe it to be easily and immediately realizable, in so far as the present state of our customs allows. It consists simply in giving back to women the civil rights which marriage alone deprives them of, which remaining single alone maintains for them. This detestable error of our legislation places woman under the covetous domination of man and transforms a married woman into an eternal minor; it might induce most young women never to marry, if they had the slightest idea about civil legislation at the time they give up their rights. It is strange that the guardians of the old order ostentatiously attach to their lying slogan the words of "family" and "property," since the marriage pact, as admired and proclaimed by them, totally destroys the property rights of one whole sex. Either property or marriage is not as holy as they declare, for two equally holy things cannot logically cancel out each other. . . .

Until civil equality is enshrined in the law there will certainly be exceptional and intolerable abuses of marital authority. The housewife and mother, still a minor at the age of eighty, is certainly in a ridiculous and humiliating situation. It is certain that the despotic powers attributed to the husband give him the right to refuse to provide for the material welfare of his wife and children; the right to commit adultery outside the home; the right to control alone, without his wife, the education of their children; a right to corrupt the latter through bad example or principles— for instance, by giving them his mistresses as governesses as has been known in illustrious families; the right to command the household and give orders to servants and maids; especially the right to insult his wife; the right to turn out the wife's parents while imposing on her his own; the right to reduce her to the hardships of poverty while squandering away her rightful income or capital on prostitutes; the right to beat her and have her complaints rejected by a court of law, if she fails to produce witnesses or recoils in the face of scandal; finally, the right to dishonor her

by unjust suspicions as well as to have her punished
for misbehavior. All these rights are barbarous, abominable, and inhumane, and I would go so far as to
say that they are the sole cause of the infidelities,
quarrels, scandals, and crimes which so often defile
the sanctuary of the family, and they will continue to
defile it, O poor human beings, until you do away
with the scaffold and prison chains for criminals, with
insults and domestic slavery, with prison and public
shame for unfaithful wives. Until that day, women
will always have the vices of the oppressed, that is to
say, the cunning ruses of slaves; and those among you
who are not in a position to be tyrants will be what so
many are today: the ridiculous slaves of these tyrants'
vengeful slaves. . . .

Yes, civil equality, equality in marriage, equality in
the family—that is what you should ask for, indeed
demand. . . . No man should obey a woman—that
would be monstrous; no man should give orders to a
woman—that is despicable.

To Gustave Flaubert:

Nohant, January 1, 1867

And then for people good at anatomy there is another
fact: there is only one sex. Men and women are so
much the same that one can hardly understand the
mass of differentiations and subtle arguments upon

413

which all societies have been nourished in this matter. I observed the childhood and the evolution of both my daughter and my son. My son was I—that is to say, a woman—much more than my daughter, who was an unsuccessful man.

To Gustave Flaubert:

Nohant, August 20, 1872

When we examine the thesis, at present upheld or contested by some very great minds, that man and woman, male and female, are essentially dissimilar beings subject to different laws, in my opinion we enter a world of conventional ideas, a world fabricated entirely of human conceits—whether imagination, study, revelation or fantasy, discovery or experiment, what difference? Science, mind, experience, or genius —you may speak, search, classify, and lay down the law as you please. It is the human mind that judges, debates, asserts. . . .

When, owing to the tendency to encompass the totality of things, one has become confirmed in belief in a dominant life force, one can no longer accept the sovereignty of convention: male dominating female or female dominating male. There is but one legitimate sovereign of their union: [natural] law. That law gives rise to males and females, females and males, who contribute by means which are not essentially different, despite what may be said, to a unique and single end—the reproduction of the species. Unity of end is the *supreme law* and adaptation of means is the consequence. Does the difference of the sexes lie in their reproductive organs? No, the sexes only express an interlocking of the organs necessary for the life-giving junction. This is obvious and perceptible in the most simple plants and the tiniest organized beings. There is but one being, split in two, so to say, aiming at that coming together which makes it whole and totally incapable of making this adaptation with a being from a different order.

Thus there is only one type in each species, a being split into two individuals whose union is necessary to reproduce life, a machine in two parts whose coupling is deliberate and necessary to produce action. . . .

So let us first do our best not to hate. It is only too true that hatred has entered love and that the relationships between men and women are often a savage struggle, a continual infringement upon ill-defined rights. Whatever stand we may take on these burning issues, let us endeavor to seek out all that tends toward a coming together of hearts, a union of intellects, bearing in mind the common goal: the child! . . .

But how? By what immediate means? I do not know! I have no ready-made theory, and if I had, I should distrust it, for fate has forced me into necessities contrary to my instincts and convictions. But I do know that the war of the sexes, as presently engaged in, does not yet seem to ask the right questions! Before I can hope for a valid solution I have to see the cause of love based upon the notions of equality before God, of similarity, or at least of assimilation, in natural law.

On Love

To Émile Paultre, friend:

Venice, June 25, 1834

Life is the most beautiful thing in the world when one is in love and the most detestable when one stops loving. In my opinion, love is all. And what do you think? You have no idea. Until now you have only loved out of necessity, and that necessity is superfluous in any true love. In true complete love, heart, mind, and body meet in understanding and embrace. Only once in a thousand years do we find these three united in perfect sympathy. But if there are only two in accord—body and mind without heart or heart and body without the mind—one imagines the existence of the third until its too painful absence destroys the links of sympathy between the other two.

From *Histoire de Ma Vie*

One of my friends, Dutheil, wishing to make the situation [with my husband] bearable, said that I could become mistress of it by becoming my husband's mistress. This was out of the question. Intimacy without love is a loathsome thing to consider. A woman who toys with her husband in order to dominate him is no better than the prostitute who does what she does for her daily bread or the courtesan for her luxury. Such reconciliation makes a husband a despicable plaything and a ridiculous dupe. . . . A complete man can only come out of a complete love. . . .

"In any case," I added, "once a human being, man or woman, has learned what complete love can be, he or she can never, and even more must never, fall back to the level of pure animality."

On Marriage

From *Lavinia*

[Lavinia to a suitor] "So far as the Count of Morangy is concerned, I have never loved him. He is one of the impotent thousands who were unable—even with my help, alas—to bring my dead heart back to life. I should not even want him for a husband. A man of his rank always sets too high a price on the protection he provides—by making you feel it. Besides, I hate marriage, I hate all men, I hate everlasting vows, promises, and plans, the future arranged in advance by contract and bargaining—at which destiny always has the last laugh."

From *Jacques*

[Jacques to his future wife] "I have not changed my mind. I am not reconciled to society, and marriage is still, to my way of thinking, one of the most barbarous institutions it has ever evolved. I do not doubt it will

be abolished if the human species makes some progress towards justice and reason. A more human and no
less sacred bond will replace it, assuring the existence
of children who will be born of a man and a woman
without forever enchaining the freedom of the one
and the other. . . .

"You are going to swear to be faithful and obedient
to me, that is, never to love anyone but me and to
obey me in everything. The first vow is absurd, the
second base. . . ."

To Hippolyte Chatiron, half-brother:

Paris, mid-February 1843

Try to prevent your son-in-law from brutalizing your
daughter on their wedding night, for many physical
weaknesses and painful childbirths among delicate
women stem from this cause alone. Men do not
sufficiently understand that their pleasure is our martyrdom. So tell him to restrain his pleasure and to wait
until he has little by little brought his wife to understanding and response. Nothing is more horrible than
the terror, the sufferings, and the revulsion of a poor
girl, ignorant of the facts of life, who finds herself
raped by a brute. As far as possible we bring them up
as saints, and then we hand them over as if they were
fillies. If your son-in-law is an intelligent man, and if
he truly loves your daughter, he will understand what

must be done, and he will not resent your talking it over with him the day before.

From *Histoire de Ma Vie*

Wealth and education, wit and polished manners, what is called "society" took on tangible forms which I could grasp. What it comes down to, I said to myself, is to become a pretty woman—smart, superior, schooled—playing a piano for people who nod approval without either listening or understanding, caring about no one, wanting to sparkle, aspiring to a rich marriage, selling her freedom and person for a carriage, a coat of arms, fine rags, and a few coins.

On Writing

From Preface to *Lettres d'un Voyageur*

. . . it is at times when my tired novelist's brain is drained of heroes and adventures that, distraught and anxious like an impresario whose company is late at curtain time, I come on stage in my dressing gown, to recite uncertainly the prologue of the awaited play. I believe that for those who take an interest in the secret processes of the human heart, certain seemingly insignificant family letters or actions of the artist would be the most explicit foreword, the clearest introduction to his work.

May the lovers of fiction nevertheless be a little forgiving. I have worked for them in several of these letters, dressing up my dull image, my poor self, in unaccustomed clothes, hiding as far as possible its physical existence behind a truer, more interesting imaginary existence. Thus, when reading these letters, one can hardly tell whether the impressions related are those of a young or old man, an adult or a child. . . . Thus, when I have spoken at times like a vagrant schoolboy, like a gouty old uncle, or like an eager young soldier,

I have in fact done nothing but portray my soul under the form it then assumed: carefree and sprightly, now tired and brooding, now young and impetuous.

From *Lettres d'un Voyageur, No. 6*

Paris, April 1835

Swept along by an inevitable destiny, neither greedy nor extravagant, the victim of unforeseen setbacks and responsible for dear, precious lives whose only bread-winner I was, I have never been a true artist, although I have felt all the weariness, ardor, enthusiasm and suffering of this hallowed profession. True glory had never crowned my efforts for rarely have I been able to wait for inspiration. Always in a hurry, forced to earn my living, I have pressed my imagination to produce, without bothering to enlist the aid of reason. When my muse refused to surrender, I have violated her and her revenge has been frigid caresses and somber revelations. . . .

Doing my best, I might never have done anything tolerable. But when the artist settles at his table to work, he believes in himself, otherwise he wouldn't do so. Then, be he great, mediocre, or worthless, he strives and hopes. But if his time is limited, if a creditor is waiting at the door, if a child who fell asleep without dinner reminds him of his misery and of the need to finish before dawn, I can assure you that, however small his talent may be, he has to make a great sacrifice and suffer deep humiliation in his own eyes. He watches others working slowly, reflectively, lovingly. He sees them carefully rereading their writings, correcting, meticulously polishing, then sprinkling them with a thousand precious gems, removing the tiniest specks of dust, and keeping them to review them again, to transcend even perfection itself. But unfortunate is he who works with trowel and spade to build a rough-hewn, formless work, at times full of vitality but always incomplete, hasty, and feverish. The ink has hardly time to dry before the manuscript must be turned in without being reread, without having even a single error corrected!

To François Buloz, editor of La Revue des Deux Mondes:

Nohant, September 15, 1841

Following your second letter, and after going over my manuscript,‡ I clearly see that you are asking something impossible. You simply want me to speak of a given period without letting my characters take part in it; I must show students of 1831 loyal to Louis Philippe's government, proletarian democrats undistressed by the restoration of the monarchy after the events of

‡ *Horace* (1842), a proletarian novel describing the massacre of students and workers in 1832 by Louis Philippe's government.

July. You want working girls who are not working girls and whose lives I must not explore. You want me to speak of the bourgeoisie without calling it stupid and unjust. I must mention society without saying that I find it ruthless and absurd. Finally, I am not allowed to have an opinion and a point of view concerning the events I recount and the settings in which I place them. You think that I am declining, but, to be honest, my poor Buloz, I am tempted to have the same opinion of you. Reread a few pages of *Jacques* or *Mauprat*. In all my books, even the most anodyne, even in the *Mosaïstes* or *La Dernière Aldini*, you will find continuous opposition to your bourgeoisie, your serious-minded men, your governments, your social inequality, and constant sympathy for men of the people. Bénédict is a peasant, Nello (from *La Dernière Aldini*) is a gondolier, Simon is also a peasant, Geneviève a working girl. If I could recall everything I have written on this subject, you would not find a single volume of mine where inequality and privilege (money being the first of these privileges) are not attacked. How is it that this has never scandalized you before and suddenly revolts you now? . . .

Even if you could prove that this will discredit me, be my undoing, ruin me, I remain stubborn on this matter and would happily ruin myself so long as I can write what I think. Until now I have been able to do so and still make a living. Even if luck has turned, I shall not turn with it, as you well know, and neither interest nor vanity can win me over. . . .

I can no longer let you deal with the rest of my

novel, unless you accept it as it is. For I cannot haggle over my freedom, which must be complete or else I shall resign. It is of course understood that when I sell this manuscript, I shall pay back the money you have advanced me.

To Henriette de La Bigottière, friend:

Paris, end of December 1842

Each to his or her task. I do what I can. As a born storyteller, I write novels; that is to say, I seek by the means of a given art form to provoke emotions, to stir, to excite, and even to shock the hearts of those among my contemporaries who are capable of emotion and who need to be provoked. Those who are not so susceptible say that I am a dispenser of poison, because I agitate the bitter sediment of the wine of their insolent self-intoxication. Those who believe, who are strong and sure, do not need my novels. They never read them. They ignore them. They are the people I admire and value most. Consequently I do not work for them, but for lesser intellects.

Those who find perversity in my writings are perverts themselves. Those who see suffering, weakness, doubts, efforts, and above all impotence, see only what I see myself. Have I ever contested these criticisms and judgments? Not at all. But I have been able to move my readers, and emotion leads to reflection and heart-searching. That is all I want. To make people question accepted lies, to call out for forgotten truths, is enough for me. My mission is no more exalted than that.

From *Histoire de Ma Vie*

I did not have the shadow of a theory when I started to write, and do not believe that I have even had one when the desire to write a novel made me take up my pen. Nevertheless, all unknowingly, my instincts have provided me with the theory which I am going to set out here, which I have generally followed, quite unaware, and which at the present moment is still under discussion.

According to this theory, a novel is as much a work of poetry as of analysis. True and even real situations and characters are needed, grouped around a character intended to sum up the feeling or the main idea of the book. The character usually embodies the passion called "love," since almost all novels are love stories. According to this theory (and as its starting point), love, and consequently the character, must be idealized and invested with all the powers one may aspire to or all the pains one has seen or felt the pangs of. But the character must never be sullied by the chance course of events. He must either die or triumph, and the writer should not fear to grant him exceptional importance in life, uncommon powers, charm, or suffering beyond what is normal for a human being, even beyond what most minds would consider credible. . . .

Is this a valid theory? I think so. But it is not, and must not be, the only one. Balzac has, with time, brought home to me the variety and power of his ideas, that the idealization of the subject could be sacrificed to the truth of the portrait, to the criticism of society and even of humanity.

Balzac summed this up completely when he replied to me: "You are seeking for human beings as they should be, I take them as they are. Believe me, we are both right. The two paths lead to a common goal. I, too, love exceptional beings; I am one myself. What is more, I have to be, to make my vulgar characters stand out, and I never sacrifice them unless I am forced to. But these vulgar beings interest me more than they interest you. I exalt and idealize them in the opposite direction, increasing their ugliness or their stupidity. I give their deformities frightening, grotesque proportions. You, you could not. You do well not to turn your attention to beings or things which might give you nightmares. To idealize the pretty and the beautiful is a woman's task."

Balzac, whose comprehensive mind, although neither infinite nor faultless, is the most complete, most capable among novelists of our time, Balzac, unequaled master in the art of depicting modern society and today's humanity, was a thousand times right to deny the existence of a single absolute system. . . . He has tried everything. He has seen and proved that all methods are good and all subjects inspiring for a flexible mind like his.

To Gustave Flaubert:

Nohant, December 18–19, 1875

I find that your school does not give attention to the substance of things, that it is too superficial. In striving after style, it gives too little account of substance and remains directed to men of letters. But, strictly speaking, there is no such thing as a "man of letters." First and foremost, one is man. We try to find man at the bottom of every story and every event. This was the weakness of *L'Éducation Sentimentale*, which I have thought so much about since, wondering why such a well-structured, solid work should have evoked such recriminations. Its weakness was the absence of positive action by the characters. They were subject to events; they never controlled them. Well, I think that the main interest of a story lies precisely in the aspect which you did not want to handle. If I were you, I would try the opposite. For the moment you are rereading Shakespeare, and this is wise! *There* is a writer who puts men at grips with events. You may notice that, for good or for evil, his characters always dominate events. They either make events or perish with them.

On Friends

Marie Dorval, Eugène Delacroix, Frédéric Chopin

*"À l'Ange Lélio"**

[*1833*]

Behold, the dawn is breaking. Come, for the dew will soon fall and you may catch cold. No, you do not fear the cold, nor the penetrating mist. But come! it is your hour, my window is open, my room full of flowers. I await you.

If you do not come soon, I shall fall asleep, for it is the hour of slumber. Ah, here you are at last! Blessed art thou, heavenly child! Give me thy forehead to kiss, let thy black hair fall across my breast, thy lovely hair a cubit long!

How beautiful is an angel with floating hair in the morning! Why do not men have such long hair?

Come, nameless one, sit by my bedside. You speak no language, you do not reveal yourself in words. How I love you thus, how well I understand you!

Angel of silence, place your cool hand on my shoul-

* Most likely Marie Dorval. See Chronology, 1833, p. xxxi.

der, warm with love, but upon which no man has ever put his lips. Only your sweet breath, your damp hair, can freshen it.

What flowers are those on your forehead, in your hands? Flowers unknown, flowers more beautiful than any woman on earth. Their perfume is intoxicating, my angel, spread them over me, cover me with leaves from your dewy crown.

Enough, my angel! I am dying! I want to live for tomorrow to see you again. Adieu, the day grows bright. Go quickly, my treasure, so that none may see you, for they would steal you from me, and then I should have to give myself to men. Adieu, let me kiss thy snowy neck and thy forehead, where shines a star. Give me a feather from thy wing that I may keep it as proof of thy visit, a souvenir of my rapture.

Why do not men have wings so that they might come at night and fly away in the morning? I prefer thistledown to any man! You blow upon it, and it is lost in the wind. No man ever becomes lighter, evanescing into spirit.

Go then, morning angel! I am falling asleep. Kiss me on the forehead and make my soul as beautiful as thine.

From *Questions d'Art et de Littérature:*

January 1837

"To have some idea of the power she [Marie Dorval] has over me," Mario† said, "you would have to know how different her nature is from mine. God has blessed her with the power to give voice to the things she feels; she can pour out her soul; she knows that she can do this; she is gifted with an expressive, expansive, powerful sensitivity, and indeed everything else which stems from a passionate heart and strong intellect. That beautiful, simple woman has learned nothing; she has divined everything. Poor, abandoned, and unappreciated as she was, nobody took the trouble to embellish her mind and guide her feelings; this is why she has made herself so great, when finally she managed to break through; this is why this great tragedienne is so true, so unchanged, so much a woman! Watch her . . . listen to her, Évan! Oh! how artless! artless and passionate! and young, and sweet, and trembling, and terrible! Now you understand how she has captivated a poor, weak, suffering heart like mine!"

"I know, Mario, that you are of a somber, intense disposition; you are said to be distrustful and haughty, but I judge you rather to be shy."

"I may be all those things," said Mario. "I do not

† In this imaginary conversation, Sand is assuming the name of Mario, addressing an equally fictional Évan.

know how to explain in a few words the cold, incomplete side of my nature; I am unable to express anything. My brain is affected by a kind of paralysis which prevents my giving expression to my feelings . . . You see, there are days when, if I could put on paper the flood of pain, anger, love, or hate which I repress within myself, I would willingly dip my pen in the last drop of my blood. Oh! if we could only say how we suffer, then perhaps we would suffer no more! For somebody else would understand us, pity and comfort us! But I can never be more than half understood, and that is not enough for me. Everything I write is dull and cold like tomorrow's afterthoughts. The spoken word is such a pale reflection of thought! To write, my friend, is the torment of life, the agony of whoever still feels a heart in his breast, a relentless struggle between desire and impotence, a man of high aspirations forever rolling a stone upon which the palace of his dreams can never be built. Oh, Sisyphus! Poor poet!

"But, listen, if, when I take my seat here, when I throw myself on these theater benches, all oppressed by the violence of my pain, burning with fever, my brain aching and heavy, my marble-cold lips smarting with bitterness, tears refusing to flow in my arid eyes, if this woman with her wasp waist, her carefree step, her sad, penetrating look, appears on the stage, do you know what I imagine?—May God forgive me this innocent conceit!—It seems to me that I am watching my own soul, that my soul has dressed up in this pale and sad and beautiful shape to show itself to me, to reveal itself to me and to humanity.

"And then this woman speaks. She cries, she curses, she invokes, she orders, she grieves! Oh, how she cries out! How she suffers! What fierce pleasure I experience seeing her cry this way! She pours out all these sensations, as pure and violent as they come to her; this soul conceives and produces at the same instant; this woman is herself that which she seems to be; in her, passion and suffering are not merely replicas, like the words I use or the sentences I write. Harsh, gripping inspiration emanates from her as pure as it comes to her; it is the fiery breath of heaven come down upon her, passing through this soul, there to cool itself."

From *Impressions et Souvenirs:*

Paris, January 1841

I have spent half my day with Eugène Delacroix. I would like to recall everything he said to me. I shall not be able to transcribe him well. He speaks better than I write. When I came upon him, I was deeply upset. I had just met that raving maniac —— who had expounded to me the strangest theories concerning drawing and color, studies which, according to him, were exclusive, one of the other.

I told Delacroix about the argument from which I have emerged with my head spinning: "Please, tell me, my friend, is this man in his right mind?"

DELACROIX: "Oh, uh, yes! He is wrong, but he does

not think he is wrong. He argues his error and he hangs on to it, believing he has hold of a truth. What can one say? He did not invent this heresy; it is taught in the highest places. M. Ingres's whole school has decreed that color is a superfluity and that it is most dangerous to fall in love with a detail detrimental to the purity of line. They have systematized this idea to the extent of valuing only Raphael's early style and of admiring the primitive masters unreservedly."

I: "I know. They profoundly despise the Venetian school, Titian first of all."

DELACROIX: "And the Dutch school too! Rembrandt is a dauber, Teniers is depraved. And all the Spanish, Velázquez included! And the great Rubens nauseates them! This makes you indignant? Oh, well! I, too, was indignant as long as I believed it to be a matter of genuine error. But this whole doctrine is in fact nothing but humbug, a eunuch's joke, and now that I know this, I laugh instead of getting angry."

I: "It is all very well for you to be philosophical. But in the meantime the public, which is no artist and understands nothing of definitions, is the dupe of silly judgments and stock phrases: 'Rubens's color work is beautiful, but he does not draw. Rembrandt achieves some happy effects, but he spoils them, he ignores line. Raphael alone knows how to draw. Michelangelo is a madman capable only of conjuring up monsters. Pure art is uniform tint and outline.' The Ingres school establishes this and the bourgeois adds: 'It seems to be the truth.' "

DELACROIX: "Oh, well! What does it matter to us if the bourgeois talks nonsense?"

I: "I care a lot. The bourgeois represents the beast we could have been, if our tastes had not been formed and our feelings elevated. Why does criticism, whose mission is to enlighten—"

DELACROIX: "Oh, criticism is usually the work of the bourgeois or of some young literary men who turn bourgeois to gain readers. Look at writers who have taste, originality, and independence! They are not understood. They are preaching in the wilderness."

I: "I am not so pessimistic as that. I am convinced that many men of letters have no fixed ideas and if art was proved to—"

DELACROIX: "Nonsense! Painting is something that not everyone can judge. It requires special talent and special training. The young men of letters who need to write articles to make a living do their best to interview a painter, and then write down what he dictates. If the painter talks nonsense, so much the worse! But please do not make me speak any more. I have a sore throat."

[SAND:] "I will leave you, apart from anything else I cannot breathe in here. But I warn you that I take my anger with me, further increased by your present indifference."

"Just a moment! You think me calmer than I am; but I have seen Ingres's *Stratonice* again and, well, I am as naïve as anybody, I find it charming."

"So much the better for you. I find it puerile and affected."

435

"That may be. It is pretentiously infantile, but with such pretty little details, such finish in the cutting up!"

"Cutting up is the word! It is made the same way as a Chinese fan, tiny ivory figures glued together. Well now, good day and good-by."

"Yes, good-by. But—why don't you talk to me without making me talk? I want to know why you dislike M. Ingres."

"I never said that. I like M. Ingres in spite of the fact that, and not because, he is systematic. He is half a genius, has immense talent and above all an elevated mind. He lacks half of painting, half of vision, half of life. This is a serious infirmity, but could be forgiven if he did not make a system out of his incapacity."

[DELACROIX:] "Oh, but wait! When we look at an *objet d'art* we should never ask ourselves what its author is thinking or saying. We must judge the work and forget the man. I know very well that, in private, M. Ingres calls me a cad and a nonentity, and that he dismisses his pupils if he thinks he perceives in them an inclination toward color. But I want to forget everything about him when I am judging his pictures."

"That is very kind of you, but when this picture further accentuates a deplorable prejudice, a haughty blindness, a mental paralysis erected into a law, I cannot stop myself from deploring the master's error and being angry with the adulatory school which confirms him in his madness."

"So you believe that *Stratonice* indicates a decline—"

"Please do not talk any more, and let me leave. It is dinner time."

"Already? Where are you dining?"

[Sand:] "At home. Will you join us?"

"Dine at your home, with your family? I am tempted! You will not let me talk?"

"We will make you hold your tongue. Get ready, I shall wait for you."

He goes into the bedroom, but leaves the door open, speaking in a loud voice and forcing me to explain what shocks me in *Stratonice!* But he does not let me tell him. The act of taking off his slippers and dressing gown restores his natural vivacity and it is no longer I but he who speaks and criticizes.

[Delacroix:] "Look! Old Ingres has done his best to be a colorist and his understanding of it is quite comical. You were wrong a few minutes ago. His prejudice is not so strong as all that! He does what he can, you can be sure! Only he confuses coloring with color. This is an old notion, extremely bourgeois, and on this subject he is as ignorant as his gatekeeper. Have you noticed that in *Stratonice* there is an abundance of very clever, very elaborate, very iridescent coloring which does not produce the least effect of color? There is a mosaic pavement, so accurate as to make a teacher of perspective despair. From foreground to background there are perhaps a thousand tiny lozenges rigorously accurate in the convergence of their lines. Which does not prevent that pavement from standing as straight as a wall. It shines like a mirror. One could use it to shave; but unless one were a fly, one would never dare to walk on it. With the tiniest touch of real color, his pavement would have receded and there would have been no need for all his thousand little lines. And yet he has tried to introduce effects of light, but again these are marked out with ruler and compass. It seems as though they have been positioned for all time and that M. Ingres's sun will never move in relation to the earth. But never mind! He has put sunlight where it is absolutely needed and I am convinced that he is very pleased. He thinks that light was made to beautify. He does not realize that it was made above all to give life. With the most delicate precision he has studied the most minor effects of daylight on marble, gildings, and materials. The only thing he forgot was reflection. Oh, yes, reflection! *There* is a thing he has never heard of. He does not suspect that everything in nature is reflection and that all color is an exchange of reflections. On all the objects in front of him he has sprinkled spots of sunlight, as though in a daguerreotype, and there is neither sun, nor light, nor air in any of it. Antiochus' bed seems to retreat into the wall; the invalid seems to have taken root in it. In vain does he struggle, by a very pretty movement, to hide his blush. It is not *Stratonice,* but the agony of being rooted to the narrow confines of his bed that makes him to writhe. The background figures suffer the same torture and make incredible efforts to detach themselves from the sticky walls. Nothing stands out and consequently nothing exists in this charming but curiously foolish picture. Oh, I know well what he must have thought! He said to himself: 'I want to create an irreproachable work; I do not only want it to teach and demonstrate; I want it to please. I will cram it with color. If it is color you want, well, color you shall get! I am going to amaze my opponents. They will have no arguments left. They will be beaten on all fronts. Come here, my pupils, and watch, I will show you what color really is!' And then, afterward, he sets about adding tone to his work, like nonpareil on a cake. He puts a red on a mantle, lilac on a cushion, green here, blue there: bright red, tender green, sky blue. He has a feel for adornment and a knowledge of dress. In hair and materials he intertwines ribbons, an exquisitely fresh lilac, trimmings, a thousand amusing ornamental trifles, none of which help in the production of color. The pale, tarnished tints of an old wall by Rembrandt are far richer than this profusion of bright tones, plastered over objects, which he will never succeed in bringing into harmony by the necessary interplay of reflections and which remain crude, isolated, cold, gaudy. You may notice that gaudy colors are always cold!"

"Speaking of cold, wrap yourself up well. It is rather chilly."

"I am ready now. I do not want to talk any more."

We arrive at my door, and despite his intention, he has not stopped jeering at the so-called color of the Ingres school. He calls them "image makers," "manuscript illuminators," *pasticheurs*. My anger is spent, but it has passed to him. Chopin joins us on the doorstep, and there they are, climbing the stairs together discussing *Stratonice*. Chopin dislikes it because the figures are mannered and without real emotion. But the finish of the painting pleases him, and, as for color, he politely says that he knows nothing about that—not aware that in so saying he is telling the truth!

Chopin and Delacroix love each other, one might almost say tenderly. Their characters are very related and they possess the same great qualities of heart and mind. But in matters of art, Delacroix understands and adores Chopin, while Chopin does not understand Delacroix. He values, loves, and respects the man; he hates the painter. Delacroix's more diversified faculties permit him to appreciate music. He knows and understands it. His taste is exquisite and discerning. He never tires of listening to Chopin, he relishes him, he knows him by heart. Chopin accepts this adoration and is touched by it; but when confronted with one of his friend's paintings, he suffers and does not know what to say to him. He is a musician, nothing but a musician. His thought can only express itself in music. He has infinite wit, finesse, and irony, but he has no understanding of painting or sculpture. Michelangelo frightens him. Rubens horrifies him. Whatever seems eccentric scandalizes him. He retreats into all that is most narrow and conventional. Strange anomaly! His genius is the most original and individual there is. But he does not want to be told so. It is true that Delacroix's taste in literature tends toward the most classical and formalistic.

There is nothing for them to argue about. I listen to them. But here comes Maurice [Sand's son, Delacroix's pupil] and opens the discussion at dessert. He wants Delacroix to explain the mystery of reflections, and Chopin listens, wide-eyed with astonishment.

The master draws a comparison between tints in painting and tones in music. "In music," he says, "harmony does not only consist in the composition of chords, but also in their relations, in their logical succession, their sequence, in what I might even call their auditive reflections. Well, painting is no different! For instance, take that blue cushion and the red carpet. Put them next to each other. You can see that where the two colors touch, they capture something from each other. The red becomes tinted with blue, the blue becomes washed with red, and in the middle purple is created. You can cram a picture with the most violent colors: if you give them the reflection that unites them, your work will never be gaudy. Is nature ever spare with colors? Does she not overflow with ferocious contrasts which never destroy her harmony? Here everything is linked by reflection. Some people claim that they can do away with this in painting; it is possible, but there is a slight drawback; they do away with painting at the same time."

Maurice remarks that the art of reflections is the most difficult in the world.

"No!" says the master. "It is as easy as A B C. This I can prove, as easily as that two plus two makes four. The reflection of a given color on another given color invariably gives a third color, as I have already told and showed you a score of times."

"Very well," says the pupil, "but what about the reflection of a reflection?"

"My God! You are really hard to please! This is asking too much in one day."

Maurice is right; the reflection of a reflection takes

us into the realms of infinity, as Delacroix well knows. But he will never be able to prove it, because he is constantly searching for it and he has admitted to me that he owes it more often to inspiration than to science. He may teach the grammar of his art; but genius cannot be taught. Color holds unfathomable mysteries, tints produced by relationships which have no names and are not to be found on any palette. There are no absolute limits to these interpenetrating reflections, and their mysterious marriage is constantly born from combinations which may accumulate without ever becoming heavy. There is no black in nature. There are no dead points in painting. Anybody in contact with another body gives out and receives flashes of color. Brighter colors dominate the less bright, but never to the extent of nullifying its effect. This is the secret of the transparency of shadows; it is also the source of the relief of objects, which Ingres's disciples totally ignore.

"I venture to convey as well as I can my appreciation," [concludes Delacroix.]

Chopin fidgets on his chair. "Please let me stop for breath," he says, "before we pass on to relief. Reflection is really quite enough for the moment. All this is ingenious; it is new to me, but it is a little like alchemy."

"No," says Delacroix, "it is pure chemistry. Tints are broken down and recombine at every instant, and reflection cannot be set apart from relief any more than a line can be separated from the model. They [the Ingres school] believe that they have invented, or at least discovered, line! That is to say, they believe they have caught the contour. Well they have not caught it at all! The contour makes fun of them, turns its back on them. Wait, Chopin! I know what you are about to say: contour is that which prevents objects from merging into one another. But nature is sparing of clear outlines. Light, which is her life and her way of existence, is constantly breaking up silhouette, and instead of drawing things flat, it raises everything to relief. If you make a line drawing of my shape on a slate, however pleasant this line may be, you will not have made a picture of my whole person. Nevertheless, if you are a colorist, you will succeed in conveying by this simple line that I have a certain density, a relief, a body. How will you manage this? By not marking the outline evenly, by making it very fine, almost interrupted in some places and marking it more strongly in other places with a second line, and, if need be, even with a third, or else with a wider, fattened line which never must be too dense, because wherever I have seen relief—and I do not know of a single, entirely flat point on the human body, be it the size of a wafer—it has never been brought out by an opaque outline. Neither the light that falls on this outline nor the shadow that creeps over it has any detectable beginning or end. If you draw a naked body, a face, or a hand, it is something quite different. Flesh is an insatiable absorber of light and an inexhaustible source of exchange of reflection. It reflects everything and is reflected on itself *ad infinitum*. Take a naked child by Rubens. It is a rainbow melted onto flesh, illuminating and penetrating it, giving it glow, relief, circulation, palpitation, life which overflows the canvas. Because, you see, painting is not only this"—he drew, in the air, a horizontal arc from his left to his right shoulder—"it is also this!" And he drew a convex arc from his forehead to his breast.

"Well, Ingres's disciples have tried to change nature! They have made man into a slate with well-defined borders, and to remove all doubts about their intentions, some of them only make flat tinted silhouettes stuck onto gilt backgrounds. I admit that this is a way of simplifying art, but an even better one would be to do away with art altogether. You, for instance, Maurice, you like to draw great numbers of human figures, and you would like to get fifty thousand on a single sheet of paper. I will teach you an excellent way to do so. Draw a wall and write on it: 'Just now five hundred thousand men are passing behind this wall!'

"You will have spared yourself the effort of learning how to draw them, and in these days you may even have more success than I, who have been stupid enough to want to learn."

Chopin is no longer listening. He is at the piano and does not notice that we are listening to him. He improvises at random. Then he stops. "Well, well," Delacroix cries out, "you are not finished yet!"

"I have not even started," [says Chopin.] "Nothing comes to me—nothing but reflections, shadows, reliefs that refuse to stay put. I am looking for the right color and I cannot even find the right line."

"You will not find the one without the other," replies Delacroix, "and you'll find them both together."

"But if all I find is moonlight?"

"Then you will have found the reflection of a reflection," says Maurice. . . .

Chopin speaks seldom and little of his art; but when he does, it is with a wonderful sharpness and soundness of judgment and intent, which could demolish any number of heresies if only he would speak out freely.

But even in private he remains reserved and his only real confidant is his piano. Nevertheless, he promises us to write a treatise wherein he will deal not only with technique but also with doctrine. Will he keep his word?

In his moments of expansiveness Delacroix also promises to write a treatise on drawing and color. But he never will, even though he writes wonderfully well. These inspired artists are condemned to be always looking ahead, with never a moment to look back.

The doorbell rings; startled, Chopin stops playing. I tell the servant that I am home to nobody.

"Oh yes," says Chopin, "you are home to him."

"Who is it then?"

"Mickiewicz."‡

"Oh yes, of course! But how do you know that it is he?"

"I do not, but I am certain of it. I was thinking of him."

It is indeed he. He shakes hands warmly with everybody, then quickly settles in a corner, begging

‡ Adam Mickiewicz (1798–1855), perhaps Poland's greatest romantic poet, lived in exile in Paris, where he became a close friend of Chopin and Sand.

Chopin to continue. Chopin continues. He is inspired, he is sublime. But the young servant rushes in terribly frightened: the house is on fire!—We go to take a look. Indeed the fire has started in my bedroom, but there is still time. Quickly we put it out. Nevertheless we are thus occupied for more than an hour. After this we ask: "What about Mickiewicz? Where can he be?" We call his name; he does not answer. We return to the drawing room, he is not there.—Oh, but yes, there he is in the little corner where we had left him. The lamp has burned out, but he has not noticed; there has been a lot of noise and movement just a pace or two from him, but he has not heard a thing; he did not even wonder why we had left him alone. He has not even realized that he was alone. He was listening to Chopin; he continued to hear him.

In somebody else this might seem like affectation. But this great poet, gentle and humble, is as simple as a child, and when he sees me laughing, he asks, "What is the matter?"

"Nothing, but the first time a house we two are in together catches on fire, my first move will be to make sure you are safe, because otherwise you would burn like a chip of wood, without even realizing it."

"Really?" he says. "I did not know!" And he leaves without another word.

Chopin escorts Delacroix home. The latter, back again in the real world, speaks of his English tailor and seems to have no other worry in the whole world than how to get clothes which are very warm without being heavy.

Notes

CHRONOLOGY

1. 1830: "Good God! What a testament! . . ." George Sand, *Correspondance*, ed. Georges Lubin, vol. 1, pp. 737–38. Cf. Joseph Barry, *Infamous Woman*, p. 109.

2. 1833: "I wept from the suffering . . ." Sand, op. cit., vol. 2, p. 375.

3. 1839: ". . . filth and prostitution . . ." Capo de Feuillide, in *Europe Littéraire*, August 9–22, 1833.

4. 1848: ". . . the heaviest load of oppression . . ." *Bulletins de la République Émanés du Ministre de l'Intérieur* (Paris, 1848), p. 45.

5. 1876: "*La Tour de Percemont* pleased me . . ." Gustave Flaubert, *Oeuvres. Correspondance*, vol. 15, p. 145.

INDIANA (1832)

1. Cf. Joseph Barry, *Infamous Woman*, p. 125.

2. George Sand, *Correspondance*, ed. Georges Lubin, vol. 2, pp. 173–74.

3. Using her pseudonym for the first time, George Sand established the practice of referring to herself as a male writer. The preface itself indicates the critical reception Sand anticipated for *Indiana*.

4. This preface was written for a low-priced, popular edition of Sand's collected works. By 1842, Sand had become a major literary force in France and the preface shows her realization of that fact.

LÉLIA (1833)

1. Both versions of *Lélia* (1833 and 1839) are contained in Pierre Reboul's meticulously annotated edition, *Lélia* (Paris: Garnier Frères, 1960).

CONSUELO and THE COUNTESS DE RUDOLSTADT (1842–44)

1. For further reading on the importance, significance, and influence of *Consuelo*—an influence that extended from Henrik Ibsen's wife, if not Ibsen himself, to Feodor Dostoevski and particularly to Walt Whitman—see Ellen Moers's *Literary Women*, especially the chapter titled, "Traveling Heroinism: Gothic for Heroines," though the entire work is rich with insight, perception, and appreciation; and Esther Shephard's *Walt Whitman's Pose* (New York: Harcourt, Brace, 1938), pp. 17 passim. Cf. Joseph Barry, *Infamous Woman*, pp. 266–68.

POLITICAL WRITINGS

1. Cf. Henri Lefebvre, *Musset*, pp. 26–27.

2. "Letter to the Rich," an essay first published in 1848, appears in George Sand, *Questions Politiques et Sociales*, pp. 225–30, a posthumous collection of articles.

3. Claude Henri de Saint-Simon (1760–1825) and his followers, brought to the fore by the July Revolution of 1830, called for the community of goods, the abolition of inheritance, and the enfranchisement of women. Soon after, they organized popular meetings urging complete equality between men and women and freedom in love instead of "the tyranny of marriage."

4. "Socialism" also appears in Sand, op. cit., pp. 258–87.

5. A Paris military drilling ground where the Republic planned to hold a popular demonstration.

6. Extract of a letter indicating Sand's political attitude late in life.

Principal Works of George Sand*

1831	Rose et Blanche (signed "J. Sand"; written with Jules Sandeau)
1832	Indiana
	Valentine
1833	Lélia
1834	Le Secrétaire Intime
	Jacques
1835	André
	Leone Leoni
1836	Simon
1837	Mauprat
	Lettres d'un Voyageur
	Lettres à Marcie (serially only, in a review)
	Les Maîtres Mosaïstes
1838	La Dernière Aldini
1839	L'Uscoque
	Spiridion
	Lélia (revised)
1840	Gabriel
	Les Sept Cordes de la Lyre
	Le Compagnon du Tour de France

* See Chronology (p. xxvii) for other works, as well as Bibliography, below.

1841	*Pauline*
1842	*Un Hiver à Majorque*
	Horace
1842–43	*Consuelo*
1843	*Fanchette*
1843–44	*La Comtesse de Rudolstadt* (sequel to *Consuelo*)
	La Politique et le Socialisme (series of four articles)
1845	*Le Meunier d'Angibault*
1846	*Isidora*
	La Mare au Diable
1847	*Le Péché de M. Antoine*
	Lucrezia Floriani
1848	"Aux Riches"
	Lettres au Peuple
	"Socialisme"
1849	*La Petite Fadette*
1850	*François le Champi*
1851	*Claudie* (play)
	Le Château des Désertes
	Le Mariage de Victorine (play)
1853	*Les Maîtres Sonneurs*
1854–55	*Histoire de Ma Vie*
1855	*Maître Favilla* (play)
1857	*La Daniella*
1858	*Les Beaux Messieurs de Bois-Doré*
1859	*L'Homme de Neige*
	Elle et Lui
1861	*Le Marquis de Villemer*
	Valvèdre
1862	*Souvenirs et Impressions Littéraires*
1863	*Mademoiselle la Quintinie*
1866	*Monsieur Sylvestre*

1867	*Le Dernier Amour*
1868	*Mademoiselle Merquem*
1870	*Pierre Qui Roule*
	Malgré Tout
1871	*Césarine Dietrich*
	Journal d'un Voyageur Pendant la Guerre
1873	*Impressions et Souvenirs*
	Contes d'une Grand-mère
1874	*Ma Soeur Jeanne*
1875	*Flamarande*
1876	*Marianne Chevreuse*

Special attention is called to these George Sand editions: *Oeuvres Autobiographiques*, edited and annotated by Georges Lubin. Pléiade Edition. 2 vols. Paris, 1970–71. Contents: *Histoire de Ma Vie, Voyage en Espagne, Mon Grand-Oncle, Voyage en Auvergne, La Blonde Phoebé, Nuit d'Hiver, Voyage Chez M. Blaise, Les Couperies, Sketches and Hints, Lettres d'un Voyageur, Journal Intime, Entretiens Journaliers avec le Très Docte et Très Habile Docteur Piffoël, Fragment d'une Lettre Écrite de Fontainebleau, Un Hiver à Majorque, Souvenirs de Mars–Avril 1848, Journal de Novembre–Décembre, 1851, Après la Mort de Jeanne Clésinger, Le Théâtre et l'Acteur* and *Le Théâtre des Marionettes de Nohant*.

Correspondance, edited by Georges Lubin. 13 vols. Paris 1964–78. Probably Sand's most important work. Each volume contains an average of 1,000 pages. Volume 13 brings the correspondence up to June 1856, inclusive. (There are more volumes to come.) For letters thereafter one must refer to other, less accurate, sources: George Sand, *Correspondance*, edited by Maurice Sand (6 vols., Paris, 1882–92); and Gustave Flaubert, *Correspondance Entre George Sand et Gustave Flaubert* (Paris, 1904).

Three posthumous Sand collections, from which extracts have been taken, should also be noted:

Questions d'Art et de Littérature (Paris, 1878).

Questions Politiques et Sociales (Paris, 1879).

Journal Intime (Paris, 1926). All parts of this collection—the Journal Intime proper, Sketches and Hints, and Entretiens Journaliers avec le Très Docte et Très Habile Docteur Piffoël—have been collated and republished by Georges Lubin in his edition of Sand's Oeuvres Autobiographiques (see above).

The French publishers of Sand's Correspondance, edited by Lubin, namely, Garnier Frères, have also brought out a number of the novels with introductory essays and annotations that are among the best new studies of Sand: Indiana, edited by Pierre Salomon (Paris, 1962); Lélia, edited by Pierre Reboul and containing both versions (Paris, 1960); Mauprat, edited by Claude Sicard (Garnier-Flammarion, Paris, 1969); Consuelo and La Comtesse de Rudolstadt, edited by Léon Cellier and Léon Guichard (3 vols., Paris, 1959); Les Maîtres Sonneurs, edited by Pierre Salomon and Jean Mallion (Paris, 1968); La Mare au Diable and François le Champi, edited by Pierre Salomon and Jean Mallion (Paris, 1962); La Petite Fadette, edited by Pierre Salomon and Jean Mallion (Paris, 1958). Also to be noted: La Daniella, edited by Annarosa Poli (Bulzoni, Rome, 1977).

Bibliographies of Works
By or About George Sand in English

GEORGE SAND'S WORKS (LISTED BY PUBLISHER)

Academy Press Ltd., Cassandra Editions, 360 North Michigan Avenue, Chicago, IL 60601

The Bagpipers
Fanchon the Cricket
Indiana
The Intimate Journal
Leone Leoni
The Letters of George Sand and Gustave Flaubert
The Master Mosaic Workers and *The Devil's Pool*
My Convent Life
She and He
Valentine
Winter in Majorca

AMS Press, Inc., 56 East 13th Street, New York, NY
10003
    Letters of George Sand (1886, 3 vols.; reprint)
    Masterpieces of George Sand (1900–2, 20 vols.; re-
    print). Contents: *Indiana, Consuelo, The Sin of
    M. Antoine, The Piccinino, The Last of the Al-
    dinis, Les Beaux Messieurs de Bois Doré, The Snow
    Man, Antonia, Nanon, A Rolling Stone, Handsome
    Laurence, The Germandre Family, The Marquis
    de Villemer, Valentine, Mauprat, She and He,
    Lavinia.* (Some novels cover two volumes.)

Blackie & Son, Ltd., 5 Fitzharding Street, London W.1,
England
    Little Fadette

Da Capo Press, 227 West 17th Street, New York, NY
10011
    Mauprat

Howard Fertig, Inc., 80 East 11th Street, New York, NY
10003
    A Companion of the Tour of France
    Indiana

Gorden Press Publishers, P.O. Box 459, Bowling Green

Station, New York, NY 10004
  Letters of George Sand (3 vols.)
  Complete Works (18 vols.)

Harper & Row, Publishers, Inc., 10 East 53d Street, New York, NY 10022
  My Life (abridged)

Haskell House Publishers, P.O. Box FF, Brooklyn, NY 11219
  The Intimate Journal of George Sand

Indiana University Press, 10th and Morton Streets, Bloomington, IN 47401
  Lélia

Shameless Hussy Press, Box 3092, Berkeley, CA 94703
  The Haunted Pool
  Lavinia

University of Nebraska Press, 901 North 17th Street, Lincoln, NE 68508
  The Country Waif

SECONDARY SOURCES

Biographical and Critical Works

Barry, Joseph. *Infamous Woman: The Life of George Sand.* Garden City, New York: Doubleday, 1977.
———. *Infamous Woman: The Life of George Sand.* Garden City, New York: Doubleday/Anchor, 1978.
Blount, Paul G. *George Sand and the Victorian World.* Athens: University of Georgia Press, 1978.
Caro, Elme Marie. *George Sand.* Trans. Gustave Masson, 1888. Port Washington, New York: Kennikat Press, 1970.

Cate, Curtis. *George Sand*. Boston: Houghton Mifflin, 1975.

———. *George Sand*. New York: Avon Books, 1976.

Doumic, René. *George Sand*. Trans. Alys Hallard, 1910. Port Washington, New York: Kennikat Press, 1972.

Edwards, Samuel. *George Sand: A Biography of the First Modern Liberated Woman*. New York: David McKay, 1972.

Ferrá, Bartolomé. *Chopin and George Sand in Majorca*. Trans. James Webb, 1936. Brooklyn, New York: Haskell House, 1974.

Hovey, Tamara. *A Mind of Her Own: A Life of the Writer George Sand*. New York: Harper & Row, 1977.

James, Henry. *French Poets and Novelists*. New York: Macmillan, 1878.

———. *Notes on Novelists*. New York: Scribner, 1914.

Jordan, Ruth. *George Sand: A Biographical Portrait*. New York: Taplinger, 1976.

Maurois, André. *Lélia: The Life of George Sand*. Trans. Gerard Hopkins. New York: Penguin Books, 1977.

Moers, Ellen. *Literary Women: The Great Writers*. Garden City, New York: Doubleday, 1976. (Notes are excellent source for research information.)

Thomson, Patricia. *George Sand and the Victorians*. New York: Columbia University Press, 1977.

Winegarten, Renée. *The Double Life of George Sand: Woman and Writer*. New York: Basic Books, 1978.

Winwar, Frances. *The Life of the Heart: George Sand and Her Times*. New York: Harper, 1945.

Conference Proceedings

Nineteenth-Century French Studies, 4, IV (1976). George Sand Colloquium, Amherst College, March 1976.

Ed. T. H. Goetz. Intro. Marie-Jeanne Pecile.

Barry, Joseph. "The Wholeness of George Sand."

Brée, Germaine. "The Fictions of Autobiography."

Lubin, Georges. "George Sand et l'Éducation."

Pecile, Marie-Jeanne. "George Sand: La Formation et l'Éducation d'une Femme Écrivain."

Hofstra University Cultural and Intercultural Studies, vol. I (1978). George Sand Conference, Hofstra University, November 1976. Intro. Henri Peyre.

Barry, Joseph. "George Sand: Our Existential Contemporary."

Blount, Paul G. "George Sand and the Victorians: Matthew Arnold as Touchstone."

Glasgow, Janis. "George Sand and Balzac."

Herrmann, Lesley S. "George Sand and Turgenev."

Jurgrau, Thelma. "The Linking of the Georges, Sand and Eliot: Critical Convention and Reality."

Karp, Carole. "George Sand and the Russians."

Lambasa, Frank. "Paris in the 1830's: The Romantic Hub of Europe."

Lubin, Georges. "George Sand en 1848."

Noland, Aaron. "Pierre-Joseph Proudhon and George Sand: A Confrontation."

O'Brien, Dennis. "George Sand and Feminism."

Pecile, Marie-Jeanne. "George Sand's Literary Encounters."

Peyre, Henri. "The Presence of George Sand Among Us."

Rogers, Nancy. "Social Protest in Her Early Works."

Roubichou, Gérard. "George Sand in 1976."

Standring, Enid. "The Lélios of Berlioz and George Sand."

Szogyi, Alex. "High Analytical Romanticism: The Narrative Voice in George Sand's *Lucrezia Floriani*."

Hofstra University Cultural and Intercultural Studies, vol.

II (1979). George Sand Conference, Hofstra University, April 1978.

Coiner, Nadia. "National Chauvinism Meets Male Chauvinism: The British Critics React to George Sand."

Daly, Pierrette. "*Consuelo:* The Artist and the Inclination to the Fantastic."

Danahy, Michael. "Growing Up Female: George Sand's View in *La Petite Fadette*."

Dixon, Sergine. "Eugène Delacroix: An Impartial Observer of George Sand's Personality."

Glasgow, Janis. "The Use of Doubles in George Sand's *Jacques*."

Greene, Tatiana. "Women and Madness in the Works of George Sand."

Hoog, Marie-Jacques. "The Will of *paraître* and the Will of *être* in George Sand."

Jones, Robert A. "George Sand, Charlotte Brontë and the Industrial Novel."

Jurgrau, Thelma. "George Sand's Attitude Towards the English."

Karp, Carole. "George Sand and the 'Men of the Forties': Bakunin, Belinsky, Herzen."

Laird, Helen. "George Sand: Social Historian and Poet."

Kraft, Barbara. "A Will to Life: Dialogues with George Sand."

Luce, Louise F. "Cities, States, and Secret Societies in *Consuelo:* Several Worlds, A Single Typology."

Pecile, Marie-Jeanne. "George Sand in America."

Richards, Carol V. "Structural Motifs and the Limits of Feminism in *Indiana*."

Rogers, Nancy E. "George Sand and Honoré de Balzac: Stylistic Similarities."

Schwartz, Lucy M. "Persuasion and Resistance: Human Relations in George Sand's Novels *Indiana* and *Lélia*."

Sourian, Eve. "Mme de Staël and George Sand."

Szogyi, Alex. "The First Translation of George Sand's Play, *Les Mississipiens*."

Yalom, Marilyn. "*Dédoublement* in the Fiction of George Sand."

Articles

Allott, Kenneth. "Matthew Arnold's 'The New Sirens' and George Sand." *Victorian Poetry*, I (1962), 156–58.

Anon. "The Romantic Realist Recovered: The Letters of George Sand." *Times Literary Supplement*, Apr. 17, 1969, pp. 413–14.

Arnold, J. V. "George Sand's *Mauprat* and Emily Brontë's *Wuthering Heights*." *Revue de Littérature Comparée*, 46 (1972), 209–18.

Baldick, Robert. "The Lady of Nohant." *Listener*, LXVI (1961), 913–14.

Barry, Joseph. "George Sand Was at Home to Life, Work and Love at Nohant." New York *Times Book Review*, July 2, 1972, 1, 13.

Baylen, Joseph O., and William E. Strickland. "Mme. Juliette Adam and George Sand: An Unpublished Souvenir." *Romance Notes*, 8 (1967), 176–82.

Bewley, V. E. A. "George Sand and Geraldine Jewsbury: An Unpublished Letter." *Revue de Littérature Comparée*, 30, (1956), 396–98.

Blount, Paul G. "George Sand and the Victorians." *Emory University Quarterly*, XX (1964), 187–92.

———. "George Sand's Misquotation of Shakespeare." *American Notes and Queries*, 12 (1973), 34–35.

Brée, Germaine. "George Sand." *The New Republic*, Aug. 21–28, 1976, 38–39.

Denommé, Robert T. "A Note Concerning the Death of George Sand." *Romance Notes*, 10 (1969), 261–64.

Jones, Howard Mumford. "American Comment on George Sand, 1837–1848." *American Literature*, III (1932), 389–407.

Juden, B., and J. Richer. "Macready and George Sand." *Revue des Lettres Modernes*, 74–75 (1962–63), 48–58.

Kappler, Richard G. "Turgenev and George Sand." *Research Studies*, XXXIV (1966), 37–45.

Leeming, David A. "Henry James and George Sand." *Revue de Littérature Comparée*, 43 (1969), 47–55.

Lombard, C. M. "George Sand's Image in America, 1837–76." *Revue de Littérature Comparée*, 39 (1965), 358–71.

McKenzie, K. A. "George Eliot and George Sand." *Journal of the Australasian Universities Language and Literature Association Proceedings*, [2] (1964), 61–62.

Rabine, Leslie. "George Sand and the Myth of Femininity." *Women and Literature*, 4, II (1976), 2–17.

Thomson, Patricia. "Elizabeth Barrett and George Sand." *Durham University Journal*, 33 (1972), 205–19.

———. "George Sand and the English Reviewers: The First Twenty Years." *Modern Language Review*, 67 (1972), 501–16.

———. "George Sand in London." *The Times Saturday Review* [London], Dec. 18, 1976.

———. "The Three Georges [Eliot, Sand, and Lewes]." *Nineteenth Century Fiction*, XVIII (1963), 137–50.

———. "*Wuthering Heights* and *Mauprat*." *Review of English Studies*, 24 (1973), 26–37.

Tomlin, E. W. F. "Dickens, Macready and George Sand." *Études Anglaises*, 28 (1975), 331–33.

Toth, Emily. "The Independent Woman and 'Free' Love." *Massachusetts Review*, 16 (1975), 647–64.

Uffenbach, Lorin A. "A Lost George Sand Letter." *Romance Notes*, 6 (1964), 37–41.

Volpe, E. L. "Prefaces of George Sand and Henry James." *Modern Language Notes*, 70 (1955), 107–8.

Winegarten, Renée. "The Reputation of George Sand." *Encounter*, XLVIII, 1 (1977), 30–38.

Dissertations

Blount, Paul G. "Reputation of George Sand in Victorian England, 1832–86." Unpublished, 1961. University Microfilms, 1970.

Glasgow, Janis M. "Psychological Realism in George Sand's Early Novels and Short Stories." *Dissertation Abstracts*, 28 (1966), No. 203A.

Gray, M. C. G. "George Sand, Gottfried Keller, George Eliot." (Unpublished M.A. thesis, Indiana University, 1965).

Jurgrau, Thelma L. " 'Pastoral' and 'Rustic' in the Country Novels of George Sand and George Eliot." *Dissertation Abstracts International*, 37 (1976), No. 284A.

Karp, Carole S. "George Sand's Reception in Russia, 1832–1881." *Dissertation Abstracts International*, 37 (1976), No. 3603A.

Kreitman, Lenore R. "George Sand's Symbolic Vision: A Fading Yet Future Fantastic." *Dissertation Abstracts International*, 37 (1976), No. 2221A.

Wall, Nancy Rogers. "The Persuasive Style of the Young George Sand." *Dissertation Abstracts International*, 35 (1974), No. 1127A.

Compiled by Nathalie Datlof
Hofstra University

Selected Bibliography
of French Publications

Adam, Juliette. *Mes Premières Armes Littéraires et Politiques.* Paris, 1904.
——. *Mes Sentiments et Nos Idées Avant 1870.* Paris, 1905.
Agoult, Marie d'. *Mémoires, 1833–1854.* Paris, 1927.
——. *Correspondance de Liszt et de la Comtesse d'Agoult.* 2 vols. Paris, 1933–34.
Balzac, Honoré de. *Béatrix.* Paris, 1962.
Barine, Arvède [pseud. of Cecile Vincens]. *Alfred de Musset.* Paris, 1893.
Blanc, Louis. *Histoire de Dix Ans, 1830–1840.* Paris, 1841–45.
Chopin, Frédéric. *Correspondance.* Ed. B. E. Sydow. 3 vols. Paris, 1953–54.
Delacroix, Eugène. *Correspondance Générale.* 5 vols. Paris, 1937–53.
——. *Journal.* 3 vols. Paris, 1950.
Didier, Charles. *Journal,* extracts, in *Revue des Sciences Humaines,* Oct.–Dec., 1959.
Dostoevski, Fyodor. *Journal d'un Écrivain.* Paris, 1904.
Evrard, Louis, ed. *Correspondance Sand–Musset.* Paris, 1956.
Flaubert, Gustave. *Correspondance Entre George Sand et Gustave Flaubert.* Paris, 1904.
——. *Oeuvres. Correspondance.* 16 vols. Paris, 1960–65.

Gavoty, Bernard. *Frédéric Chopin*. Paris, 1974.

Goncourt, Edmond and Jules de. *Journal*. 3 vols. Paris, 1888.

Heine, Heinrich. *Lutèce*. Paris, 1855.

Houssaye, Arsène. *Les Confessions: Souvenirs d'un Demi-Siècle*. 6 vols. Paris, 1885–91.

Karénine, Wladimir [pseud. of Varvara Komarova]. *George Sand*. 4 vols. Paris, 1899–1926.

Lefebvre, Henri. *Musset*. Paris, 1970.

Lubin, Georges. *George Sand en Berry*. Paris, 1967.

———. *Album Sand*. Paris, 1973.

Mariéton, Paul. *Une histoire d'Amour*. Paris, 1903.

Marix-Spire, Thérèse. *Les Romantiques et la Musique: Le Cas George Sand, 1804–1838*. Paris, 1955.

Martellet, Adèle Colin. *Dix Ans Chez Alfred de Musset*. Paris, 1899.

Musset, Alfred de. *Correspondance, 1827–1857*. Paris, 1907.

———. *Poésies Complètes*. Paris, 1957.

———. *Théâtre Complet*. Paris, 1958.

Musset, Paul de. *Lui et Elle*. Paris, 1859.

Pailleron, Marie-Louise. *George Sand*. 2 vols. Paris, 1938–42.

Plauchut, Edmond. *Autour de Nohant*. Paris, 1897.

Poli, Annarosa. *L'Italie dans la Vie et dans l'Oeuvre de George Sand*. Paris, 1960.

———. *George Sand et les Années Terribles*. Bologna-Paris, 1975.

Pommier, Jean. *Autour du Drame de Venise*. Paris, 1958.

Pontmartin, Armand de. *Mes Mémoires*. Paris, 1882, 1886.

Regard, Maurice. *Gustave Planche*. 2 vols. Paris, 1955.

Rocheblave, Samuel. *George Sand et Sa Fille*. Paris, 1905.

Sainte-Beuve, Charles-Augustin. *Correspondance Générale*. 16 vols. Paris, 1935–70.

Salomon, Pierre. *George Sand*. Paris, 1953.

Sandeau, Jules. *Marianna*. Paris, 1865.

Ségu, Frédéric. *Un Maître de Balzac Inconnu: H. de Latouche*. Paris, 1928.

Sellards, John. *Dans le Sillage du Romantisme: Charles Didier*. Paris, 1933.

Silver, Mabel. *Jules Sandeau*. Paris, 1936.

Vier, Jacques. *La Comtesse d'Agoult et Son Temps*. 6 vols. Paris, 1955–63.

Vigny, Alfred de. *Journal d'un Poète*. Paris, 1935.

Vincent, Louise. *George Sand et le Berry*. 2 vols. Paris, 1919.

Of the above works, the following are also available in English translation:

Balzac, Honoré de. *Béatrix*. Trans. Beth Archer. Englewood Cliffs, N.J.: Prentice-Hall, 1970.

Barine, Arvède [pseud. of Cécile Vincens]. *Alfred de Musset*. Trans. Charles Conner Hayden. New York: E. C. Hill, 1906.

Blanc, Louis. *The History of Ten Years, 1830–40*. Trans. 1845; reprint. New York: A. M. Kelley, 1969.

Chopin, Frédéric. *Selected Correspondence of Fryderyk Chopin*. Abr. from B. E. Sydow ed. Trans., ed. Arthur Hedley. New York: McGraw-Hill, 1963.

Delacroix, Eugène. *Selected Letters, 1813–1863*. Sel. and trans. Jean Stewart from *Correspondance Générale*. New York: St. Martin's Press, 1971.

———. *The Journal of Eugène Delacroix*. Trans. Walter Pach. New York: Covici Friede, 1937.

Dostoevski, Fyodor. *The Diary of a Writer*. Trans. and annot. Boris Brasol. New York: Braziller, 1954.

Flaubert, Gustave. *The George Sand-Gustave Flaubert Letters*. Trans. Aimee L. McKenzie, 1921; reprint. New York: Liveright, n.d.

———. *Complete Works*. New York: M. W. Dunne, 1904.

Gavoty, Bernard. *Frédéric Chopin*. Trans. Martin Sokolinsky. New York: Scribner, 1977.

Goncourt, Edmond and Jules de. *The Goncourt Journals, 1851–1870.* Trans. Lewis Galantière. Garden City, New York: Doubleday, 1937.

Heine, Heinrich. *Lutèce.* Trans. Charles Godfrey Leland, Thomas Brooksbank, and Margaret Armour. London: Heineman, 1903.

Houssaye, Arsène. *Man About Paris: The Confessions of Arsène Houssaye.* Sel., trans., and ed. Henry Knepler. New York: Morrow, 1970.

Musset, Alfred de. *Complete Plays.* Trans. R. Pellissier, W. B. Thompson, and M. H. Dey. New York: E. C. Hill, 1905.

———. *Complete Poems.* Trans. M. A. Clarke. New York: E. C. Hill, 1905.

Acknowledgments

"Acknowledgment" is too weak a word for the gratitude, appreciation, and immense affection we who write, read, or think about George Sand feel for Georges Lubin, who has devoted his life (and often his wife) to editing and annotating her masterwork, the endless *Correspondance*. No one shares his findings more graciously than he. Such too is the generous attitude of Sandists in general, and I think particularly of Nathalie Datlof and Alvin Lundquist, to whom go these warm public thanks. Neel Randsholt and Howard Brabyn deserve special credit for the help and back-and-forth criticism indispensable for the translation, for which, of course, I must take the full blame. No less to Elizabeth Frost Knappman of Anchor Press who asked for this George Sand reader and patiently coaxed it into being. To Georgiana Remer, as well, whose copy editing can only be called "exquisite." And to Liliane Lassen always, for the man-woman dialogue permitting a man to understand a woman and himself, and, so he hopes, George Sand.

Index

467